RECONCEPTUALISING STRICT LIABILITY FOR THE TORT OF ANOTHER

This book adopts a novel approach to resolving the present difficulties experienced by the courts in imposing strict liability for the tort of another. It looks beyond the traditional classifications of 'vicarious liability' and 'liability for breach of a non-delegable duty of care' and, for the first time, seeks to explain all instances of strict liability for the tort of another in terms of the various relationships in which the courts impose such liability. The book shows that, despite appearances, there is a unifying feature to the various relationships in which the courts currently impose strict liability for the tort of another. That feature is authority. Whenever the courts impose strict liability for the tort of another, the defendant is either vested with authority over the person who committed a tort against the claimant or has vested or conferred a form of authority upon that person in respect of the claimant. This book uses this feature of authority to construct a new expositive framework within which strict liability for the tort of another can be understood.

Volume 31 in the series Hart Studies in Private Law

Reconceptualising Strict Liability for the Tort of Another

Christine Beuermann

·HART·
OXFORD · LONDON · NEW YORK · NEW DELHI · SYDNEY

HART PUBLISHING

Bloomsbury Publishing Plc

Kemp House, Chawley Park, Cumnor Hill, Oxford, OX2 9PH, UK

HART PUBLISHING, the Hart/Stag logo, BLOOMSBURY and the Diana logo are trademarks of Bloomsbury Publishing Plc

First published in Great Britain 2019

A catalogue record for this book is available from the British Library.

A catalogue record for this book is available from the Library of Congress.

ISBN: HB: 978-1-50991-753-2
ePDF: 978-1-50991-755-6
ePub: 978-1-50991-754-9

Typeset by Compuscript Ltd, Shannon
Printed and bound in Great Britain by CPI Group (UK) Ltd, Croydon CR0 4YY

MIX
Paper from responsible sources
FSC® C013604

To find out more about our authors and books visit www.hartpublishing.co.uk. Here you will find extracts, author information, details of forthcoming events and the option to sign up for our newsletters.

I dedicate this book to my grandmother, Stella Leonie Neller, who died in 2018 aged 105 – she would have done amazing things if given the same opportunities I have been lucky enough to receive

Cases do not unfold their principles for the asking. They yield up their kernel slowly and painfully. The instance cannot lead to a generalisation till we know it as it is. That in itself is no easy task. For the thing adjudged comes to us oftentimes swathed in obscuring dicta, which must be stripped off and cast aside.

Benjamin N Cardozo, *The Nature of the Judicial Process* (1921) 29

ACKNOWLEDGEMENTS

This book took longer to publish than I anticipated. The continuous struggles of the highest courts when imposing strict liability for the tort of another, however, provided fertile ground for refining the arguments presented herein and the book is all the better for the delay.

I am indebted to Professors Jane Stapleton and Peter Cane. It is no small thing to reteach a person how to think. They remain my intellectual heroes and inspiration and I can only hope to be a similar beacon to my own students, encouraging them to push the boundaries and re-examine the established learning about private law.

To my family and friends, 'thank you' simply does not do justice. You've been the wind beneath my wings and I share this with you all.

TABLE OF CONTENTS

TABLE OF CASES

TABLE OF LEGISLATION

Commonwealth

New South Wales

Victoria

Western Australia

United Kingdom

British Columbia (Canada)

1

Introduction

The cases in which strict liability is imposed on a defendant for a tort committed by another person appear inconsistent and often contradictory. An employer, for example, can be held liable for a crane driver who negligently harms an employee,[1] but not for a tool manufacturer who negligently harms an employee.[2] A school can be held liable for a teacher who sexually assaults a student,[3] but not for a janitor who sexually assaults a student.[4] Explaining such distinctions has proved difficult throughout the common law world.[5]

This book takes an important first step towards developing a convincing justification for the strict liability imposed on a defendant for the tort of another which is capable of accommodating such distinctions. It shows that, despite appearances, there is a unifying feature to the various cases in which the courts impose such liability. That feature is authority. Whenever the courts impose strict liability on a defendant for the tort of another, the defendant is either vested[6] with authority over the person who committed the tort or has conferred[7] a form of authority upon that person in respect of the claimant.[8] This book uses this feature of authority to construct a new expositive framework within which the strict liability imposed on a defendant for the tort of another can be better understood.

Part I of the book will start by identifying the circumstances in which the courts currently impose strict liability on a defendant for the tort of another. It shows that the range of circumstances in which such liability has been imposed by the courts has narrowed over time, such that the imposition of strict liability for the tort of another is largely restricted to three main types of relationships:[9]

1. the *employment relationship* (the relationship between an employer and an employee);

[1] *Kondis v State Transport Authority* (1984) 154 CLR 672.
[2] *Davie v New Merton Board Mills Ltd* [1949] AC 604.
[3] See, eg, *Bazley v Curry* (1999) 174 DLR (4th) 45 and *Lister v Hesley Hall Ltd* [2002] 1 AC 215.
[4] *G(ED) v Hammer* (2003) 230 DLR (4th) 554.
[5] Particularly in Australia and England and Wales which is the focus of this book. See below.
[6] The term 'vested' is used throughout this book to refer to the creation of new authority.
[7] The term 'conferred' is used throughout this book to refer to authority previously vested in one person being given to another.
[8] Such authority may be either to enter into legal relations with the claimant or to direct the claimant or their property more generally.
[9] Though includes analogous relationships, discussed further in chs 4 and 8.

2. the *school relationship* (the relationship between a school[10] and a student); and
3. the *agency relationship* (the relationship between a principal and a contractual agent[11]).

The feature of authority is common to all three relationships. Importantly, the recent introduction by the courts in England and Wales of new tests for both vicarious liability[12] and so-called 'liability for breach of a non-delegable duty of care'[13] has yet to see any expansion of the circumstances in which strict liability is imposed on a defendant for the tort of another beyond relationships of which authority is a feature.[14]

Part II of the book uses this feature of authority to construct a new expositive framework for the strict liability imposed on a defendant for the tort of another. Three separate forms of strict liability are identified and explained:

1. strict liability for the tort of a person upon whom authority has been conferred in relation to another or *conferred authority strict liability* (found in the employment and school relationships[15]);
2. strict liability for the tort of an employee or *employee strict liability* (found in the employment relationship only); and
3. strict liability for the tort of an agent or *agent strict liability* (found in the agency relationship only).

Each form of strict liability is shown to reflect differences in the nature of the authority present in each of the relationships by reason of which strict liability is imposed on a defendant for a tort committed by another person.

Part III of the book sets out the advantages of the proposed expositive framework. It demonstrates how that expositive framework makes clear the boundaries between the different forms of strict liability for the tort of another and how it can be used to explain what appear to be miscellaneous examples of the liability.

[10] Defined broadly to include both privately and publicly operated educational institutions, excluding institutions providing child care for younger children and universities.

[11] Although there is no generally agreed definition of the term 'agent', this book will confine the definition to a person who has been vested with authority by a principal to effect legal relations on the principal's behalf; that is, an agent in the contractual sense. This is because it is generally only when an agent has been vested with authority in the contractual sense, that a principal will be held strictly liable for the wrongdoing of the agent. See further ch 6.

[12] The change from the more 'process'-based *Salmond* test to the more 'rule'-based 'close connection test' in *Lister v Hesley Hall Ltd* [2002] 1 AC 215 has loosened the restrictions on imposing vicarious liability. This has resulted in pressure to expand the scope of vicarious liability but not necessarily the relationships by reason of which it is imposed. This theme will be revisited throughout this book. See also C Beuermann, 'The abstraction of form and the associated dangers for the English courts: the case study of vicarious liability', paper presented at Obligations IX, Melbourne Law School, 18 July 2018.

[13] *Woodland v Essex County Council* [2014] AC 537.

[14] Although it has affected the scope of the liability imposed within those relationships. Consider *Mohamud v WM Morrisons Supermarkets plc* [2016] AC 677, discussed further in ch 7. In terms of relationships, the foster carer relationship by reason of which liability was imposed by the Supreme Court of the United Kingdom in *Armes v Nottinghamshire Shire Council* [2018] AC 355 is closely analogous to the school relationships and is discussed further in ch 4.

[15] And relationships which are closely analogous. See further chs 4 and 8.

It is argued, in conclusion, that the proposed expositive framework is capable of providing new insights into both the justification for the strict liability imposed on a defendant for the tort of another and the structure of the law of torts more generally.

To start, however, it is first necessary to consider the nature of the strict liability imposed on a defendant for the tort of another and the framework within which such liability is currently understood.

I. What is 'Strict Liability for the Tort of Another'?

The phrase 'strict liability for the tort of another' is used in this book to describe any form of liability imposed in tort which exhibits the following two characteristics. First, the liability is imposed in respect of a tort committed by a person other than the defendant against the claimant. Secondly, the liability is imposed regardless of whether the defendant also personally engaged in any conduct[16] in respect of the claimant to which liability in tort might attach.[17] It is not that the defendant did not commit a tort against the claimant, but that the claimant does not need to provide evidence of such a tort in order to succeed against the defendant.[18] Instead, it is sufficient for a claimant to show that:

1. a person other than the defendant committed a tort against the claimant;
2. the defendant was party to a relationship (whether with the claimant or the person who committed the tort against the claimant) which had the requisite features to attract strict liability; and
3. the commission of the tort by the other person was sufficiently connected[19] with that relationship for strict liability to be imposed.

'Strict liability for the tort of another' is therefore imposed by reason of the relationship to which the defendant is party rather than by reason of anything the defendant did or did not do (other than enter into the relationship by reason of which liability is imposed).[20]

By definition, the phrase 'strict liability for the tort of another' excludes any form of liability triggered by a tort committed by a person other than the defendant which is only imposed once a claimant adduces evidence of conduct personally

[16] Defined broadly to include both acts and omissions.

[17] P Cane, 'Responsibility and Fault: a Relational and Functional Approach to Responsibility' in P Cane and J Gardner (eds), *Relating to Responsibility* (Oxford, Hart, 2001) 81, 99.

[18] *Bernard v The Attorney General of Jamaica* [2005] IRLR 398, [21] (Lord Steyn): 'Vicarious liability is a principle of strict liability. It is a liability for a tort committed by an employee not based on any fault of the employer. There may, of course, be cases of vicarious liability where employers were at fault. But it is not a requirement'.

[19] Various terms have been used to describe the extent of the necessary connection, including 'close', 'scope' and 'course', with the extent of the necessary connection being discussed in detail in ch 7.

[20] P Cane, *The Anatomy of Tort Law* (Oxford, Hart, 1997) 46–47.

engaged in by the defendant which is itself capable of attracting liability in tort. The liability imposed on a defendant in such circumstances is personal, rather than strict. An example of personal liability for the tort of another is the duty of care recognised by the House of Lords in *Home Office v Dorset Yacht Co Ltd*.[21] In that case, notwithstanding that the tort of trespass was committed by the escaped borstal boys, the liability sought to be imposed on the Home Office was liability for its own negligence in allowing the escape (of which proof was required). The liability imposed by the High Court of Australia in *Geyer v Downs*[22] is another example of personal liability for the tort of another. In that case, a school was held liable when a student was 'accidentally struck on the head by a softball bat' held by another student.[23] Once again, notwithstanding that the tort of battery had been committed by one student against another, the school was held liable for its own negligence in not adequately supervising the playground at the time the incident occurred and proof of that negligence had to be adduced by the claimant in order for liability to be imposed.

As this book is solely concerned with strict liability for the tort of another, it does not examine any of the various forms of liability which require a claimant to adduce evidence of conduct personally engaged in by the defendant which attracts liability in tort. Personal liability is not ignored altogether, but the consideration of personal liability is limited to the final chapter which briefly explores the implications of this book on the explanation of personal liability arising within the same relationships and the structure of the law of torts more generally.

The phrase 'strict liability for the tort of another' also excludes any form of strict liability triggered by a tort committed by another person against the claimant which is imposed for reasons *other than* a relationship with the requisite features to which the defendant is party (whether with the claimant or the person who committed the tort against the claimant). Consider the liability imposed in *Rylands v Fletcher*.[24] In that case, the defendant land owner engaged an independent contractor to construct a dam which subsequently collapsed into a series of subterranean mine shafts, flooding a neighbouring property. Although the defendant land owner was held liable for the damage, it can be argued that it was not the defendant land owner's relationship with the independent contractor that attracted liability, but the defendant land owner's 'non-natural' use of land which created a reasonably foreseeable risk of harm to the neighbouring property.[25] Specifically, the decision of the land owner to construct and maintain a dam which had the consequence of causing water to escape to the neighbouring property.

[21] [1970] AC 1004.
[22] (1977) 138 CLR 91.
[23] Ibid 92.
[24] (1866) LR 1 EX 265; (1868) LR 3 HL 330.
[25] (1868) LR 3 HL 330, 339 (Lord Cairns). Although the High Court of Australia has since suggested that the liability imposed under the so-called rule in *Rylands v Fletcher* is a form of personal liability; see *Burnie Port Authority v General Jones Pty Ltd* (1992) 179 CLR 520, 556. cf *Cambridge Water Co v Eastern Counties Leather* [1994] 2 AC 264.

As this book is principally concerned with strict liability for the tort of another which arises *by reason* of a relationship to which the defendant is party, this book does not examine any of the various forms of strict liability which arise for reasons other than that relationship.

Although this book is limited to examining 'strict liability for the tort of another', the analysis may extend to strict liability imposed for other forms of liability,[26] such as liability for breach of the duty of confidence[27] or liability for breach of the statutory prohibition against harassment.[28] The scope and/or limits of strict liability for the tort of another need first to be determined before examining the extent to which such strict liability might be extended to forms of liability beyond the law of torts.

II. Existing Terminology

The presence of strict liability for the tort of another is typically indicated by use of the labels 'vicarious liability' or 'liability for breach of a non-delegable duty of care'. Unfortunately, such labels are imprecise and their use has been problematic.

First, the labels used to describe strict liability for the tort of another have not always been limited to describing *only* strict liability for the tort of another. This is a particular problem in respect of the label 'liability for breach of a non-delegable duty of care'. Sometimes, the holder of what is currently called a 'non-delegable duty of care' is held liable because the holder of the so-called 'duty' personally engaged in conduct in respect of the beneficiary of that 'duty' which attracts liability in tort. Consider an employee injured as a result of her employer failing to establish a safe system of work. This failure will constitute a breach of the so-called 'non-delegable duty' owed by the employer to the employee if it can be shown that a reasonable employer would have installed such a system.[29] Liability in this type of situation is imposed because the employer personally engaged in conduct towards an employee which attracts liability in tort and the employee has provided evidence of that conduct.[30] Such liability is outside the scope of this book.

Yet the holder of a so-called 'non-delegable duty of care' is held liable at other times in circumstances in which no evidence is adduced by the beneficiary of the 'duty' of conduct personally engaged in by the holder of the 'duty' to which liability in tort might attach. Consider the decision of the High Court of Australia

[26] Defined in its broadest sense.

[27] *Various Claimants v Wm Morrisons Supermarkets plc* [2018] 3 WLR 691.

[28] *Majrowski v Guy's and St Thomas' NHS Trust* [2007] 1 AC 224.

[29] See, eg, *McLean v Tedman* (1984) 155 CLR 306 in which an employer was held liable for failing to provide a reasonable system of rubbish bin collection.

[30] Tort liability for these purposes is not restricted to the tort of negligence.

in *Kondis v State Transport Authority.*[31] In that case, an employee was negligently injured by an independent contractor[32] engaged by the employer to use a crane to dismantle a structure on the employer's property. Despite no evidence of the employer personally engaging in any conduct to which liability in tort might attach (other than enter into the relationship with the person who did commit the tort), the employer was held to have breached the so-called 'non-delegable duty' owed to the employee. Such liability was imposed regardless of whether the defendant also personally engaged in any conduct that attracted liability in tort and is the type of liability with which this book is concerned. The label 'liability for breach of a non-delegable duty of care' appears, therefore, to be used in different circumstances to describe different forms of liability.

Secondly, neither the label 'vicarious liability' nor 'liability for breach of a non-delegable duty of care' gives a clear indication as to *why* strict liability for the tort of another is imposed or the concern to which the strict liability is responding. This creates difficulties in situations where both labels can be used to describe the strict liability arising in a single factual circumstance. Consider the recent series of cases involving the historic sexual abuse of children by the employees of institutions charged with their care (the *child sexual assault cases*).[33] In those cases, there was the possibility of holding the institutions 'vicariously liable' for the sexual assaults perpetrated by the employee or holding that the sexual assaults constituted a breach of the so-called 'non-delegable duty of care' owed by the institution to the child. Judges found it difficult to distinguish between the two forms of strict liability for the tort of another and received little guidance in their efforts from the labels used to describe the different forms of strict liability.[34] The absence of any clear direction as to why either 'vicarious liability' or liability for breach of a so-called 'non-delegable duty of care' were imposed made it particularly difficult to determine the boundary between the two forms of strict liability for the tort of another. Faced with these difficulties, a majority of judges seemingly opted to impose the more familiar 'vicarious liability' rather than address the longstanding difficulties associated with determining the nature and incidence of the strict liability that might be imposed for breach of a so-called 'non-delegable duty of care'.[35] This, in turn, necessitated the unfortunate finding that the deliberate and

[31] (1984) 154 CLR 672.

[32] Or more correctly, the employee of an independent contractor engaged to dismantle the structure.

[33] Starting in Australia with the decision of the High Court of Australia in *New South Wales v Lepore* (2003) 212 CLR 511 (McHugh J and Gaudron J). The first decision in England and Wales was the decision of the House of Lords in *Lister v Hesley Hall Ltd* [2002] 1 AC 215 (Lord Hobhouse). Note also that the requisite status of employee has been challenged in England and Wales; *Various Claimants v Catholic Child Welfare Society* [2013] 2 AC 1.

[34] See, eg, *New South Wales v Lepore* (2003) 212 CLR 515 in which both forms of liability were considered by different judges. See also *Armes v Nottinghamshire County Council* [2018] AC 355.

[35] Glanville Williams once famously said of the non-delegable duty: 'the cases are decided on no rational grounds, but depend merely on whether the judge is attracted by the language of non-delegable duty'. G Williams, 'Liability for Independent Contractors' (1956) *Cambridge Law Journal* 180, 186. Indeed, in England and Wales, the imposition of such liability would have been quite difficult until

self-serving[36] act of sexually assaulting a child could occur within the 'course of employment'[37] as it was 'closely connected'[38] with that employment.

The failure of the labels 'vicarious liability' and 'liability for breach of a non-delegable duty of care' to reflect the reasons why strict liability for the tort of another is imposed also creates difficulties in situations where a single label is used to describe the strict liability arising in different factual circumstances. The label 'vicarious liability', for instance, is used to describe both the strict liability imposed on an employer for the tort of an employee and the strict liability imposed on a principal for the tort of an agent. The use of a single label to describe liability in both circumstances suggests that the reasons for liability in both circumstances are the same. It is difficult to reconcile this conclusion, however, with the traditional rule that an employer cannot be held 'vicariously liable' for the tort of an independent contractor.[39] This is because although an agent may be an employee, an agent may also be an independent contractor or have been acting gratuitously. This inconsistency has led some commentators to challenge whether what is currently called 'vicarious liability' should be recognised outside the employment relationship;[40] but it does not necessarily follow that just because an employer cannot be held 'vicariously liable' for a tort committed by an independent contractor that a principal cannot be held strictly liable for a tort committed by an agent at all. It may be that the reasons for imposing liability in the two situations differ. Unfortunately, this possibility has been obscured by the use of a single label to describe the liability imposed in both circumstances.

As can be seen, the labels 'vicarious liability' and 'non-delegable duty of care' are vague and confusing and add little to the current understanding of strict liability in tort for the harm caused by another. This book therefore proposes to abandon such labels and devise more appropriate terminology to describe the different forms of strict liability for the tort of another that are imposed by the courts.

III. Existing Explanation(s)

It is not just the terminology currently used to describe strict liability for the tort of another which is problematic. At present, there does not appear to be any convincing way of explaining why strict liability for the tort of another might be imposed.

the Supreme Court laid down a test for determining the existence of a 'non-delegable duty of care' in *Woodland v Essex County Council* [2004] AC 537.

[36] P Cane, 'Vicarious Liability for Sexual Abuse' (2000) 116 *Law Quarterly Review* 21, 21.

[37] The so-called *Salmond* test. FV Robert and RA Buckley, *Salmond & Heuston on the Law of Torts* (21st ed, London, Sweet & Maxwell, 1996) 443.

[38] *Lister v Hesley Hall Ltd* [2002] 1 AC 215.

[39] *Quarmann v Burnett* 1840) 6 M&W 499; 151 ER 509. Although the rule has recently been challenged with the extension of vicarious liability in England to relationships 'akin to employment'. See *Various Claimants v Child Catholic Welfare Society* [2013] 2 AC 1. Also *Barclays Bank plc v Various Claimants* [2018] EWCA Civ 1670.

[40] See R Stevens, 'Why Do Agents "Drop out"?' [2005] *Lloyd's Maritime and Commercial Law Quarterly* 101.

A. Strict Liability for the Tort of Another Arising by Reason of the Employment Relationship

Attempts have been made to justify the strict liability imposed on an employer for a tort committed by an employee on various grounds. Early explanations tended to focus on the capacity of an employer to exert a degree of control over an employee's work. The problem with this type of explanation, as Atiyah pointed out, is that control is neither a necessary nor sufficient condition of the strict liability.[41] It is not necessary because an employer can be held strictly liable for a tort committed by *any* employee, even though the degree of control exercised by an employer diminishes as the skill level of each individual employee increases.[42] Control is also not a sufficient condition because control is exercised over other individuals for whom strict liability does not arise. A school, for instance, is not always held strictly liable for a tort committed by a student even though the school might be in a position to exert some control over the behaviour of that student.[43]

More modern explanations of the strict liability imposed on an employer for a tort committed by an employee focus on the benefit an employer derives from an employee's work. It is argued that just as an employer takes the benefit of an employee's work in terms of profit, so too should that employer bear the burden of any damage caused by an employee in the course of earning that profit.[44] Such accounts struggle to explain why an employer is only held strictly liable for a tort committed by an employee and not for a tort committed by an independent contractor who might also deliver the employer a benefit.[45] There is also the problem of explaining why an employer is only held strictly liable for damage caused by an employee that constitutes a tort, as opposed to being held strictly liable for *all* damage caused by an employee.[46] That an employer takes the benefit of an employee's work cannot explain why liability is imposed in one situation but not the other.

Further explanations of the strict liability imposed on an employer for a tort committed by an employee have been devised from the typically superior capacity of an employer to pay for the damage caused by an employee. It is argued, for instance, that an employer has 'deeper pockets' than an employee and can ensure that an injured claimant receives the compensation to which she is entitled. This does not explain, however, why it is the employer rather than any other

[41] Ibid 15–17.

[42] Hence control is no longer the sole criterion for identifying an employer relationship. See *Stevens v Brodribb Sawmilling Company Pty Ltd* (1986) 160 CLR 16.

[43] The capacity to exert such control depends, to a large extent, on the child's age. See further ch 4.

[44] See J Stapleton, *Product Liability* (London, Butterworth & Co, 1994) 193.

[45] It has been argued that employees might be distinguished from independent contractors on the grounds that the benefit to be delivered by an independent contractor will generally be limited by the terms of the contract under which the contractor has been engaged, whereas the benefit to be delivered by an employee is unlimited. See Stapleton ibid. See also PS Atiyah, *Vicarious Liability in the Law of Torts* (London, Butterworth & Co, 1967) 18.

[46] Atiyah, ibid 28.

well-resourced institution, such as the government, which is required to compensate the claimant.[47] Alternatively, it is argued that an employer is better positioned to distribute the cost of compensation through the employer's enterprise. But this does not explain why charities or other institutions that are unable to distribute losses are also held strictly liable.[48]

B. Strict Liability for the Tort of Another Arising by Reason of the Agency Relationship

It has already been noted that the strict liability imposed on a principal for a tort committed by an agent is explained in similar terms to the strict liability imposed on an employer for a tort committed by an employee. Specifically, it is explained in terms of an agent's representative capacity.[49] An agent acts as representative of the principal and not on the agent's own behalf. As the principal is the beneficiary of the agent's work, it is argued that the principal should also bear the burden of any damage caused by the agent in obtaining that benefit.[50] Both the principal and the employer must take the good with the bad.

As the strict liability imposed on a principal for a tort committed by an agent is explained in similar terms to the strict liability imposed on an employer for a tort committed by an employee, similar problems exist with the explanation's use. That a principal takes the benefit of an agent's work, for instance, does not explain why a principal is only held strictly liable for some damage caused by an agent, as opposed to being held strictly liable for *all* damage caused by an agent. There is also the further problem, discussed above, of reconciling the explanation with the general rule that an employer cannot be held 'vicariously liable' for a tort committed by an independent contractor (in the terms in which that liability is currently described).

[47] JW Neyers 'A Theory of Vicarious Liability' (2004) 43 *Alberta Law Review* 287, 293–98.

[48] Ibid.

[49] *Colonial Mutual Life Assurance Society Ltd v Produce and Citizens Cooperative Assurance Company of Australia* (1931) 4 CLR 1, 48–49 (Dixon J): 'In most cases in which a tort is committed in the course of the performance of work for the benefit of another person, he cannot be vicariously responsible if the actual tortfeasor is not his servant and he has not directly authorised the doing of the act which amounts to a tort. The work, although done at his request and for his benefit, is considered as the independent function of the person who undertakes it, and not as something which the person obtaining the benefit does by his representative standing in his place, and, therefore, identified with him for the purpose of liability arising in the course of its performance. The independent contractor carries out his work, not as a representative, but as a principal. But a difficulty arises when the function entrusted is that of representing the person who requests its performance in a transaction with others, so that the very services to be performed consists in standing in his place and assuming to act in his right and not in an independent capacity'.

[50] GE Dal Pont, 'Agency: Definitional Challenges through the Law of Tort' (2003) 11 *Torts Law Journal* 6, 16–17.

C. Strict Liability for the Tort of Another Arising by Reason of Relationships which Give Rise to a so-called 'Non-Delegable Duty of Care'

There are a variety of relationships in which the courts recognise a so-called 'non-delegable duty of care'. They have been said to include relationships between 'adjoining owners of land in relation to work threatening support or common walls; master and servant in relation to a safe system of work; hospital and patient; school authority and pupil; and (arguably), occupier and invitee'.[51] The use of the label 'non-delegable duty' in each of those relationships is typically taken to indicate that strict liability for the tort of another can be imposed. This proposition will be challenged in chapter 2.

Assuming for the moment that strict liability for the tort of another is imposed by reason of each of the above relationships, attempts have been made to justify such liability on the basis of an 'assumption of responsibility'.[52] The holder of the so-called 'non-delegable duty' is said to undertake not just to use reasonable care in respect of the beneficiary of the duty, but to 'ensure' that reasonable care is taken.[53] Once such an 'assumption of responsibility' is found to exist, it is argued that the person who assumed responsibility should be held liable for any torts committed by the person over whom responsibility was assumed, regardless of whether the defendant also personally engaged in conduct to which liability in tort might attach.[54]

There are several difficulties in using the concept of an 'assumption of responsibility' to explain the strict liability imposed for the tort of another within the various relationships in which a so-called 'non-delegable duty of care' is recognised. First, the courts have failed to use the notion of an 'assumption of responsibility' with any consistency. As Kit Barker has demonstrated, the concept is used in a variety of senses: sometimes it indicates an implied promise by the defendant to take care; sometimes it means the defendant has assumed the legal risk of the consequences of her actions; and on yet other occasions, it means nothing more than the defendant has voluntarily chosen to act in a particular way.[55] As judges

[51] *Burnie Port Authority v General Jones Pty Limited* (1994) 179 CLR 520, 550–51. A similar list was outlined by Lord Sumption in *Woodland v Essex County Council* [2014] AC 537, 576.

[52] *Kondis v State Transport Authority* (1984) 154 CLR 672, 687 (Mason J): 'because the person on whom it is imposed has undertaken the care, supervision or control of the person or property of another or is so placed in relation to that person or his property as to assume a particular responsibility for his or its safety, in circumstances where the person affected might reasonably expect that due care will be exercised'. See also R Stevens, 'Non-Delegable Duties and Vicarious Liability' in J Neyers, S Pitel and E Chamberlain (eds), *Emerging Issues in Tort Law* (Oxford, Hart, 2007) 331. J Murphy, 'Juridical Foundations of Common Law Non-Delegable Duties' in J Neyers, S Pitel and E Chamberlain (eds), *Emerging Issues in Tort Law* (2007) 369.

[53] *Kondis v State Transport Authority* (1984) 154 CLR 672, 687.

[54] Ibid.

[55] K Barker, 'Unreliable Assumptions in the Modern Law of Negligence' (1993) 109 *Law Quarterly Review* 461.

do not always articulate the sense in which they are using the concept, the concept can appear little more than a label for the particular conclusion a judge wants to reach.

Secondly, it is not always clear how an 'assumption of responsibility' in any of the senses in which it is used above, might arise in the various relationships by reason of which a so-called 'non-delegable duty of care' is recognised.[56] Take, for instance, the relationship between adjoining land owners when working on a party wall or foundations at the boundary of a property. It is difficult to see a land owner making an 'assumption of responsibility' in terms of an implied promise when there may not have been any communication between the adjoining land owners. It is also not uncommon for the relationship between land owners to be relatively informal so that it is unlikely that any intention to make a legally binding promise could be found.[57] Similarly, it is somewhat artificial to say that a landowner will have necessarily assumed the legal risk of the work being done when she has appointed an appropriately qualified contractor to do the work as the land owner might have structured her relations with that contractor in such a way as to avoid liability to the adjoining land owner.[58] The most that can be said is that legal risk might have been assumed by reason of the hazardous nature of the work being conducted. But there has been very little judicial support for the more general idea that legal liability should attach to extra-hazardous activities[59] or clarity as to when an activity will be sufficiently hazardous for such liability to attach.[60] It is also not clear why a landowner should be subject to strict liability for the tort of another for voluntarily choosing to engage an independent contractor to work on the party wall or foundations at the boundary of the property[61] when other decisions by a landowner to engage an independent contractor to do work on the premises more generally do not attract similar liability.[62]

Finally, even if it is possible to give some appropriate meaning to the concept, an 'assumption of responsibility' does not always appear to be sufficient to impose strict liability for the tort of another in the various relationships in which a

[56] This may be one reason why Lord Sumption sought to separate cases of extra-hazardous activities from other cases of so-called 'non-delegable duties' in *Woodlands v Essex County Council* [2014] AC 537, 583.

[57] Ibid 466.

[58] Ibid 471. This was the case in *Bower v Peate* (1876) LR 1 QBD 321, where the land owner authorised the independent contractor to do the work 'only on the condition of his preventing it from causing injury to this plaintiff, and only so far as it could be done consistently with the safety of the premises of the latter' (at 325).

[59] See *Read v J Lyons & Company* [1947] AC 156, 181–182 (Lord Simonds): 'I would reject the idea that, if a man carries on a so-called ultra-hazardous activity on his premises, the line must be drawn so as to bring him within the limit of strict liability for its consequences to all men everywhere'. More recently, Lord Sumption commented that the line of cases involving so-called 'non-delegable duties of care' imposed in response to extra-hazardous activities might need to be reconsidered; *Woodland v Essex County Council* [2014] AC 537, 573.

[60] eg the High Court of Australia considered welding to be an extra-hazardous activity in *Burnie Port Authority v General Jones Pty Limited* (1994) 179 CLR 520 but not fixing a stove in *Northern Sandblasting Pty Ltd v Harris* (1997) 188 CLR 313.

[61] Barker, 'Unreliable Assumptions in the Modern Law of Negligence' (n 55) 474.

[62] eg hiring an electrician, as in *Northern Sandblasting Pty Ltd v Harris* (1997) 188 CLR 313.

so-called 'non-delegable duty of care' is recognised. Take, for instance, the relationship between a school and a student. Where the student attends a private school, it might be possible to say that the contract for education between the student's parents and the school contains an implied promise to ensure that reasonable care of the student will be taken. In the child sexual assault cases, however, schools were found strictly liable for sexual assaults committed by some employees, but not all.[63] Similarly, an employer will not always be liable to an employee injured as a result of the negligence of an independent contractor engaged by the employer. It has never been suggested, for instance, that an employer should be liable for the negligent driving of a taxi driver engaged to transport an employee in the course of employment. An 'assumption of responsibility' cannot explain why a school or employer would be held strictly liable in one situation and not the other.

It might be that the concept of an assumption of responsibility is simply in need of refinement. John Murphy, for instance, has sought to extend the situations in which an 'assumption of responsibility' will be recognised so that an assumption of responsibility can be found not only where a defendant has undertaken to take care of a claimant, but where the defendant has created an exceptional risk by which the claimant is injured.[64] Rob Stevens has suggested the opposite and sought to restrict the situations in which an 'assumption of responsibility' can be found.[65]

Regrettably, such attempts to refine the scope of an 'assumption of responsibility' have done little more than confirm that the explanatory power of the concept is, and always has been, limited. Although both Murphy and Stevens adopt different approaches to setting the scope of an 'assumption of responsibility', the result reached by Murphy and Stevens is largely the same. For Murphy, strict liability for the tort of another can be imposed where there has been an 'assumption of responsibility' and an 'assumption of responsibility' can be found where a defendant has undertaken to care for the claimant or the defendant has created a situation of exceptional risk. For Stevens, an 'assumption of responsibility' can only be found where a defendant has undertaken to care for the claimant (expressly or impliedly), but strict liability for the tort of another can be imposed for a number of reasons, including an 'assumption of responsibility' or the creation of an 'abnormal risk' by the defendant.[66] It seems, therefore, that strict liability for the tort of another can still arise regardless of the scope of any 'assumption of responsibility' made by the defendant.

[63] See *B v Order of the Oblates of Mary Immaculate* (2005) 238 DLR (4th) 385 in which a school was found not liable for the sexual assault of a student by a baker employed by the school. Similarly, in *G(ED) v Hammer* (2003) 230 DLR (4th) 554 a school was held not to be liable for the sexual assault of a student by a janitor employed by the school. See further ch 4.

[64] Murphy, 'Juridical Foundations of Common Law Non-Delegable Duties' (n 52) 380–87.

[65] R Stevens, *Torts and Rights* (Oxford, OUP, 2007) 122. The text actually says 'where the defendant has voluntarily assumed responsibility for the defendant's care', but the second reference to defendant should presumably be a reference to the plaintiff.

[66] Ibid 331.

Nor have such refinements provided much guidance as to why the existence of an 'assumption of responsibility' is not always sufficient for strict liability for the tort of another to be imposed. Murphy has argued that for such liability to arise, it is also necessary for the courts to impose an affirmative duty on the defendant to act.[67] Murphy, however, does not attempt to explain when or why such an affirmative duty will arise. Stevens argues that the existence of an 'assumption of responsibility' will always be a 'matter of construction'; so that it might be that the defendant has qualified or somehow limited the extent of responsibility she has assumed.[68] Again, he provides little guidance as to when such a qualification might be considered to have been made.

IV. A New Expositive Framework

The framework within which strict liability for the tort of another is currently understood is flawed. The terminology with which such liability is described is vague and confusing and there is no convincing explanation as to why such liability is imposed. As a result, there is very little guidance for judges when deciding cases, creating uncertainty and inconsistency in the law.

It is therefore submitted that the existing framework for understanding strict liability for the tort of another should be abandoned. In its place, this book proposes a new expositive framework within which the liability can be understood. This framework is derived not from the labels currently used by the courts to describe the liability but from an analysis of the relationships by reason of which strict liability for the tort of another is currently imposed.

The foundations for the new expositive framework are laid down in part I of this book. Chapter 2 identifies the relationships which are thought to give rise to strict liability for the tort of another and considers whether different forms of strict liability for the tort of another arise by reason of those relationships. The chapter shows that there are only three main types of relationships which regularly give rise to strict liability for the tort of another: the employment relationship; the school relationship; and the agency relationship. Various forms of strict liability for the tort of another appear to be imposed by reason of those relationships.

Chapter 3 analyses in detail the three relationships by reason of which strict liability for the tort of another is currently imposed. It shows that authority is a common feature of all three relationships. In the employment relationship, an employer is vested with authority to direct the conduct of an employee and can exercise that authority for the employer's own benefit. In the school relationship, a school is vested with authority to direct the conduct of a student, although such authority is exercised for the benefit of the students. In the agency relationship,

[67] Murphy (n 52) 387–90.

[68] Stevens, *Torts and Rights* (n 65) 123.

a principal vests an agent with authority to effect legal relations on the principal's behalf. This feature of authority can be used to construct a new expositive framework within which strict liability for the tort of another can be understood. Different forms of strict liability for the tort of another will be shown to reflect differences in the nature of the authority present in each of the relationships which currently give rise to such liability.

Part II of this book sets out the details of the new expositive framework for strict liability for the tort of another. The framework comprises three separate forms of liability. The first form of liability is strict liability for the tort of a person upon whom authority has been conferred in relation to another or *conferred authority strict liability*. This form of strict liability is found in both the employment and school relationships and is explained in chapter 4. The basis of this liability is the authority vested in both an employer and a school to direct the conduct of an employee or a student.

The cases show that where an employer or school confers its authority to direct the conduct of an employee or student upon another person and that person commits a tort against the employee or student in the course of exercising that authority, the employer or school will be held strictly liable to the injured employee or student in respect of the tort committed by the person upon whom authority has been conferred.[69] The conferral of authority by an employer or a school is significant because it creates a power relationship between the person upon whom authority has been conferred and the employee or student which did not previously exist. This power relationship enables the person upon whom authority has been conferred to direct the conduct of an employee or student and creates an expectation that the employee or student will obey. The power relationship is therefore subject to abuse. A teacher, for instance, can use the authority conferred upon them by a school to direct a student into a private room in order to perpetrate a sexual assault.

It is submitted that it is the potential for the person upon whom authority has been conferred to abuse the power relationship created by the employer or school that attracts the concern and the intervention of the law. Conferred authority strict liability responds to this potential for abuse by holding an employer or school liable (regardless of the employer or school personally engaging in any conduct to which liability in tort might attach) whenever a person upon whom authority has been conferred by an employer or school to direct the conduct of an employee or student commits a tort against that employee or student in the course of exercising the conferred authority.

A second form of strict liability for the tort of another within the new expositive framework proposed by this book is strict liability for the tort of an employee or *employee strict liability*. This form of strict liability is limited to the employment relationship and is explained in chapter 5. The basis of this liability is the authority vested in an employer to direct the conduct of an employee which, though similar

[69] See, eg, *Wilsons & Clyde Coal Co v English* [1938] AC 57.

to that vested in a school to direct the conduct of a student, can be distinguished on the grounds that the authority vested in an employer can be exercised by the employer for the employer's own benefit.

The cases show that where an employee commits a tort against a stranger to the employment relationship whilst acting within the course of employment, the employer will be held strictly liable to the injured stranger in respect of the tort committed by the employee.[70] The authority vested in an employer to direct the conduct of an employee is significant not only because an employer can exercise that authority for its own benefit, but because failure by an employee to follow the employer's directions carries with it a potential threat of immediate disciplinary action should the employee decide not to follow the employer's directions. Due to the potential threat of immediate disciplinary action by an employer, an employee may unduly prioritise compliance with the employer's directions rather than give due weight to any alternate considerations that might reasonably lead the employee to conduct herself differently in the circumstances. It follows that the exercise of authority by an employer over an employee is subject to abuse. An employer, for instance, may direct an employee to undertake a specific number of jobs at different locations which will be difficult to perform unless the employee speeds whilst travelling between jobs, putting members of the public at risk.

It is submitted that it is the potential for an employer to abuse the authority to direct the conduct of an employee by putting an employee in a position that the employee unduly prioritises compliance with the directions of the employer that attracts the concern and the intervention of the law. Employee strict liability responds to the potential for abuse of the authority vested in an employer to direct the conduct of an employee by holding an employer liable (regardless of the employer personally engaging in any conduct to which liability in tort might attach) whenever an employee commits a tort against a stranger to the employment relationship within the course of her employment.

A third form of strict liability in tort for the harm caused by another within the new expositive framework proposed by this book is strict liability for a tort committed by an agent or *agent strict liability*. This form of strict liability is limited to the agency relationship and is explained in chapter 6. The basis of this liability is the authority vested in an agent by a principal to effect legal relations on the principal's behalf.

The cases show that where an agent commits a tort against a party wishing to effect legal relations with the principal (the *transactional party*) in the course of effecting legal relations between the principal and the transactional party, the principal will be held strictly liable to the transactional party in respect of the tort committed by the agent.[71] The vesting of authority by a principal in an agent is significant. An agent uses that authority to effect legal relations on behalf of the principal in circumstances in which the transactional party is not expected to

[70] See, eg, *Bugge v Brown* (1919) 26 CLR 110.
[71] See, eg, *Hern v Nichols* (1708) 1 Salk 289; 91 ER 256.

confirm with the principal the details of those legal relations. The authority vested in an agent by a principal to effect legal relations on the principal's behalf is therefore subject to abuse. An agent, for instance, can use the authority vested in them by a principal to misrepresent the nature of property being sold by the principal to a transactional party. It is submitted that it is the potential for an agent to abuse the authority vested in them by a principal that attracts the concern and the intervention of the law. Agent strict liability responds to this potential for abuse by holding a principal liable (regardless of the principal personally engaging in any conduct to which liability in tort might attach) whenever an agent commits a tort against a transactional party in the course of effecting legal relations between the principal and the transactional party.

By focusing on the feature of authority present in each of the relationships which give rise to strict liability for the tort of another, the new expositive framework proposed by this book presents a clearer understanding of the liability. Strict liability for the tort of another can now be seen to respond to the potential for abuse of the authority present in the relationships by reason of which the liability is imposed. Importantly, the liability operates at the relationship level. It is the *potential* for an abuse of authority to occur within a relationship which attracts the concern and intervention of the law, rather than the *actual* abuse of authority which might occur in a specific case. It follows that a defendant will not necessarily escape strict liability for the tort of another by adducing evidence that an abuse of authority did not take place.[72]

Having outlined a new expositive framework for strict liability for the tort of another, the third part of this book sets out the advantages of the framework. Chapter 7 demonstrates how the new expositive framework proposed by this book makes clear the boundaries between the different forms of strict liability for the tort of another. It can now be seen that although different forms of strict liability for the tort of another appear to arise in a single factual situation, the different forms of liability vary in scope so that the potential for overlap between the different forms of strict liability for the tort of another is actually quite limited. Employee strict liability, for instance, is limited to a tort committed by an employee within the course of her employment.[73] As a general rule, an employee is only considered to be acting within the course of her employment when she is acting in accordance with her employer's *actual* directions immediately prior to the tort occurring (whether express or implied).[74] This is because it is only when an employee is acting in accordance with her employer's actual directions that there is the potential for

[72] Though, in certain circumstances, the defendant might seek an indemnity from the other person in respect of whose tort the defendant is being held liable. See further chs 4, 5 and 6.

[73] Although in Canada the 'course of employment' requirement is now satisfied by considering the closeness of the connection between the employment and the tort (see generally *Bazley v Curry* (1999) 174 DLR (4th) 45) and in England and Wales has been replaced by the requirement for a 'close connection' (see generally *Lister v Hesley Hall Ltd* [2002] 1 AC 215). The test has been retained in Australia (see generally *Prince Alfred College v ADC* (2016) 258 CLR 134. Discussed further in ch 5.

[74] See further ch 5.

the employer to abuse its authority by putting the employee in a position that she unduly prioritises compliance with her employer's directions rather than give due weight to any alternate considerations that might reasonably lead the employee to conduct herself differently.

In contrast, conferred authority strict liability is limited to circumstances in which the person upon whom authority has been conferred by an employer or school commits a tort against the employee or student in the course of exercising the conferred authority. As a general rule, whether a person upon whom authority has been conferred by an employer or school to direct the conduct of an employee or student commits a tort against the employee or student in the course of exercising the conferred authority is determined by reference to the terms of the *apparent* authority conferred by the employer or school, as opposed to the terms of the actual authority conferred by the employer or school.[75] This is because an employee or student over whom authority has been conferred will deal with the person upon whom authority has been conferred on the basis of the terms of the apparent authority which has been conferred by the employer or school. It is the terms of the apparent authority therefore which shapes the power relationship between an employee or student and the person upon whom authority has been conferred. The difference in scope between the different forms of strict liability for the tort of another is particularly important in imposing strict liability for intentional torts.[76]

Chapter 8 demonstrates how the new expositive framework proposed by this book can be used to explain what appear to be miscellaneous examples of the liability. A partner, for instance, can be held strictly liable for a tort committed by a co-partner.[77] Under the new expositive framework, such liability can be seen as a form of agent strict liability since partners confer authority upon one another as agents to effect legal transactions on each other's behalf in order to conduct the business of the partnership. Similarly, there are cases in which a bailee has been held strictly liable for a tort committed by a person upon whom authority has been conferred by the bailee to deal with a bailor's goods.[78] Under the new expositive framework, such liability can be seen as a form of conferred authority strict liability, there being no real distinction between authority which is conferred in respect of a person or the person's goods. The only miscellaneous form of strict liability for the tort of another which does not appear to fit within the new expositive framework is the strict liability imposed on the owner of a motor vehicle for a tort committed by a person driving the vehicle for the owner's purposes.[79]

[75] See further ch 4.

[76] Notwithstanding the problematic nature of the term 'intentional torts'. See generally C Beuermann, 'Are the Torts of Trespass to the Person Obsolete? Part 1 – Historical Development' (2017) 25 *Tort Law Review* 103 and C Beuermann, 'Are the Torts of Trespass to the Person Obsolete? Part 2 – Continued Evolution' (2018) 26 *Tort Law Review* 6.

[77] Such liability, though founded in tort, is now recognised by statute. See further ch 8.

[78] See *British Road Services Ltd v Arthur V Crutchley & Co Ltd* [1968] 1 Lloyd's Rep 271. See further ch 8.

[79] See *Launchbury v Morgans* [1973] AC 127. See further ch 8.

Although the driver of a vehicle might be acting on the vehicle owner's behalf, the owner of a vehicle does not generally confer any authority upon a driver in respect of another person or her goods. Current cases indicate, however, that the courts are not as willing as they once were to impose such liability.[80]

V. Limits of the Book

This book demonstrates, for the first time, that there is a common feature to the various relationships in which the courts impose strict liability for the tort of another. On this basis, the book constructs a new expositive framework for strict liability for the tort of another which can provide judges with much needed guidance and promote certainty and consistency in the law. The outstanding question is *why* strict liability for the tort of another is imposed.

The new expositive framework shows that what attracts the concern and intervention of the law is the potential for abuse of the authority which exists in the relationships in which strict liability for the tort of another is imposed. Similar concerns can be seen elsewhere in the law. Consider the fiduciary duty. A fiduciary is in a position of power in respect of the beneficiary of the duty and, to the extent that such a position of power can be abused, is subject to enhanced responsibilities.[81] This book speculates in the final chapter as to why the law imposes strict liability for the tort of another in response to concerns about the potential for an abuse of the authority which exists in the relationships by reason of which such liability is imposed. It does so by examining more broadly the significance of a relationship between the parties to the imposition of liability in the law of torts more generally. This book does not, however, produce a full normative justification for the liability. This is a considerable project for which there is insufficient space within the scope of this book. The question though is an important one, and to this extent, the book has exposed a whole new field of inquiry.

It has been suggested that the introduction of new tests for imposing 'vicarious liability' and liability for breach of a so-called 'non-delegable duty' by the courts in England and Wales indicates that strict liability for the tort of another is 'on the move'.[82] It is significant, in this respect, that the Australian courts have so far refused to abandon the existing tests for imposing strict liability for the tort of another.[83] It is argued in the final chapter that the new tests introduced by the courts in England and Wales have resulted from confusion as to the differences between the various types of strict liability for the tort of another and that the new expositive framework proposed by this book provides the means to overcome that confusion and set the law back on track.

[80] See *Scott v Davis* (2000) 204 CLR 333.
[81] eg the no conflict rule.
[82] Lord Phillips in *Various Claimants v Catholic Child Welfare Society* [2013] 2 AC 1, [19].
[83] *Prince Alfred College Inc v ADC* (2016) 258 CLR 134.

VI. Methodology

This book was developed from an examination of cases concerning strict liability for the tort of another decided by the highest courts in primarily Australia and England and Wales. Selected cases from other jurisdictions were also considered where particularly illustrative. The book is current as at 18 October 2018 and includes cases up until the decision of the Supreme Court of the United Kingdom in *Armes v Nottinghamshire County Council*.[84]

The object in examining the cases was not necessarily to scrutinise the reasons given by judges for their decisions but to try and isolate particular factual circumstances which could better explain the decisions ultimately reached.[85] This approach was taken because judicial reasoning in respect of strict liability in tort for the harm caused by another has proved largely inadequate. As illustrated at the beginning of this chapter, such reasoning has been unable to explain either the nature or incidence of strict liability for the tort of another. The vague and confusing terminology currently used to describe strict liability for the tort of another has further obfuscated judicial reasoning.

As strict liability for the tort of another is typically discussed in the context of the relationships in which it arises,[86] this book has instead focused on examining the features of those relationships. As a result of this approach, it has been possible to discern a common feature of the relationships which currently give rise to strict liability for the tort of another. On this basis, a new expositive framework for strict liability for the tort of another has been constructed which provides a more satisfying explanation of the liability.

VII. Conclusion

Strict liability for the tort of another has proved notoriously difficult to rationalise despite wide-ranging and concerted efforts across multiple jurisdictions. For the first time, this book offers a way through the confusion. It provides a new expositive framework for the liability based on the one feature which each of the relationships which give rise to strict liability for the tort of another have in common – the feature of authority.

[84] [2018] AC 355.

[85] The only exception in this regard is ch 2, which explores the relationships within which strict liability for the tort of another was historically imposed in the context of the reasons historically given for the imposition of such liability.

[86] Cane, *The Anatomy of Tort Law* (n 20) 46–47.

PART I

Current Approach

2

Relationships which Give Rise to Strict Liability for the Tort of Another

At present, the relationships which give rise to strict liability for the tort of another are thought to be identified through use of the labels 'vicarious liability' and 'liability for breach of a non-delegable duty of care'. Typically, those relationships are as follows:

Table 1 Relationships giving rise to strict liability for the tort of another

'Liability for Breach of a Non-Delegable Duty of Care'[1]	**'Vicarious Liability'**
Employment relationship	Employment relationship
Relationship between adjoining land owners in relation to work threatening support or common walls	Agency relationship
Relationship between hospital and patient	
School relationship	
Relationship between occupier and invitee (arguably)	

Following the recent decision of the Supreme Court of the United Kingdom in *Armes v Nottinghamshire County Council*,[2] one further relationship might be added; the relationship between the state and a foster child in respect of a tort committed against the foster child by a foster carer in whose charge the foster child had been placed by the state (the *foster care relationship*). That the foster care relationship might give rise to strict liability for the tort of another was previously accepted by the New Zealand Court of Appeal,[3] but denied by the Supreme Court of Canada.[4] All lower court judges in *Armes* also denied liability.[5] Given that the possibility that the foster care relationship has only recently been recognised and a general consensus that the relationship does indeed give rise to strict liability for the tort of another has yet to be formed, the foster care relationship will not

[1] *Burnie Port Authority v General Jones Pty Limited* (1994) 179 CLR 520, 550–51.
[2] *Armes v Nottinghamshire County Council* [2018] AC 355.
[3] *S v Attorney-General* [2003] 3 NZLR 450.
[4] *KLB v British Columbia* [2003] 2 SCR 403.
[5] See generally C Beuermann, 'Up in *Armes:* The Need for a Map of Strict Liability for the Wrongdoing of another in Tort' (2018) 25(1) *Torts Law Journal* 1.

be considered in this chapter. Instead, it will be examined in chapter 4, along with the possibility that, as a relationship which is closely analogous to the school relationship, the foster care relationship might give rise to conferred authority strict liability.

Whether Table 1 correctly identifies the relationships which do give rise to strict liability for the tort of another (apart from the foster care relationship), depends upon whether the labels currently used by the courts to describe the liability are sound. As demonstrated in the previous chapter, the labels 'vicarious liability' and 'liability for breach of a non-delegable duty of care' are imprecise and their use has been problematic. It therefore cannot be assumed that the relationships set out in the Table 1 are the relationships that actually give rise to strict liability for the tort of another.

The object of this chapter is to develop a clear understanding of the relationships that do give rise to strict liability for the tort of another as that liability is *currently* imposed by the courts. To this end, this chapter will examine the liability imposed by the courts by reason of each of the above relationships using the labels 'vicarious liability' and 'liability for breach of a non-delegable duty of care'. The object of that examination is twofold. First, to determine whether each of the above relationships currently gives rise to strict liability for the tort of another and, secondly, where a relationship does give rise to strict liability for the tort of another, to determine whether the relationship attracts different forms of the liability. The chapter will demonstrate that the relationships which give rise to strict liability for the tort of another have narrowed over time. Strict liability for the tort of another now appears limited to three main types of relationships:[6] the employment relationship, the school relationship and the agency relationship. Furthermore, different forms of strict liability for the tort of another appear to be imposed by reason of those relationships.

Strict liability for the tort of another will be described throughout this chapter using existing labels. Although flawed, the use of such labels is appropriate given that the chapter describes what it is the courts currently do. In due course, the labels will be replaced with new terminology which more accurately describes the liability being imposed.

I. Employment Relationship

The labels 'vicarious liability' and 'liability for breach of a non-delegable duty of care' are both used by the courts to describe strict liability for the tort of another imposed by reason of an employment relationship.

[6] And relationships which are closely analogous.

A. 'Vicarious Liability'

There are numerous cases in which the courts have recognised that an employer might be held strictly liable for a tort committed by an employee. As early as 1691, Chief Justice Holt held in *Boson v Sandford* that:[7]

> whoever employs another is answerable for him and undertakes for his care all that make use of him.

The concept of vicarious liability can be traced to Roman law and the well-documented liability of a master for the unlawful activity of a slave.[8] In Roman law, this was because the slave was the property of the master and could therefore be viewed as an extension of the master himself. Similar reasoning underpinned the liability in Roman law of a husband for the unlawful activity of his wife and a father for the unlawful activity of a child. The Roman conception of liability for the unlawful activity of another was used by Blackstone to identify and explain the strict liability that might be imposed on a master for the tort of a servant in the *Commentaries*.[9]

Various Latin terms have been used to describe the strict liability that might be imposed on an employer for the tort of an employee. Blackstone adopted the Roman description of the liability: *qui facit per alium facit per se* ('he who acts through another does the act himself').[10] Another common descriptor commonly utilised by the courts was *respondeat superior* ('let the master answer').[11] The term 'vicarious liability' is of more recent origin, having allegedly been coined by Pollock in the 1880s.[12] The label has been used consistently by the courts since that time to describe the strict liability imposed on an employer for the tort of an employee.

B. 'Liability for Breach of a Non-Delegable Duty of Care'

In contrast to 'vicarious liability', liability imposed under the label 'liability for breach of a non-delegable duty of care' is of more recent origin.

Historically, there was very little prospect of an employee holding an employer liable in tort for harm suffered at work. This is because employees were seen as having voluntarily assumed any risks which the employee knew or should have known to be part of her job. An employee required to work with dangerous machinery, for instance, was thought to have accepted the risk of being injured by

[7] 2 Salk 440; 91 ER 382. Cited by P Giliker, *Vicarious Liability in Tort: A Comparative Perspective* (Cambridge, CUP, 2010).

[8] See generally PS Atiyah, *Vicarious Liability in the Law of Torts* (London, Butterworth & Co, 1967).

[9] W Blackstone *Commentaries on the Laws of England* (3rd ed, Clarendon Press, 1768) Vol 3, 429.

[10] Ibid 429. Presumably the source of the 'master's tort' theory of vicarious liability. See R Stevens, 'Vicarious Liability or Vicarious Action' (2007) 123 *Law Quarterly Review* 30.

[11] eg Lord Kenyon CJ in *Ellis v Turner* (1800) 8 Term Reports 531; 101 ER 1529.

[12] Ibid.

that machinery when the employee took on the position. For this reason, although a stranger to the employment relationship could use 'vicarious liability' to hold an employer strictly liable for the tort of an employee, an employee injured by the tort of a fellow employee could not. Under the doctrine of common employment, an employee was taken to have assumed the risk of being harmed by a fellow employee on entering into the employment contract.[13]

Towards the end of the nineteenth century, there was a shift away from the view that employees freely entered into and accepted all risks associated with an employment contract. Legislation was introduced in the United Kingdom to protect the interests of employees.[14] Around the same time, the courts adopted a range of measures which made it easier for an employee to sue an employer in tort.

First, the courts enumerated a number of specific duties owed by an employer to an employee. Those duties were a duty to provide a safe place of work, a duty to provide safe tools and equipment with which to work, a duty to establish a safe system of work for the employee to operate under and a duty to select competent staff.[15] An employer could be found personally liable to an employee for a breach of any of those duties which interfered with the employee's bodily integrity. A breach occurred when an employer failed to use the standard of care that a reasonable employer might have used in fulfilling those duties.

Secondly, in *Smith v Baker*[16] the House of Lords substantially weakened the idea that an employee could be taken to have voluntarily assumed the risks of employment. In that case, an employee who worked in a quarry was injured when a rock being manoeuvred overhead by a crane dropped and fell on him. The employer argued that no liability arose because the employee accepted such risks when agreeing to work in a quarry. The House of Lords held, however, that the employer was liable. The work the employee agreed to do was not so inherently dangerous that the employee could be taken to have accepted such risks when entering into the employment. The work only became dangerous because the employee was required to work beneath a negligently operated crane. This was a specific risk which the employee could not be taken to have consented to simply by entering into and remaining in his employment.

Finally, and for present purposes most relevantly, the courts designated the specifically enumerated duties of care owed by an employer to an employee as 'non-delegable'. In so doing, the courts were able to side-step the doctrine of common employment which prevented an employee from using so-called 'vicarious liability' to hold an employer liable for the tort of a fellow employee. This was achieved by holding the employer liable for a breach of its own, so-called 'personal' duty of care, as opposed to holding the employer 'vicariously liable' for

[13] JG Fleming, *The Law of Torts* (9th ed, Sydney, Law Book Company, 1998) 570–71.

[14] See Employers' Liability Act 1880 (UK) c 1036. See also Workmen's Compensation Act 1897 (UK) c 37. See generally Fleming ibid, ch 10.

[15] *Wilsons & Clyde Coal Co v English* [1938] AC 57.

[16] [1891] AC 325.

the tort of the employee.[17] The House of Lords decision in *Wilsons & Clyde Coal Company Limited v English*[18] provides a good example. In that case the employer coal company had delegated the responsibility of devising a safe system for the operation of the mine to the mine manager, being required to do so by statute.[19] When an employee was later injured as a result of the system of work initiated by the mine manager being negligently devised, the employer was held liable to the employee. The House of Lords held that the implementation of the negligently devised system by the mine manager was a breach of the employer's own duty to provide a safe system of work. Such liability arose even though what is currently called 'vicarious liability' could not be imposed on the employer in respect of the negligence of the mine manager due to the doctrine of common employment.

Viewed in its historical context, the so-called 'non-delegable duty of care' owed by an employer to an employee appears to have been recognised as part of a concerted effort to increase the responsibility of employers to employees. More specifically, it was used as a device by the courts to overcome the problematic doctrine of common employment. The difficulties presented by the doctrine of common employment have since been addressed more directly with the doctrine being abolished by statute in England and Wales and a number of Australian states.[20]

C. Does the Employment Relationship Currently Give Rise to Strict Liability for the Tort of Another?

There is very little doubt that the liability currently imposed by the courts by reason of an employment relationship using the label 'vicarious liability' is a form of strict liability for the tort of another. Such liability is imposed on an employer as a matter of course where an employee commits a tort within the course of employment.[21] No evidence of the employer personally engaging in any conduct to which liability in tort might attach need be adduced for such liability to be imposed.

Whether strict liability for the tort of another is imposed by reason of an employment relationship using the label 'liability for breach of a non-delegable duty of care' is not so clear. This is because the so-called 'non-delegable duty of care' has historically been described as a 'personal' duty. This can be seen in the judgment of Lord Wright in *Wilsons*:[22]

> What is the extent of the duty attaching to the employer? Such a duty is the employer's personal duty, whether he performs or can perform it himself, or whether he does not perform it or cannot perform it save by servants or agents. A failure to perform such a duty is the employer's personal negligence.

[17] *Kondis v State Transport Authority* (1984) 154 CLR 672, 678–79.
[18] [1938] AC 57 ('*Wilsons*').
[19] Coal Mines Act 1911 (UK) c 50.
[20] Fleming, *The Law of Torts* (n 13) 570 (fn 102).
[21] Issues as how the scope of employment is determined will be addressed in ch 5.
[22] [1938] AC 57, 83–84.

The so-called 'non-delegable duty of care' was most likely described in such terms to avoid the appearance that courts were simply side-stepping the doctrine of common employment by finding yet another way to hold an employer strictly liable for the tort of an employee.[23]

The use of the word 'personal' to describe the so-called 'non-delegable duty' has tended to confuse the nature of the liability imposed in the event of a breach. For genuine personal liability to be imposed on an employer for breach of a so-called 'non-delegable duty', it must be shown that the employer personally failed to take reasonable measures for the safety of the employee and that such measures would have prevented the employee from being injured. Such a failure would have to be clearly established by the evidence and pleaded in the case. There are numerous cases, however, where no such liability has been established. Instead, it appears that proof of a tort committed by some other person was sufficient for the liability of the employer to be established, as was the case in *Wilsons* itself.

Consider the decision of the High Court of Australia in *Kondis v State Rail Authority*.[24] In that case an employee was injured as a result of the negligence of the operator of a crane hired by the employer to dismantle a structure on the employer's property. No evidence of the employer personally engaging in any conduct to which liability in tort might attach was adduced. Despite the absence of such evidence, the employer was found to have breached the so-called 'non-delegable duty' owed to the employee. In the circumstances of the case, the employer's liability can only be described as a form of strict liability for the tort of another. Evidence of the tort of the crane operator was sufficient for liability to be imposed on the employer under the label 'liability for breach of the non-delegable duty of care'.

The House of Lords decision in *McDermid v Nash Dredging & Reclamation Company Limited*[25] provides another example of strict liability for the tort of another being imposed on an employer using the label 'liability for breach of a non-delegable duty of care'. In that case, the employee had been directed by his employer to work with the employer's parent company and was injured whilst untying a ship from a dredger as a result of negligent directions given by the ship's captain. Once again, no evidence of the employer personally engaging in any conduct to which liability in tort might attach was adduced; evidence of the tort committed by the ship's captain was sufficient for liability to be imposed.

Cases such as *Kondis* and *McDermid* indicate that the courts do impose strict liability for the tort of another by reason of an employment relationship using the label 'liability for breach of a non-delegable duty of care'. As both cases are relatively recent (decided in the 1980s), they also indicate a willingness on behalf of the courts to continue to impose such liability. The cases also confirm that there is more than one form of strict liability for the tort of another which the courts impose by reason of an employment relationship, since neither the liability imposed in

[23] See section I.B above.
[24] (1984) 154 CLR 672 ('*Kondis*').
[25] [1987] AC 906 ('*McDermid*').

either *Kondis* nor *McDermid* can be described as what is currently called 'vicarious liability'. In *Kondis*, the crane operator was the employee of an independent contractor for whom the defendant employer could not be held 'vicariously liable'. In *McDermid*, the defendant employer was held liable to the injured employee even though the captain who gave the negligent directions was employed by the defendant employer's parent company and was, again, not a person for whom the defendant employer could be held 'vicariously liable'. It follows that the employment relationship is not only a relationship which currently gives rise to strict liability for the tort of another, but is a relationship which appears to attract two different forms of the liability.

II. Relationship between Adjoining Land Owners in Relation to Work Threatening Support or Common Walls

The label 'liability for breach of a non-delegable duty of care' is not only used by the courts to describe liability imposed by reason of an employment relationship, but is also used to describe liability imposed by reason of the relationship between adjoining land owners in relation to work threatening support or common walls (the *relationship between adjoining land owners*).

A. 'Liability for Breach of a Non-Delegable Duty of Care'

The so-called 'non-delegable duty of care' owed by adjoining land owners in relation to work threatening support or common walls was first recognised in *Bower v Peate*.[26] The case concerned a defendant land owner who had engaged a building contractor to demolish an existing house and construct a new one. The foundations for the new house were excavated to a level beneath those of the foundations of the building on the adjoining property. As a result of the building contractor failing to adequately underpin the foundations of the building, the building was damaged. The owner of the adjoining property succeeded in suing the defendant land owner to recover his loss. The court held that the defendant land owner could not 'relieve himself of his responsibility'[27] for the construction by engaging someone else to do the work.

The decision in *Bower v Peate* was approved by the House of Lords in *Dalton v Angus*,[28] a case also concerning damage to an adjoining property caused by a building contractor failing to adequately underpin building foundations. In *Hughes v Percival*,[29] the House of Lords extended the liability of a defendant land owner to

[26] [1876] LR 1 QBD 321.
[27] Ibid.
[28] (1881) 6 App Cas 740.
[29] (1883) 8 App Cas 443.

cover damage caused by the negligence of a building contractor to a common wall shared with an adjoining land owner. The duty owed by the defendant land owner was described as one that the land owner 'could not get rid of responsibility [for] by delegating the performance of it to a third person'.[30]

To understand what led the courts to recognise the so-called 'non-delegable duty of care' owed by adjoining land owners in relation to work threatening support or common walls, it is necessary to examine the legal context in which the duty was established. When *Bower v Peate* was decided in 1876, negligence was in its formative stages. A duty of care had been recognised in respect of the 'common callings', and the language of 'duty' and 'reasonableness' was starting to be applied to other situations. It was therefore open to the courts to find that a defendant land owner owed a duty to use reasonable care when carrying out construction work.[31] Such a duty might have been breached, for instance, by the defendant land owner failing to adequately supervise the construction work or failing to put in place appropriate systems to enable the construction work to be undertaken safely. Any liability imposed for breach of such a duty would have been personal in nature, only being imposed once evidence of the personal failure of the defendant land owner to conduct themselves reasonably had been adduced. Such an approach would have been in keeping with the general rule that a person could not be held liable for the tort of an independent contractor, which was well established by that time.[32]

Liability for breach of a duty to use reasonable care was not, however, the only type of liability that could be imposed on a defendant land owner in 1876 in relation to work threatening support or common walls of adjoining properties.[33] Where buildings had been in place for a period of at least 20 years, for instance, a defendant land owner could be held liable for removing an adjoining land owner's 'right of support'[34] whether or not the defendant land owner was personally responsible for removing the support.[35] A defendant land owner could also be held liable for private nuisance on the basis that the material damage caused by the construction work commissioned by the defendant land owner constituted an unreasonable use of land.[36] As with liability for removing a 'right of support', it was sufficient for such liability to be imposed to show that damage had been caused by the construction work without it being necessary to show that the defendant land owner had personally caused that damage.

[30] *Hughes v Percival* (1883) 8 App Cas 443 (Lord Blackburn).

[31] Ibid 449 (Lord Watson): 'I agree with your Lordships that it was the duty of the appellant in carrying out his building operations to see that reasonable precautions were taken in order to protect from injury the eastern wall of his tenement, of which the respondent was part owner'.

[32] *Quarman v Burnett* (1840) 6 M&W 499; 151 ER 509.

[33] See Fleming (n 13) 367–68. See also JR Spencer, 'Motor-cars and the Rule in *Rylands* v *Fletcher*: a Chapter of Accidents in the History of Law and Motoring' (1983) 42 *Cambridge Law Journal* 65.

[34] This 'right of support' was acquired by prescription. See *Dalton v Angus* (1881) 6 App Cas 740.

[35] Ibid.

[36] *St Helen's Smelting Co v Tipping* (1865) 11 HL Cas 642.

The court in *Bower v Peate* was consequently faced with a confusion of legal principles and the difficulty of determining which set of legal principles to apply to the facts of the case. For guidance on how to resolve this problem, the judges looked to the earlier decision of *Pickard v Smith*.[37] In that case, the court had faced a similar confusion of legal principles in deciding whether the lessee of a coal cellar at a railway station could be held liable to a passer-by who fell into the coal cellar through a trapdoor which had been left open and unguarded by a coal merchant delivering coal to the lessee. At the time *Pickard v Smith* was decided, there were cases to say that an occupier owed a duty to use reasonable care to guard or fence hazards on her premises and could be held liable when the occupier's failure to do so caused personal injury.[38] Such liability was accompanied by the general rule that no liability could arise for the negligence of an independent contractor. But there were also cases which said that where a failure to guard or fence hazards amounted to a public nuisance, the occupier could be held liable even if the occupier had engaged an independent contractor to rectify the nuisance and the independent contractor had negligently failed to do so.

The court in *Pickard v Smith* resolved the confusion of legal principles by recognising a so-called 'non-delegable duty of care'.[39] That the court was concerned with reconciling different legal principles in recognising this 'non-delegable duty' can be seen in the judgment of Williams J:[40]

> the defendant became the occupier of the cellar and hold subject to the use of the platform overhead by passengers, and he knew that it would be so used, and he knew that the hole with the door open would be in effect a trap to catch such passengers. It was his obvious duty, therefore, if he used the hole in a way necessarily to create such danger, to take reasonable precautions not to injure persons lawfully using the platform; *sic utere tuo ut alienum non laedas*. No sound distinction in this respect can be drawn between the case of a public highway and a road which may be and to the knowledge of the wrongdoer probably will in fact be used by persons lawfully entitled so to do.

As *Pickard v Smith*[41] was the main authority relied upon by the court in *Bower v Peate*, the 'non-delegable duty of care' in *Bower v Peate* appears to have been recognised for similar reasons. The court was faced with a confusion of legal principles and was looking for a way to rationalise the law. Recognising a so-called 'non-delegable duty' provided the court with the means to do this. It enabled the court to follow established cases without detracting from the developing law of negligence.

[37] (1861) 1 CB (NS) 470.

[38] These cases involved defendant land owners who had been held liable for failing to take reasonable steps to guard or fence a variety of hazards such as coal chutes, trapdoors and other openings on their property into which unsuspecting plaintiffs had fallen. See *Southcote v Stanley* (1856) 1 Hurlstone and Norman 247; 156 ER 1195.

[39] See generally FH Newark, 'The Boundaries of Nuisance' (1949) 64 *Law Quarterly Review* 480.

[40] *Pickard v Smith* (1861) 1 CB (NS) 470, 479.

[41] *Pickard v Smith* has now been credited as the 'source of the concept of the non-delegable duty as applied to a common law duty of care'; *Kondis v State Transport Authority* (1984) 154 CLR 672, 684 (Mason J).

B. Does the Relationship between Adjoining Owners of Land in Relation to Work Threatening Support or Common Walls Give Rise to Strict Liability for the Tort of Another?

There is little doubt that the liability originally imposed by the courts for breach of the so-called 'non-delegable duty of care' owed by adjoining land owners in relation to work threatening support or common walls was a form of strict liability for the tort of another. In cases such as *Bower v Peate*, once evidence of a tort being committed by the building contractor was adduced there was generally no further investigation into whether the defendant land owner had personally engaged in any conduct to which liability in tort might attach. Commission of a tort by the building contractor was therefore sufficient for the liability of the defendant land owner to be established. This can be seen from the following passage in *Bower v Peate*:[42]

> there is, on the other hand, good ground for holding him liable … *no matter through whose default* the omission to take the necessary measures for such prevention may arise.

Although strict liability for the tort of another was originally imposed for breach of the so-called 'non-delegable duty of care' owed by adjoining land owners, it does not necessarily follow that modern courts are similarly willing to impose such liability. For a number of reasons, it now appears unlikely that a defendant land owner will be held strictly liable for the tort of a building contractor in relation to work threatening the support or common walls of an adjoining land owner.

First, there has only been one higher court decision in either Australia or England and Wales since the end of the nineteenth century to consider the so-called 'non-delegable duty' owed by adjoining land owners and in that case the court refused to impose strict liability on the defendant land owner for the tort of the building contractor. In *Stoneman v Lyons*,[43] the High Court of Australia reviewed the reasons why strict liability for the tort of a building contractor might be imposed on the defendant land owner and, finding those reasons unacceptable, decided to apply instead the general rule that a person cannot be held strictly liable for the tort of an independent contractor (as opposed to the tort of an employee).[44]

The facts of *Stoneman v Lyons* are very similar to those that were before the court in *Bower v Peate*. The defendant land owner had engaged a building contractor to construct a supermarket on his land. In the process of digging foundation trenches for the supermarket, the building contractor failed to take appropriate measures to underpin the foundations of the building on the adjoining property. After a night of heavy rain, the wall of the building on the adjoining

[42] (1876) LR 1 QBD 321, 327 (emphasis added).
[43] (1975) 133 CLR 550.
[44] *Quarman v Burnett* (1840) 6 M&W 499; 151 ER 509.

property closest to the foundation trenches collapsed and the owner of the adjoining property sued the defendant land owner to recover his loss. No negligence on the part of the defendant land owner was established.

After reviewing previous cases, the High Court identified two possible reasons why a defendant land owner might be held strictly liable for the tort of a building contractor in relation to work threatening the support or common walls of an adjoining land owner. The first was that the construction work undertaken by the defendant land owner might be considered an extra-hazardous activity. In *Bower v Peate*, Cockburn CJ said:[45]

> a man who orders a work to be executed, from which, in the natural course of things, injurious consequences to his neighbour must be expected to arise, unless means are adopted by which such consequences may be prevented, is bound to see to the doing of that which is necessary to prevent the mischief, and cannot relieve himself of his responsibility by employing someone else – whether it be the contractor employed to do the work from which the danger arises or some independent person – to do what is necessary to prevent the act he has ordered to be done from becoming wrongful.

The High Court was not convinced, however, that the undertaking of 'extra-hazardous' activities was a sufficient basis upon which to impose strict liability on a defendant land owner for the tort of a building contractor. Although such a principle had received some support in the lower courts,[46] the principle had not yet been recognised by the High Court of Australia[47] and the House of Lords had strongly disapproved of the principle in *Read v J Lyons & Co.*[48] Even if such a principle could be found (and the High Court did not ultimately decide this question), a majority of the High Court decided that the construction of a shopping centre could not be considered an extra-hazardous activity so that the defendant land owner in *Stoneman v Lyons* could not be held strictly liable for the tort of the building contractor on that basis.[49] The Supreme Court of the United Kingdom has recently reiterated the concern about whether the undertaking of 'extra-hazardous' activities is sufficient to impose strict liability for the tort of another in *Woodland v Essex County Council.*[50]

A second reason identified by the High Court of Australia as to why a defendant land owner might be held strictly liable for the tort of a building contractor in

[45] (1876) LR 1 QBD 321, 326.

[46] See *Honeywill & Stein Ltd v Larkin Bros (London's Commercial Photographers) Ltd* [1934] 1 KB 191.

[47] The High Court of Australia had previously refrained from ruling on the existence of the principle in *Torette House Pty Ltd v Berkman* (1940) 62 CLR 637.

[48] [1947] AC 156, 181–82 (Lord Simonds): 'and I would reject the idea that, if a man carries on a so-called ultra-hazardous activity on his premises, the line must be drawn so as to bring him within the limit of strict liability for its consequences to all mean everywhere'. See also *Biffa Waste Services Ltd v Maschinenfabrik Ernst Hese GmbH* [2009] QB 725.

[49] (1975) 133 CLR 550, 575 (Mason J with whom both Barwick CJ and Gibbs J agreed): 'it would be wrong to classify the demolition and erection of a building (necessarily involving an excavation) in immediate proximity to the wall of an adjoining building as an extra-hazardous act'. Stephen J made a comment to a similar effect at 566.

[50] [2014] AC 537, 573.

relation to work threatening the support or common walls of an adjoining land owner was the possibility that the adjoining land owner had acquired a right of support by prescription after 20 years of uninterrupted use.[51] This was a much more limited basis by which to explain any strict liability which had been imposed on adjoining land owners as such liability could only arise after buildings on the adjoining land owner's property had been in existence for longer than 20 years.

Although the existence of a right of support was not pleaded in *Stoneman v Lyons*, Stephen J considered and rejected the possibility that the existence of a right of support justified the imposition of strict liability on a defendant land owner for the tort of a building contractor. In his view, such a rule was 'clearly ill-adapted to conditions in modern cities'[52] and the liability of a defendant land owner when undertaking construction work on her property was instead governed by the tort of negligence.[53] It followed that a defendant land owner had a duty to undertake any such construction work with reasonable care and could not 'excavate up to his own boundary regardless of the effect upon his neighbour's building' even if the building had been in existence for less than 20 years.[54]

The only other judge to consider whether a right of support could be used as a basis for imposing strict liability on a defendant land owner for the tort of a building contractor in relation to work threatening the support or common walls of an adjoining land owner was Mason J. He did not discuss the issue in any detail but commented that:[55]

> The respondents pointed to cases in which a landowner has been held to be subject to a higher duty than that imposed by the ordinary duty of care. However, they are cases … in which the defendant infringed the plaintiff's rights by interfering with his right of support (*Bower* v *Peate*; *Dalton* v *Angus*) or by interfering with a party wall (*Hughes* v *Percival*). In each case it may be seen that the defendant was in breach of a duty which he owed to the plaintiff.

Although this rather ambiguous statement might indicate that Mason J considered that strict liability could be imposed on a defendant land owner for the tort of a building contractor on the basis of the adjoining land owner's right of support, it is submitted that this is unlikely in light of his subsequent judgment in *Kondis v State Rail Authority*.[56] In that case, Mason J sought to explain all categories of so-called 'non-delegable duties' (including that owed by adjoining land owners) on the basis that the holder of the so-called 'non-delegable duty' had 'assumed responsibility'

[51] *Dalton v Angus* (1881) 6 App Cas 740. The High Court of Australia had also affirmed the existence of a right of support by prescription in *Delohery v Permanent Trustee Co of New South Wales Ltd* (1904) 1 CLR 283, notwithstanding the existence of the Torrens land system in Australia.

[52] (1975) 133 CLR 550, 567.

[53] A view now confirmed by the statutory abolition of rights of support in many Australian states. See F Burns, 'The Future of Prescriptive Easements in Australia and England' (2007) 31 *Melbourne University Law Review* 3.

[54] (1975) 133 CLR 550, 567.

[55] *Stoneman v Lyons* (1975) 133 CLR 550, 575–76.

[56] (1984) 154 CLR 672.

for the safety or care of the beneficiary of the duty. If Mason J was stating in *Stoneman v Lyons* that a defendant land owner could be held strictly liable for the tort of a building contractor because of an adjoining land owner's right of support, it would follow that he somehow thought that a defendant land owner 'assumed responsibility' to an adjoining land owner for the safety of a building where that building had been in place for 21 years but did not 'assume responsibility' to an adjoining land owner for a building that had only been in existence for 19 years. This would be somewhat surprising given the arbitrariness of the 20-year period.

In addition to the refusal of the High Court of Australia in *Stoneman v Lyons* to impose strict liability on a defendant land owner for the tort of a building contractor in relation to work threatening the support or common walls of an adjoining land owner, recent developments in the tort of private nuisance also make it unlikely that modern courts will impose strict liability for the tort of another for breach of the so-called 'non-delegable duty of care' owed by adjoining land owners. When the so-called 'non-delegable duty of care' owed by adjoining land owners was first recognised, liability for private nuisance was imposed as a general rule regardless of whether the defendant land owner had acted reasonably. As previously noted, such liability was at odds with the developing tort of negligence which required proof of the defendant's personal failure to act with reasonable care to be adduced for liability to be imposed. More recently, however, the courts have been restricting liability in nuisance to circumstances in which a claimant can adduce evidence of some sort of personal conduct by the defendant to which liability in tort might attach. For instance, a defendant land owner who neither creates nor continues a nuisance emanating from her land cannot be held liable for that nuisance unless the defendant land owner otherwise failed to act reasonably.[57] This covers the situation in cases such as *Bower v Peate*. It follows that a defendant land owner cannot be held liable for a private nuisance created by a building contractor unless it can be shown that the defendant land owner directly authorised the conduct constituting the tort or was somehow aware of the problems with the construction work and failed to take reasonable steps to protect the adjoining property from damage. This change in the nature of the liability imposed for private nuisance removes the conflict which originally existed between the tort of private nuisance and the tort of negligence. The original reason for imposing strict liability for the tort of another for breach of the so-called 'non-delegable duty of care' owed by adjoining land owners consequently no longer exists.

The consistent refusal of the courts to hold an occupier strictly liable for the tort of an independent contractor more generally provides another reason why it is unlikely that modern courts will impose strict liability for the tort of another for breach of the so-called 'non-delegable duty of care' owed by adjoining land owners. In *Torette House Pty Ltd v Berkman*,[58] the High Court of Australia refused

[57] See *Sedeigh-Denfield v O'Callaghan* [1940] AC 880.
[58] (1940) 62 CLR 637.

to hold the defendant land owner liable for damage caused to an adjoining property which was flooded when a plumber engaged by the defendant land owner negligently turned on a stopcock. Similarly, in *Northern Sandblasting Pty Limited v Harris*[59] the High Court refused to hold the defendant landlord liable to the daughter of a tenant who was electrocuted when an electrician engaged by the landlord negligently repaired a stove. In light of such cases, it is not clear that there is anything particularly special about a building contractor which can justify continuing to hold a defendant land owner strictly liable for the tort of a building contractor in relation to work threatening the support or common walls of an adjoining land owner, but not liable in relation to damage caused to an adjoining land owner by other types of contractors engaged by the defendant. At the very least, such a feature has yet to be identified by the courts.

The only exception in this regard appears to be the decision of the High Court of Australia in *Burnie Port Authority v General Jones Limited*,[60] where the defendant land owner was held liable to the owner of an adjoining property destroyed by fire due to the negligence of a welder engaged by the defendant land owner. The liability of the defendant land owner in that case was, however, determined in accordance with ordinary negligence principles[61] and can be viewed as personal liability since the defendant land owner was aware that the welder would be welding in the vicinity of highly flammable material and took no steps to reduce the foreseeable risk of harm to the adjoining property.[62]

A final reason it is now unlikely that moderns courts will impose strict liability for the tort of another for breach of the so-called 'non-delegable duty of care' owed by adjoining land owners is the increased regulation of construction projects by government. Since *Bower v Peate* was decided, a variety of different regulatory regimes have been instituted, each of which place varying degrees of responsibility upon a defendant land owner for damage to an adjoining property. As a result, there is no clear policy direction provided by legislatures justifying the continued imposition of strict liability for the tort of another on a defendant land owner for the tort of a building contractor in relation to work threatening the support or common walls or an adjoining land owner. In England and Wales, for instance, the Party Wall etc Act 1996 gives land owners certain rights to perform work on party

[59] (1995–97) 188 CLR 313.

[60] (1994) 179 CLR 520.

[61] Ibid 560.

[62] Ibid 559 (Mason CJ, Deane, Dawson, Toohey and Gaudron JJ): 'In the present case, the particular qualities of EPS made the stacked cardboard containers of Isolite in the roof area of the Authority's premises a dangerous substance in the sense that, if one of the cardboard containers were accidentally set alight, an uncontrollable conflagration would almost inevitably result. Clearly, the introduction of more than twenty of those cardboard containers called for special precautions to be taken to avoid any risk of that happening. A fortiori, the carrying out of welding activities in the premises within which the cardboard containers of Isolate were stacked was itself a dangerous activity in that it was reasonably foreseeable that, unless special precautions were taken, sparks or molten metal might fall upon one of the containers and set the cardboard alight. As has been seen, the evidence established that the Authority (through one of its employees) was aware that the cardboard containers of Isolite were being stored in the roof area near where welding work was to be carried out by W&S'.

walls but in exchange for these rights makes the land owner liable for damage to the owner of an adjoining property which is caused by such work.[63] This liability appears to arise whether the damage is caused by the negligence of the land owner or an independent contractor engaged by the land owner. In contrast, the Conveyancing Act 1919 in New South Wales acknowledges the existence of a general right of support but imposes on land owners an ordinary duty of care not to interfere with that right of support so that it is unlikely that a land owner could be held liable for the negligence of an independent contractor under the section.[64] A compromise position is reached by the Building Act 1993 in Victoria under which land owners are permitted in certain circumstances to undertake construction work in the vicinity of the foundations or a party wall shared with an adjoining property but only after the land owner has first taken out insurance which will cover the owner of the adjoining property in the event of any damage.[65]

As can be seen, there are a number of reasons why modern courts are unlikely to impose strict liability for the tort of another for breach of the so-called 'non-delegable duty of care' owed by adjoining land owners. The most telling is the fact that no higher court in Australia or England and Wales has imposed such liability since the end of the nineteenth century, although the other reasons go some way to explaining why this has occurred. It therefore appears unlikely that the relationship between adjoining land owners in relation to work threatening support or common walls is any longer a relationship that gives rise to strict liability for the tort of another.

III. Relationship between Hospital and Patient

As with the relationship between adjoining owners of land in relation to work threatening support or common walls, the label 'liability for breach of a non-delegable duty of care' has been used to describe liability imposed by reason of the relationship between hospital and patient (the *hospital relationship*). The so-called 'non-delegable duty of care' owed by a hospital to a patient was recognised much later than in either the employment relationship or the relationship between adjoining land owners and is typically traced to a trilogy of cases decided by the England and Wales Court of Appeal in the middle of the twentieth century.

A. 'Liability for Breach of a Non-Delegable Duty of Care'

The first suggestion that the duty of care owed by hospital to patient was 'non-delegable' is found in the judgment of Lord Greene MR in *Gold v Essex County*

63 Party Wall etc Act 1996 (UK) c 40, s 7(2).
64 Conveyancing Act 1919 (NSW), s 177.
65 Building Act 1993 (Vic) s 93.

Council.[66] In that case, a five-year-old girl required treatment for warts on her face. On attending at the hospital, she was seen by a visiting dermatologist who suggested the warts be treated by the application of Grenz rays. She was then sent to the radiology department where she was treated by a competent radiologist employed by the hospital. On the sixth treatment, the radiologist forgot to cover the unaffected parts of the young girl's face with a protective, lead-lined rubber cloth. As a result, the girl's face was 'permanently disfigured'.[67]

Had *Gold* been decided today, the case would have been relatively straightforward. What is currently called 'vicarious liability' would have been imposed as a matter of course once it was established that the radiologist was an employee of the hospital and was acting in the course of his employment at the time the negligence occurred. At the time *Gold* was decided, however, there was some doubt as to whether a hospital could be held 'vicariously liable' for the negligence of a doctor or other any other medical practitioner employed by the hospital. Medical practitioners were not thought of as 'servants in the proper sense of the word'.[68] This was because a hospital could not control a medical practitioner in the performance of her duties due to her special skill and knowledge. As Farwell LJ commented in *Hillyer v The Governors of St. Bartholomew's Hospital*:[69]

> This is … essential to the success of operations; no surgeon would undertake the responsibility of operations if his orders and directions were subject to the control of or interference by the governing body.

Faced with these difficulties, Lord Greene MR held in *Gold* that the duty of care owed by the hospital to the patient was 'non-delegable'. He argued that, as the hospital had undertaken to care for the patient, the hospital could not escape liability for negligence in the course of that care by delegating that care to another person (in that case, the radiologist).[70] In his view, because the hospital had 'assumed responsibility' for the care of the patient, it followed that the hospital was liable to the patient for the negligence of the radiologist whether or not the radiologist was an employee.[71]

The other two members of the court, however, chose to deal with the issue much more directly. Lord Justice MacKinnon did not accept the views expressed in *Hillyer* and held that what is currently called 'vicarious liability' could be imposed on an employer for the negligence of an employee even if that employee was a medical practitioner and exercised skill beyond the control of the employer. Lord Justice MacKinnon said:[72]

> (1) One who employs a servant is liable to another person if the servant does an act within the scope of his employment so negligently as to injure that other … (2) That

[66] [1942] 2 KB 293 ('*Gold*').
[67] Ibid 294.
[68] *Hillyer v The Governors of St. Bartholomew's Hospital* [1909] 2 KB 820, 825 (Farwell LJ).
[69] Ibid 826.
[70] *Gold v Essex County Council* [1942] 2 KB 293, 301.
[71] Ibid 303.
[72] Ibid 304–05.

> principle applies even though the work which the servant is employed to do is of a skilful or technical character as to the method of performing which the employer is himself ignorant, for example, a shipowner and the certified captain who navigates the ship.

Lord Justice Goddard also suggested that whether or not a hospital could be held strictly liable for the negligence of a medical practitioner depended on whether the medical practitioner was employed under a contract *of* service as opposed to a contract *for* service.[73] Consequently, both MacKinnon LJ and Goddard LJ imposed what is currently called 'vicarious liability' on the hospital in *Gold* following a straightforward application of 'vicarious liability' principles; the radiologist was an employee who had been negligent in the course of his employment.

The question of whether the duty of care owed by a hospital to a patient could be considered 'non-delegable' was next considered by the England and Wales Court of Appeal in *Cassidy v Ministry of Health*.[74] In that case, the patient was a general labourer who had been admitted to hospital for a procedure on his hand. The procedure involved keeping the patient's hand in a rigid splint for 14 days. On removal of the splint at the end of the period, the patient was unable to use his fingers. Subsequent treatment did not lead to any improvement and the patient effectively lost the use of the hand. Although the patient faced evidential difficulties in identifying the actual cause of his problems, the court was prepared to rely on the *res ipsa loquitur* doctrine and all judges found the hospital liable to the patient. Lord Justice Somervell and Singleton LJ based their decision on the fact that all the medical practitioners involved in the treatment of the patient at the hospital were employees of the hospital. As a result, what is currently called 'vicarious liability' was imposed on the hospital in accordance with ordinary principles.[75]

In contrast, Denning LJ persisted with Lord Greene MR's view in *Gold* that a hospital owed a patient a so-called 'non-delegable duty of care'. Lord Justice Denning said:[76]

> I take it to be clear law as well as good sense, that, where a person is himself under a duty to use care, he cannot get rid of his responsibility by delegating the performance of it to someone else, no matter whether the delegation be to a servant under a contract of service or to an independent contractor under a contract for services.

On the facts of the case, that duty had been breached as a result of the negligence of the hospital's employees. It was therefore not necessary to recognise a so-called 'non-delegable duty' and no such duty was recognised by the other judges.

[73] Ibid 313 (Goddard LJ): 'Hospital managers, be they local authorities or governors of voluntary institutions, nowadays have in their service many specialists – solicitors, accountants, engineers, electricians and the like. I can see no sound reason why they should be responsible for the acts of these servants and not for those of nurses who are equally in their service. That they are not liable for the doctor's negligence is due simply and solely to the fact that he is not their servant. I desire, however, to say that for the purpose of this judgment I am not considering the case of doctors on the permanent staff of the hospital. Whether the authority would be liable for their negligence depends, in my opinion, on whether there is a contract of service and that must depend on the facts of any particular case'.

[74] [1951] 2 KB 343 ('*Cassidy*').

[75] Ibid (Somervell LJ) 351 and (Singleton LJ) 354–55.

[76] Ibid 363.

Lord Justice Denning once again resorted to the idea that the duty of care owed by a hospital to a patient was 'non-delegable' in *Roe v Minister of Health*.[77] In that case the hospital was found not liable to the patient. This was because all members of the court found that the medical practitioners in question had not been negligent. If the medical practitioners had been negligent though, it is not entirely clear that the other members of the court would have been prepared to find that the duty of care owed by the hospital to the patient was 'non-delegable'. Lord Justice Somervell was of the view that what is currently called 'vicarious liability' could have been imposed on the basis that the medical practitioners were employed by the hospital and were acting in the course of their employment at the relevant time.[78] Lord Justice Morris quoted extensively from the judgment of Lord Greene MR in *Gold*, but he also found the medical practitioners in question to be employees.[79]

It is very difficult from an analysis of *Gold*, *Cassidy* and *Roe* to say that the courts actually recognised a so-called 'non-delegable duty of care' within the hospital relationship. The supposedly 'non-delegable' nature of the duty established in those cases was at best the view of a few minority judges, with the remaining judges using what is currently called 'vicarious liability' as the basis for their decision. Despite this, the High Court of Australia has suggested in dicta on at least two occasions that the duty of care owed by a hospital to a patient is 'non-delegable'.[80] Similar comments have been made by the House of Lords[81] and the Supreme Court of the United Kingdom[82] and there are also a handful of lower court cases in which a hospital has been found to be in breach of such a duty.[83] Consequently, it appears to have been assumed that hospitals owe patients a so-called 'non-delegable duty of care', although the basis of this assumption is not particularly convincing.

B. Does the Relationship between Hospital and Patient Give Rise to Strict Liability for the Tort of Another?[84]

The difficulties in determining whether hospitals owe patients a so-called 'non-delegable duty of care' have translated into difficulties in determining the nature of the liability imposed in the event of a breach. The cases suggest that it was at least envisaged that strict liability for the tort of another should be able to be imposed

[77] [1954] 2 QB 67 ('*Roe*').

[78] Ibid 79–80.

[79] Ibid 88.

[80] See *Kondis v State Transport Authority* (1984) 154 CLR 672, 685 and *Burnie Port Authority v General Jones Pty Limited* (1994) 179 CLR 520, 550.

[81] *X (Minors) v Bedfordshire County Council* [1995] 2 AC 633, 740 (Lord Browne-Wilkinson).

[82] *Woodland v Essex County Council* [2014] AC 537, 583.

[83] See below.

[84] Section reproduced in C Beuermann, 'Do Hospitals Owe a so-called "Non-Delegable Duty of Care" to their Patients?' (2018) 26 *Medical Law Review* 1.

for breach of the so-called 'non-delegable duty of care' owed by a hospital to a patient. In the initial trilogy of cases, each patient sought to hold a hospital liable for the negligence of one or more medical practitioners. In *Gold*, for instance, the question was whether the hospital could be held liable for the radiologist. In *Roe*, it was whether the hospital could be held liable for an anaesthetist. It is less clear from the cases, however, whether such liability was or continues to be imposed.

First, there have only been a small number of cases which have actually considered the so-called 'non-delegable duty' owed by hospital to patient. Lord Phillips of Worth Matravers MR suggested in *A v Ministry of Defence*[85] that in the United Kingdom this was because the 'authorities administering the NHS ceased to take issue on the extent of their liability for treatment negligently administered'.[86] Consequently, the whole question of the liability of a hospital for the negligence of a medical practitioner (whether employees or independent contractors) became somewhat of a non-issue. Substantial access to medical indemnity funds can perhaps explain the small number of cases in Australia. The availability of such funds means that where the negligent medical practitioner is a doctor, a claim brought directly against the negligent doctor can be easily satisfied.[87] In New Zealand, the no-fault insurance scheme covers medical negligence and removes the capacity for any such claims to be made.[88]

Secondly, in the cases in which courts have purported to hold a hospital strictly liable for breach of the so-called 'non-delegable duty' owed to a patient, most have involved the negligence of at least one medical practitioner employed by the hospital or, alternatively, personal negligence on the part of the hospital itself.[89] Accordingly, the liability imposed on a hospital in these cases can be described as what is currently called 'vicarious liability' or, alternatively, personal liability. In *Samios v Repatriation Commission*,[90] for instance, the patient sued the Repatriation Commission when he attended a hospital operated by the Commission on at least three occasions and the medical practitioners he saw failed to diagnose and treat his dislocated shoulder. Jackson SPJ found a doctor employed by the Commission to be negligent as well as the radiologists of a clinic that had been engaged by

[85] [2005] QB 183.

[86] That is, after the enactment of The National Health Service Act 1977 (UK) c 49. Ibid 198. Further information about the strategy of NHS to resolving claims can be found at www.resolution.nhs.uk.

[87] A similar suggestion has been made to explain the situation in Canada. Blair JA said in *Yepremian v Scarborough General Hospital* (1980) 110 DLR (3d) 513, 560: 'What all the cases reveal is the procedural convenience and administrative simplicity of holding hospitals liable only for the negligence of doctors employed by them and making other doctors on their staffs directly answerable to their patients for their negligence. The uniformity of this practice has a practical explanation well known to the legal profession. Under the present regime of public insurance for medical expenses, hospitals and doctors bill the insurance authority separately. In addition, hospitals have no "deeper" pockets than doctors from which to pay damages because of the universality of medical liability insurance coverage'.

[88] RP Balkin and JLR Davis, *Law of Torts* (4th ed, Sydney, LexisNexis, 2009) 407–10.

[89] See *Albrighton v Royal Prince Alfred Hospital* [1980] 2 NSWLR 542 in which the negligent orthopaedic surgeon was found to be an employee. See also *Bull v Devon Area Health Authority* [1993] 4 Med LR 117 in which the hospital was found personally liable.

[90] [1960] WAR 219.

the Commission to provide support services whilst its own radiologists were on vacation.[91] The liability of the Commission in that case can therefore be explained by reason of the Commission's 'vicarious liability' for the doctor it employed. It was also suggested, though not proved, that personal liability might also be imposed on the Commission by reason of the Commission's inadequate systems.[92]

The only case in which liability has been imposed on a hospital for the tort of a medical practitioner where the liability could not be described as 'vicarious' or personal appears to be the decision of a single county court judge in *M v Calderdale & Kirklees Health Authority*.[93] In that case, the patient had been referred by a Community Health Centre operated by the health authority to a hospital in the local area for an abortion. The abortion was performed negligently, and the patient successfully sued the health authority for breach of its so-called 'non-delegable duty of care' when the hospital that performed the operation became insolvent. Of this decision, Lord Phillips of Worth Matravers MR said in *A v Ministry of Defence*:[94]

> The exception is the finding of the existence of a non-delegable duty of care made by Judge Garner as one of the grounds of his decisions in *M* v *Calderdale and Kirklees Health Authority*. This finding did not represent the current state of English law.

Given such comments, *Calderdale* hardly provides convincing evidence that strict liability for the tort of another can be imposed on a hospital for breach of the so-called 'non-delegable duty of care' owed to a patient.

Thirdly, there have been a number of cases in which the courts have refused to impose strict liability on a hospital for breach of the so-called 'non-delegable duty of care' owed to a patient. In *Ellis v Wallsend District Hospital*,[95] for instance, a majority of the New South Wales Court of Appeal found that a hospital could not be held liable for the negligence of an honorary medical officer who used the hospital's operating theatres for his own patients. Samuels JA, with whom Meagher JA agreed, examined the initial trilogy of English cases and noted that it was a minority view that a hospital owed a so-called 'non-delegable duty of care' to a patient. Despite this, he felt bound to acknowledge that the duty of care owed by a hospital to a patient was 'non-delegable' given the High Court of Australia's support for such a duty in the above-mentioned dicta.[96] He was not, however, prepared to find the hospital liable for the negligence of the honorary medical officer in the circumstances of the case. Samuels JA tightly circumscribed the type of medical practitioner for whom a hospital could be held liable under a so-called 'non-delegable duty of care' and held that, as the honorary medical officer in

[91] Ibid 228.

[92] Ibid (Jackson SPJ). 'For this, I think, Dr Traub must take primary responsibility, but perhaps the hospital system itself should not escape some criticism'.

[93] [1998] Lloyds Law Reports: Medical 157 ('*Calderdale*').

[94] [2005] QB 183, 203.

[95] (1989) 17 NSWLR 553.

[96] See above n 80.

the case was 'engaged in his own business and not the hospital's',[97] the liability of the hospital under its so-called 'non-delegable duty of care' did not extend to the particular honorary medical officer.

The England and Wales Court of Appeal also refused to impose strict liability on a hospital for breach of the so-called 'non-delegable duty of care' owed to a patient in *A v Ministry of Defence*.[98] The patient in that case was the small child of a soldier stationed in Germany who had sustained severe brain damage at the time of his birth due to the negligence of a German obstetrician at a German hospital. The Ministry of Defence was sued for breach of a so-called 'non-delegable duty of care' owed to the child on the basis that the Ministry of Defence had previously operated its own hospitals in Germany for military personnel and their families. Those hospitals were later closed for financial reasons. In their stead, the Ministry of Defence had made arrangements with a number of German hospitals to provide medical treatment to military personnel and their families in accordance with English standards. Lord Phillips of Worth Matravers MR (with whom the other judges agreed) found that the Ministry of Defence was not liable to the child even though the Ministry of Defence had undertaken to provide medical care. In his view, the Ministry of Defence could not be held liable for the negligence of the German obstetrician at a German hospital which was not operated by the defendant.

A similar decision was reached by the England and Wales Court of Appeal in *Farraj v King's Healthcare NHS Trust*.[99] The patient in that case resided in Jordan. She was pregnant and wanted to test that her unborn baby had not contracted a genetic disease carried by both parents. A sample of foetal tissue was sent to the defendant's hospital in London for testing. The defendant hospital subcontracted the testing to an external laboratory which negligently confirmed that the sample was 'all clear'. The court found that the hospital was not liable to the patient even though the hospital had arranged for the testing to be undertaken. Once again the court held that the hospital could not be held strictly liable for the tort of an external service provider.

It might be that cases such as these can be explained by reference to specific facts which made it inappropriate in each of the cases to impose strict liability on the hospital for breach of the so-called 'non-delegable duty of care' owed to the patient.[100] If so, they are not particularly significant. The problem is that it is very difficult to draw from the reasoning of the judges in those cases any convincing factual distinctions which would justify imposing strict liability on a hospital for breach of the so-called 'non-delegable duty of care' owed to a patient in one situation but not the other. In *Ellis*, for instance, the court was concerned that the honorary medical officer was involved in carrying on his own business and

[97] (1989) 17 NSWLR 553, 599.
[98] [2005] QB 183.
[99] [2010] 1 WLR 2139.
[100] R Stevens, *Torts and Rights* (Oxford, OUP, 2007) 117–19, 123.

not that of the hospital. This was evidenced by the fact that the honorary medical officer was not paid by the hospital. Although the honorary medical officer 'accepted a degree of management'[101] from the hospital, because he was not paid by the hospital he could be considered to be carrying on his own business. This reasoning seems to contradict that in *A v Ministry of Defence* where the fact that the Ministry of Defence *did pay* for the negligent medical services was thought significant in *refusing* to impose liability for the tort of another for breach of the so-called 'non-delegable duty of care'. In *Farraj v King's Healthcare NHS Trust*, it was said to be significant that the plaintiff was not an in-patient of the hospital.[102] But at the same time, Dyson LJ was using examples to justify his decision which would have denied liability even if the plaintiff had been an in-patient. For instance, Dyson LJ was of the view that the purchaser of a car could not sue the manufacturer where damage was sustained as a result of defects in the steel used in the car's construction after the steel had been sent to an appropriately skilled independent contractor for testing.[103] Similarly, he thought a building owner could not sue the building developer for damage caused by defects in concrete used in the building which had been sent to an appropriately skilled independent contractor for testing.[104] It would follow from Dyson LJ's examples that whether a patient is an in-patient or not, once material has been sent to a reputable, external independent contractor for testing, no liability for the hospital could arise.

Lord Sumption tried to navigate these difficulties in *Woodland* by wording his five-stage test for a 'non-delegable duty of care' in such a way that could satisfactorily explain why strict liability for the tort of another was not imposed on the hospitals in these cases, regardless of the actual reasoning used by the judges in those cases. He consequently emphasised requirements such as the need for a patient to be in the 'actual custody, charge or care'[105] of the hospital and the need for the function delegated to the third party to be an 'integral part'[106] of the duty 'assumed'[107] by the hospital towards the patient. The decision in *Farraj* was therefore correct, according to Lord Sumption, on the basis that the claimant was not an in-patient of the defendant hospital.[108] What is not clear from Lord Sumption's decision is whether, in his view, the result should have been different if the claimant was an in-patient of the defendant hospital. What if the hospital regularly subcontracted out such testing because it didn't have the facilities to do it? Even though such testing would arguably have been 'integral' to the patient's treatment, could it then be argued that the hospital had not 'assumed responsibility' for such testing? It was on this basis that Lord Sumption agreed with the

[101] (1989) 17 NSWLR 553, 599.
[102] [2010] 1 WLR 2139, 2163–64.
[103] Ibid 2165. At least at common law, cf Consumer Protection Act 1987 (UK) c 43.
[104] Ibid.
[105] [2014] AC 537 (UKSC), 583.
[106] Ibid.
[107] Ibid.
[108] Ibid 584.

decision in *A v Ministry of Defence*, though not the reasoning. In Lord Sumption's view, the Ministry of Defence had not 'assumed responsibility' for the provision of medical treatment to the soldiers and their families. But what does 'assumed responsibility' mean in this context? Is it that the hospital impliedly promised to perform that particular duty or function, or that the hospital assumed the legal risk of the consequences of the duty or function not being performed, or more simply that the hospital voluntarily chose to act in a particular way.[109] It is difficult to dismiss the unwillingness of the courts to impose strict liability in cases such as *Farraj* and *A v Ministry of Defence* as fact-dependent when the test employed by the courts for imposing a 'non-delegable duty' rest on concepts as imprecise and contestable as an 'assumption of responsibility'.[110]

Taking into account each of the above points, there is no clear authority showing that courts do impose strict liability on a hospital for breach of the so-called 'non-delegable duty of care' owed to a patient. Where the courts purport to impose strict liability on a hospital for breach of the so-called 'non-delegable duty', they do so in circumstances in which 'vicarious liability' (as it is currently described) can also be imposed. Where the courts refuse to impose strict liability on a hospital for breach of the so-called 'non-delegable duty', they do so on the basis of distinctions which do little more than establish that the negligent medical practitioner was an independent contractor as opposed to an employee of the hospital (hence the focus on features such as payment and control). On this basis, it is very difficult to say that the hospital relationship is a relationship which itself gives rise to strict liability for the tort of another. Instead, what appears to attract strict liability for the tort of another is a co-existing employment relationship.[111]

Whilst courts in Australia and England and Wales have been slow to recognise that a hospital relationship does not attract strict liability for the tort of another,[112] courts in Canada appear to have now reached this conclusion. In *Yeprehemian v Scarborough General Hospital*,[113] Arnup JA of the Ontario Court of Appeal cautioned against blindly following the English cases on the question of hospital liability because the interrelationships of the state, the medical profession, the hospitals and patients had developed along different lines from those in Ontario since the introduction of 'nationalised medicine'.[114] A majority of the court then

[109] K Barker, 'Unreliable Assumptions in the Modern Law of Negligence' (1993) 109 *Law Quarterly Review* 461.

[110] See discussion in previous chapter.

[111] For an explanation of how the hospital relationship differs from other relationships which attract strict liability for the tort of another, see Beuermann, 'Do Hospitals Owe a so-called "Non-Delegable Duty of Care" to their Patients?' (n 85).

[112] Though the problems are starting to be acknowledged more readily. See *Farraj v King's Healthcare NHS Trust* [2010] 1 WLR 2139 in which Smith LJ assumed but did not decide that hospitals owe their patients a non-delegable duty of care after noting that the existence of such a duty was only ever a minority position.

[113] (1980) 110 DLR (3d) 513.

[114] Ibid 533.

went on to find that a hospital could only be held strictly liable for the negligence of medical practitioners employed by the hospital and not for the negligence of medical practitioners associated with the hospital by other means.[115] No subsequent Canadian case appears to have contradicted the decision.

IV. School Relationship

The school relationship is another relationship by reason of which the courts impose liability using the label 'liability for breach of a non-delegable duty of care'. The so-called 'non-delegable duty' owed by a school to a student was recognised in similar circumstances and for similar reasons as the so-called 'non-delegable duty' owed by a hospital to a patient.

A. 'Liability for Breach of a Non-Delegable Duty of Care'

There is some debate as to when the so-called 'non-delegable duty of care' owed by a school to a student was first recognised. In *Commonwealth of Australia v Introvigne*,[116] Mason J traced the so-called 'non-delegable duty' to the decision of the House of Lords in *Carmarthenshire County Council v Lewis*,[117] where it was held that the duty of care owed by a school to its students was 'not discharged by merely appointing competent teaching staff and leaving it to the staff to take appropriate steps for the care of the children'.[118] The difficulty with attributing the so-called 'non-delegable duty' to *Carmarthenshire*, however, is that the issue in the case was not the liability of the school to its students, but the liability of the school to a truck driver who had collided with a telegraph pole after swerving to avoid a young child who had ran out of the school and out onto the road. It is also not immediately evident from *Carmarthenshire* whether the school was held liable for its own negligence in failing to install appropriate locks on gates, or strictly liable for the conduct of the teacher who was looking after the child immediately prior to the child running out onto the road, particularly given that a number of the judges were of the view that the teacher had not been negligent in the circumstances.[119]

Despite some uncertainty as to the effect of the decision in *Carmarthenshire*, the High Court of Australia did subsequently confirm in *Ramsay v Larsen*[120] that the duty of care owed by school to student was 'non-delegable'. *Ramsay v Larsen* concerned a student who had been climbing a tree in the school grounds in order

[115] Ibid 540.
[116] (1982) 150 CLR 258.
[117] [1955] AC 549.
[118] (1982) 150 CLR 258, 270.
[119] *Carmarthenshire County Council v Lewis* [1955] AC 549, 568–69 (Lord Reid).
[120] (1964) 111 CLR 16.

to retrieve a set of keys. Although the student had been previously told by a teacher to get down, the student had returned to climb the tree once more. The teacher then tried to assist the student recover the keys by instructing the student to swing a rope over the branch where the keys were located so that the branch could be shaken in order to dislodge the keys. Using this method, the student successfully recovered the keys. Unfortunately, the student fell whilst trying to get back down to the ground, injuring both his legs and arms. The student subsequently claimed that the teacher had been negligent in giving him directions in respect of climbing the tree and sued the school in respect of that negligence.

Had *Ramsay v Larsen* been decided today, there would have been little difficulty in imposing what is currently called 'vicarious liability' on the school for the teacher's negligence. The teacher was an employee of the school and had been acting in the course of his employment immediately before the negligent conduct occurred. As with the cases in which the so-called 'non-delegable duty of care' owed by a hospital to a patient was first recognised, however, there were difficulties in establishing that a school had sufficient control over the activities of the teacher for the teacher to be considered an 'employee' for the purposes of the liability. Such difficulties stemmed from the decision in *Hole v Williams*[121] in which the full court of the Supreme Court of New South Wales had held that a school could not be 'vicariously liable' for the tort of a teacher for teachers, along with medical practitioners, had sufficient discretion in undertaking tasks to preclude them being considered an employee.[122]

Faced with the decision in *Hole v Williams*, two of the judges in *Ramsay v Larsen* dealt with it directly and overruled it.[123] Justice Kitto held that the concerns about what is currently called 'vicarious liability' expressed in *Hole v Williams* were no longer well founded due to the subsequent findings in *Gold* and *Cassidy* that such liability could be imposed on a hospital for the negligence of medical practitioners it employed.[124] As a result, it was possible to find the school 'vicariously liable' for the negligence of the teacher and both Kitto and McTiernan JJ sought to hold the school liable on that basis.

A majority of the High Court preferred, however, to find that the school owed its students a so-called 'non-delegable duty of care' and that, in the circumstances of the case, there was a possibility that the duty had been breached due to the negligence of the teacher.[125] Justice Taylor, with whom Owen and Windeyer JJ agreed, cited with approval the following comments made in the case by Ferguson J of the full court of the Supreme Court of New South Wales:[126]

> I prefer the view that a public school teacher in the exercise of his functions as such is exercising an authority delegated to him by the Crown in respect of obligations

[121] (1910) 10 SRNSW 638.
[122] Ibid 648.
[123] (1964) 111 CLR 16, 26 (McTiernan J) and 30 (Kitto J).
[124] Ibid 29.
[125] The majority ordered a new trial.
[126] (1964) 111 CLR 16, 38.

> assumed by the Crown. At common law where a person has assumed a legal duty towards another he cannot escape liability for a breach of that duty by delegating its performance to somebody else.

Authority for this general proposition was derived from the cases concerning the so-called 'non-delegable duty of care' owed by a hospital to a patient, a duty which was seen by the judges as closely analogous.[127] The supposedly 'non-delegable' nature of the duty of care owed by a school to a student can be seen, therefore, to have emerged from similar difficulties to those which led to the 'non-delegable duty' being recognised in the hospital relationship.

B. Does the School Relationship Give Rise to Strict Liability for the Tort of Another?

There is little doubt that the liability imposed by the High Court of Australia in *Ramsay v Larsen* for breach of the so-called 'non-delegable duty of care' owed by a school to a student was a form of strict liability for the tort of another. The only question in that case was whether the school could be held liable for the tort of the teacher and no evidence of any personal conduct which might attract liability in tort by the school was adduced. It remains in issue, however, whether it is the school relationship or a co-existing employment relationship which attracts such strict liability. This is because, in most cases, the teacher who tortiously injured the student will also have been an employee of the defendant school or school authority.[128]

The best way to determine whether the school relationship itself gives rise to strict liability for the tort of another is to see if there are any cases in which strict liability for the tort of another has been imposed on a school in circumstances in which so-called 'vicarious liability' could not also be imposed. The decision of the High Court of Australia in *Commonwealth of Australia v Introvigne*[129] provides an example of such a case. The student in the case was injured when he and some friends were playing in the vicinity of a flagpole. At the time of the incident, there was only one teacher on playground duty, the remaining teachers having been called to a meeting to be informed of the headmaster's unexpected death. The student succeeded in suing the Commonwealth government, as the government responsible for schools in the Australian Capital Territory, for breach of the so-called 'non-delegable duty' owed by the Commonwealth government to the student. The liability imposed in the case could only be described as a form of strict liability for the tort of another as no evidence of a tort having been committed by the Commonwealth government was adduced.

[127] Ibid 34–35.

[128] Cf *Woodland v Essex County Council* [2014] AC 537 where the issue arose as to whether a school could be held liable for the negligence of a swimming teacher who had been engaged as an independent contractor.

[129] (1982) 150 CLR 258 ('*Introvigne*').

Introvigne is significant because the Commonwealth government did not personally administer schools in the Australian Capital Territory. Instead, it had appointed the New South Wales state government to administer the schools on its behalf and it was the New South Wales state government that had employed the negligent teachers. As the Commonwealth government did not employ the negligent teachers, the liability imposed in the case could not have been based on an employment relationship. It follows, that the liability must been imposed by reason of the school relationship.

The more recent decision of the Supreme Court of the United Kingdom in *Woodland v Essex County Council*[130] is to similar effect. The claimant, a 10-year-old schoolgirl, had been participating in swimming lessons organised by her school at the local Council pool when she was found 'hanging vertically' in the water.[131] Although she was successfully resuscitated after being dragged from the pool, she sustained 'severe hypoxic brain injuries'.[132] The claimant sued the school in respect of her injuries. The swimming lesson had been conducted by a swimming instructor and a lifeguard employed by an independent contractor engaged by the Council to conduct swimming lessons at the pool. As neither the swimming instructor nor the lifeguard were employed by the school, there was no scope for holding the school 'vicariously liable' for their alleged negligence. Instead, the claimant asserted that the duty of care owed by the school to her was 'non-delegable' and that liability for breach of such a duty extended to the alleged negligence of the swimming instructor and lifeguard. The defendant applied for the claim to be struck out on the basis that the duty of care owed by a school to its students had not been previously recognised as 'non-delegable' in England and Wales. The strike-out action succeeded at trial and was not overturned by the Court of Appeal. The Supreme Court, however, overturned the successful strike out application and found that the duty of care owed by a school to its students was indeed 'non-delegable'.[133]

The decisions in *Introvigne* and *Woodland* demonstrate that the courts do impose strict liability for the tort of another by reason of the school relationship under the label 'liability for breach of a non-delegable duty of care'. As the cases are relatively recent, it also indicates a willingness on behalf of the courts to continue to impose such liability. This willingness can also be seen in the child sexual assault cases.[134] Justice McHugh said in *New South Wales v Lepore*, for example:[135]

> In my opinion a State education authority owes a duty to a pupil to take reasonable care to prevent harm to the pupil. The duty cannot be delegated. If, as is invariably the

[130] [2014] AC 537.

[131] Ibid 541.

[132] Ibid.

[133] On being sent back to trial to determine the actual claim, it was found that the school was in breach of the non-delegable duty of care owed to the claimant by virtue of the negligence of the swimming instructor and/or lifeguard.

[134] See *New South Wales v Lepore* (2003) 212 CLR 511 (McHugh J and Gaudron J). See also *Lister v Hesley Hall Ltd* [2002] 1 AC 215 (Lord Hobhouse).

[135] (2003) 212 CLR 511, 562.

> case, the State delegates the *performance* of the duty to a teacher, the State is liable if the teacher fails to take reasonable care to prevent harm to the pupil … It is the State's duty to protect the pupil, and the conduct of the teacher constitutes a breach of the State's own duty.

It does not matter for these purposes that most judges in the child sexual assault cases who were prepared to find a school or similar institution liable for a sexual assault commissioned by a teacher chose to impose liability on the defendant institution using the label 'vicarious liability' rather than 'liability for breach of a non-delegable duty of care'.[136] This is because the principal question in respect of the so-called 'non-delegable duty of care' in those cases was whether liability for breach of the duty extended to cover intentional misconduct of a teacher.[137] No questions were raised as to whether the so-called 'non-delegable duty of care' actually existed or whether strict liability for the tort of another could be imposed in the event of a breach.

V. Relationship between Occupier and Invitee (Arguably)

The final relationship by reason of which the courts impose liability using the label 'liability for breach of a non-delegable duty of care' is the relationship between occupier and invitee. The High Court of Australia noted the existence of the so-called 'non-delegable' duty owed by an occupier to an invitee in *Burnie Port Authority v General Jones Limited*.[138] Recognition of the 'non-delegable duty' was qualified, however, with the word 'arguably',[139] reflecting the considerable uncertainty surrounding the existence of the so-called 'non-delegable duty' and the nature of the liability imposed in the event of a breach.

A. 'Liability for Breach of a Non-Delegable Duty of Care'

Some 100 years after it was first suggested in *Pickard v Smith* that the duty of care owed by a lessee of premises to a passer-by was 'non-delegable', the House of Lords held in *Thomson v Cremin*[140] that the duty of care owed by an occupier to an invitee was also 'non-delegable'.

The passage of time between the decisions in *Pickard v Smith* and *Thomson v Cremin* is significant because the state of the law prior to each of the cases differed

[136] See further ch 4.
[137] See *New South Wales v Lepore* (2003) 212 CLR 511, 601–03 (Gummow and Hayne JJ).
[138] (1994) 179 CLR 520.
[139] Ibid 550–51.
[140] (1953) 2 All ER 1185.

considerably. As noted in section II of this chapter, the law prior to *Pickard v Smith* was in a state of development and there was a confusion of legal principles as to whether a lessee could be held liable to a passer-by regardless of having personally engaged in any conduct to which liability in tort might attach. In contrast, the principles governing the liability of an occupier to an invitee were relatively settled by the time *Thomson v Cremin* was decided. In *Indermaur v Dames*,[141] it had been held that an occupier owed discrete duties to different categories of entrants depending on their status: a relatively low duty was owed to a trespasser who was thought should bear the consequences of any injury since the trespasser had no right to be there;[142] a higher duty was owed to a licensee who the occupier was required to advise of any dangers known to the occupier;[143] and an even higher duty was owed to an invitee, which required the occupier to 'use reasonable care to prevent damage from unusual danger which [the occupier] knows or ought to know'.[144] Each of those duties, as the language of *Indermaur v Dames* suggests, was at best a duty to use reasonable care. *Thomson v Cremin*, therefore, was a significant change in how the liability of an occupier to an invitee had previously been determined.

Thomson v Cremin concerned a cargo of grain on a ship being unloaded by a firm of stevedores when a heavy wooden shore attached to the hull of the ship fell on one of the stevedore's employees. The wooden shore was found to have been negligently fixed to the hull when the ship was loaded in Australia by a firm of Australian stevedores. The injured employee successfully sued the shipowner for his injuries even though the shipowner was unaware of the problem with the wooden shore and had used reasonable care in selecting the Australian stevedores. The basis of the liability was said to be the so-called 'non-delegable nature of the duty of care' owed by the occupier to the invitee. In this respect, Lord Wright held:[145]

> The duty of the invitor towards the invitee is, in my opinion, a duty personal to the former, in the sense that he does not get rid of the obligation by entrusting its performance to independent contractors. It is true that the invitor is not an insurer: he warrants, however, that due care and skill to make the premises reasonably safe for the invitee have been exercised, whether by himself, his servants, or agents or by independent contractors whom he employs to perform his duty. He does not fulfil the warranty merely by leaving the work to contractors, however reputable or generally competent. His warranty is broken if they fail to exercise the proper care.

In reaching this conclusion, Lord Wright expressly considered the decision in *Pickard v Smith* and decided that the liability of the occupier should be determined in the same way.[146] A similar analogy had been made by Luxmoore J in the

141 (1865–66) LR 1 CP 274.
142 See *Norman v Great Western Railway Company* [1915] 1 KB 584, 592.
143 *Indermaur v Dames* (1865–66) LR 1 CP 274, 288.
144 Ibid.
145 (1953) 2 All ER 1185, 1191–92.
146 Ibid.

England and Wales Court of Appeal decision in *Wilkinson v Rea*,[147] to which Lord Wright also referred. *Wilkinson v Rea* concerned coal being loaded onto a ship in dry dock by a coal merchant whilst a number of minor repairs were being carried out by the employees of a repair company. In order to load the coal it was necessary to leave a hatch in the galley open. An employee of the repair company fell down the hatch after the ship's engineer turned off the lights in the galley at the request of a Lloyd's surveyor who was testing those lights. In finding the ship owner liable to the employee, Luxmoore LJ found, as it had been in *Pickard v Smith*, that a danger was created when the hatch in the galley was opened by the coal merchants and that the shipowner could not avoid liability for that danger by leaving it to the coal merchants to take steps to guard against that danger.

Given the analogies to *Pickard v Smith*, what appears to have been driving the decision in *Thomson v Cremin* and the establishment of the so-called 'non-delegable duty of care' owed by an occupier to an invitee was a concern with the different legal treatment of people injured as a result of the condition of an occupier's property. The court was struggling to see why an occupier might be found liable to a passer-by injured as a result of the negligence of an independent contractor, but not to an invitee. This was a valid concern. It is not clear, however, whether at this point in time it was the decision in *Pickard v Smith* which was out of line with authority or the decision in *Indermaur v Dames*. Significantly, Luxmoore J was the only judge in *Wilkinson v Rea* to rely on *Pickard v Smith* in reaching his decision. The other judges had based the liability of the shipowner in that case on a breach of the statutory duty imposed on the shipowner under the Shipbuilding Regulations 1931 to efficiently light 'all parts of a ship where work is being carried on'.[148] Furthermore, the period between *Pickard v Smith* and *Thomson v Cremin* had seen a significant change in the willingness of the courts to hold one person liable for the tort of another. A matter of weeks before the Lords heard *Thomson v Cremin*, the England and Wales Court of Appeal held in *Haseldine v C A Daw and Son Limited*[149] that the duty owed by an occupier to an invitee was a duty to use reasonable care only and that an occupier could not be found liable to an invitee who was injured as a result of the negligence of an independent contractor engaged by the occupier. In reaching that decision, Scott LJ (who was also a member of the court in *Wilkinson v Rea*) noted:[150]

> To put on the occupier any higher measure of duty than that of care, seems to me to depart from first principles … to put on him a so-called 'strict liability' similar to the responsibility of an insurer seems to be unjust unless there be present other circumstances which give rise to an exceptional measure of duty or make it right that the particular action should be at the peril of the actor.

[147] [1941] 1 KB 688.
[148] Shipbuilding Regulations 1931 (UK) (St R & O, No 133), regs 42(a) and (b).
[149] [1941] 2 KB 343.
[150] Ibid 353.

B. Does the Relationship between Occupier and Invitee Give Rise to Strict Liability for the Tort of Another?

There is little doubt that the liability imposed by the House of Lords in *Thomson v Cremin* was a form of strict liability for the tort of another since there was no evidence of a tort being personally committed by the occupier in the case. As the negligent party was an independent contractor, it must also have been the relationship between the occupier and invitee which gave rise to the strict liability. Just because the relationship between occupier and invitee historically gave rise to strict liability for the tort of another, however, does not necessarily mean that modern courts are similarly willing to impose such liability.

One reason it seems unlikely that modern courts will impose strict liability for the tort of another for breach of the so-called 'non-delegable duty of care' owed by an occupier to an invitee is that it now appears unlikely that *Pickard v Smith* would be decided the same way today. *Pickard v Smith* was strongly influenced by public nuisance principles. The tort of public nuisance was created in the sixteenth century to afford a remedy to members of the public who were injured as a result of an 'interference with a public or common right'.[151] Although initially a crime, it was subsequently reasoned that a member of the public particularly damaged by an interference with a public right of way should be able to have an action in tort just as would a private land owner whose private right of way was interfered with.[152] This reasoning was flawed. As Professor Newark[153] and others[154] have noted, there was nothing but a superficial resemblance between the circumstances giving rise to an action for a private nuisance and the newly created tort of public nuisance. The circumstances giving rise to the two torts were, more importantly, fundamentally different because one responded to interferences in land and the other responded to interferences in personal integrity. It follows that the tort of public nuisance was nothing more than an action in negligence 'born before its due time'.[155]

It has taken almost 500 years to recognise that a mistake was made, but in *Hunter v Canary Wharf Ltd*[156] the House of Lords finally restored the tort of private nuisance to a tort that protects against interferences with land and not against interferences with personal security.[157] It can now be seen that by relying on *Pickard v Smith* and imposing strict liability in *Thomson v Cremin* on an occupier for the tort of another for breach of a so-called 'non-delegable duty of care',

[151] Fleming (n 13) 460.
[152] YB 27 Hen 8 Mich Pl 10 cited in Newark, 'The Boundaries of Nuisance' (n 39) 483.
[153] Ibid.
[154] eg WTS Stallybrass, *Salmon's Law of Torts* (9th ed, London, Sweet & Maxwell, 1936) 229.
[155] Newark (n 39) 485.
[156] [1997] AC 655.
[157] Although the Supreme Court of the United Kingdom is yet to take the step of denying the existence of a tort of public nuisance on this basis.

the House of Lords compounded this initial mistake. The Lords themselves seemed to subsequently realise their error and sought to distance themselves from the decision in *Thomson v Cremin*. In *Davie v New Merton Board Mills Ltd*,[158] for instance, Lord Reid 'dismissed as dicta the remarks about the responsibility of an invitor for the negligence of a contractor'.[159] Lord Hodson in *Riverstone Meat Co Pty Ltd v Lancashire Meat Co Pty Ltd*[160] also suggested that the decision in *Thomson* v *Cremin* 'may have to be reconsidered'.[161] It is also not insignificant for these purposes that the decision in *Thomson v Cremin* took some 12 years to be published after it was decided.

Changes in the law since *Thomson v Cremin* provide another reason why it is unlikely that modern courts will impose strict liability for the tort of another for breach of the so-called 'non-delegable duty of care' owed by an occupier to an invitee. In England and Wales, the effect of *Thomson v Cremin* has been reversed by legislation. The Occupiers' Liability Act 1957 not only collapsed the different duties owed by an occupier to entrants into a single duty owed to the occupier's visitors,[162] but also expressly provided that an occupier was not strictly liable for damage to a visitor caused by an independent contractor engaged by the occupier if the occupier had acted reasonably in 'entrusting the work to an independent contractor'.[163]

The position in Australia is not so clear. Although some states and territories have enacted legislation similar to the legislation in England and Wales,[164] only the legislation in Western Australia provides that an occupier will not generally be held strictly liable for the negligence of an independent contractor unless the conduct of the occupier might of itself personally attract liability in tort.[165] More important is the decision of the High Court of Australia in *Australian Safeway Stores Pty Ltd v Zaluzna*.[166] In that case, the High Court held that occupiers in Australia owe a single duty to all categories of entrant on their property to use reasonable care.[167] As can be seen from the quote by Lord Wright in *Thomas v Cremin* above, what was thought to be 'non-delegable' was the duty of an occupier to an invitee, not the duty of an occupier to the other possible categories of entrant. Now that this specific duty no longer exists, any finding that an occupier owed a so-called 'non-delegable duty' would necessarily extend to all possible entrants, exceeding the liability imposed upon an occupier prior to *Zaluzna*. At a time where strict liability for the tort of another is the exception rather than the rule, this seems quite a leap.

[158] [1959] AC 604.
[159] *Voli v Inglewood Shire Council* (1963) 110 CLR 74, 97 (Windeyer J).
[160] [1961] AC 807.
[161] *Voli v Inglewood Shire Council* (1963) 110 CLR 74, 97 (Windeyer J).
[162] Occupiers' Liability Act 1957 (UK) c 31, s 2(1).
[163] Ibid s 2(4)(b).
[164] Victoria, South Australia, Western Australia and the Australian Capital Territory.
[165] Occupiers Liability Act 1985 (WA), s 6.
[166] (1987) 162 CLR 479 ('*Zaluzna*').
[167] Although the court arguably left open the question of what duty was owed by an occupant to a contractual entrant.

With the benefit of hindsight, the addition of the word 'arguably' by the High Court of Australia when describing the so-called 'non-delegable duty of care' owed by occupier to invitee now seems appropriate. It now seems unlikely that the relationship between an occupier and an invitee gives rise to strict liability for the tort of another.

VI. Agency Relationship

The final relationship to be examined by this chapter is the agency relationship. Courts impose liability by reason of the agency relationship using the label 'vicarious liability'. For the purposes of this book, an agency relationship is defined as a relationship in which one person (the *agent*) is vested with authority to effect legal relations on behalf of another (the *principal*).[168] This can be justified on the basis that, as a general rule, it is only when an agent is acting in this narrow, contractual sense that the courts consistently impose what is currently called 'vicarious liability'. The definition of agency will be discussed further in chapter 6.

A. 'Vicarious Liability'

As with the employment relationship, courts have imposed so-called 'vicarious liability' by reason of the agency relationship since medieval times. Just as a master could be held liable for a slave who acted tortiously in the course of her duties, so too could a master be held liable for a slave who acted tortiously whilst entering into a contract on the master's behalf.[169] As actions in debt developed, such liability was taken beyond the domestic sphere and businesses more generally were held liable for employees who acted tortiously whilst entering into contracts on an employer's behalf. The liability was finally extended to agents who were not employees but independent contractors. This was first done in cases in which the independent contractor was acting on behalf of an undisclosed principal.[170]

B. Does the Agency Relationship Give Rise to Strict Liability for the Tort of Another?

It is not too difficult to find cases in which a principal has been held strictly liable for the tort of an agent. Consider *Hern v Nichols*.[171] In that case, a factor selling

[168] These definitional difficulties were recently canvassed by the High Court of Australia in *Sweeney v Boylan Nominees Pty Limited* (2006) 226 CLR 161.

[169] OW Holmes Jr, 'Agency Part II' (1891) 5 *Harvard Law Review* 1, 2.

[170] See, eg, *Gurratt v Cullum* T. 9 Anne, cited by Holmes ibid 3.

[171] (1708) 1 Salk 289 [91 ER 256].

silk on behalf of the defendant principal misrepresented the quality of the silk. The defendant principal was held liable for the misrepresentation even though no evidence of personal conduct amounting to a tort on behalf of the principal was established. It may be, however, that it is not the agency relationship which gives rise to such strict liability but a co-existing employment relationship, given that an agent may also be an employee. This same issue arose in the context of both the hospital and school relationships.

In this regard, *Hern v Nichols* is particularly significant. The factor in the case was not an employee, but an independent contractor. It follows that it must have been the agency relationship which gave rise to the strict liability imposed on the principal. Consider also *Udell v Atherton.*[172] In that case, the defendant principal was held strictly liable for a misrepresentation made by an agent appointed by the defendant principal to sell timber on a commission basis. Once again, as the agent was not an employee, the only relationship which could have given rise to the strict liability imposed on the principal was the agency relationship.

Hern v Nichols and *Udell v Atherton* both demonstrate that the agency relationship gives rise to strict liability for the tort of another. Although both cases are quite old, they are commonly referred to by judges and *Hern v Nichols* was approved relatively recently by the House of Lords in *Armagas Ltd v Mundogas SA.*[173] There is no reason to think that such liability would not continue to be imposed today.

VII. Conclusion

A number of conclusions can be drawn from the analysis in this chapter. First, the labels currently used by the courts to describe strict liability for the tort of another are inadequate. Use of the labels does not necessarily indicate the presence of strict liability for the tort of another, nor do the labels adequately distinguish between different forms of the liability. Consider the hospital relationship. Although it has long been recognised that a hospital owes a so-called 'non-delegable duty' to its patients, the hospital relationship does not itself appear to give rise to strict liability for the tort of another. Instead such liability appears to be based on a co-existing employment relationship. The school relationship, in contrast, does give rise to strict liability for the tort of another. Such liability, however, might also be based on a co-existing employment relationship and there is very little guidance to determine which relationship might trigger the liability in the particular circumstances of a case.

Secondly, the willingness of the courts to impose strict liability for the tort of another has narrowed over time. Consider the relationship between adjoining

[172] (1861) 7H & N 172.
[173] [1986] AC 717.

land owners in relation to work threatening support or common walls. Although the relationship historically gave rise to strict liability for the tort of another, courts no longer appear willing to impose such liability.

Finally, there are very few relationships which *currently* give rise to strict liability for the tort of another. Of all the relationships identified in the table at the beginning of this chapter, the only relationships (apart from the foster care relationship) which generally give rise to strict liability for the tort of another are the employment relationship, the school relationship and the agency relationship. Within those relationships, different forms of strict liability for the tort of another can be seen to exist. The labels used to describe such liability, however, give few clues as to why those forms of liability arise or how they might be different.

As can be seen, strict liability for the tort of another as it is currently imposed by the courts is very different from the strict liability indicated by use of the labels 'vicarious liability' and 'liability for breach of a non-delegable duty of care'. It is no real surprise then, that current efforts to explain strict liability for the tort of another have failed. Such theories have sought to explain a form of liability which no longer exists.

PART II

Reconceptualising the Law

3

The Common Feature of Authority

Having developed a clear understanding of strict liability for the tort of another as that liability is currently imposed by the courts, it is now possible to examine the principal relationships which give rise to strict liability for the tort of another to see what it is about those relationships which attracts the concern and intervention of the law.

To this end, this chapter will analyse in detail the employment, school and agency relationships. It will show that authority is a common feature of all three relationships. Furthermore, it will show that the feature of authority is capable of distinguishing the cases in which the courts impose strict liability for the tort of another from the cases in which the courts do not. This chapter will then use the feature of authority to outline a new expositive framework for strict liability for the tort of another which will provide judges with much needed guidance and promote certainty and consistency in the law. Different forms of strict liability for the tort of another will be shown to reflect differences in the nature of the authority present in the three principal relationships by reason of which such liability is imposed.

I. The Relationships

In order to determine what it is about the employment, school and agency relationships that attracts strict liability for the tort of another, it is first necessary to consider why such relationships exist and how they function.

A. Employment Relationship

The employment relationship plays an important role in society. It enables employers to secure long-term access to human resources on set terms without the associated costs and risks of continual contract negotiations.[1] It does this by way

[1] This is not to suggest that employment does not have its disadvantages, eg increased cost of regulatory compliance, as evidenced by the trend towards a degree of vertical disintegration; H Collins, 'Independent Contractors and the Challenge of Vertical Disintegration to Employment Protection Laws' (1990) 10 *Oxford Journal of Legal Studies* 3. However, at the very least, employment does offer the core advantage suggested above.

of the contract of employment. Under the contract of employment, an employee voluntarily submits to the authority of the employer by agreeing to do what is asked by the employer in return for a regular wage. This will include complying with express instructions given by an employer as well as any other policies, incentives or penalties instituted by an employer to shape how an employee performs their tasks (collectively, '*directions*'). Any failure to comply with such directions is capable of being addressed by the employer as a breach of contract or through some other form of disciplinary action.

The authority vested in an employer to direct the conduct of an employee is broad in scope. Under a typical employment contract, an employer is given authority by the employee to direct all of the employee's conduct in the course of employment for the purposes of the employer's business.[2] This authority continues until the employment relationship is brought to an end by one of the parties. An employee is consequently at her employer's disposal for an indefinite period.[3] Also significant is the fact that the terms of that authority are put in place at the beginning of the employment relationship and need not[4] be reviewed for the duration of the employment relationship. This can be contrasted with any of the other types of contracts that might be entered into by an employer in order to secure the use of human resources. For example, an employer may engage a person to do a particular thing, such as write a report or build a structure. These types of contracts have increased with the need of employers for flexibility in managing their human resources. Under these contracts, although some type of authority may be given by the person to the employer, it will necessarily be limited by reference to the task and its duration and the need to enter into a new contract if those parameters are exceeded.

The authority vested in an employer to direct the conduct of an employee is therefore an important component of the employment relationship. Such authority enables an employer to achieve the commercial objectives which led to the employment relationship being created in the first place.

[2] Such authority might, however, be limited by the particular role the employee was appointed to perform where there is an express or implied term in the contract that the employee can only be asked to do a certain type of work, although redundancy laws mean that employees can be redeployed throughout a business even if their initial contract was to perform a particular task.

[3] Even where an employment contract is for a fixed period, it can be distinguished from a contract with an independent contractor for a similar duration as such a contract would not generally be limited by reference to the task to be undertaken, but by time. This means that much broader use can be made of the employee by the employer than the independent contractor whose task will be much more tightly prescribed by the contract (see below). For example, contrast a lecturer employed on a one-year contract to a specialist brought in to deliver and teach a particular course. The employer would generally only be able to direct the specialist with respect to things like when, where and how the course must be taught. In contrast, the employer would be able to direct the employee as to a broad range of other activities, including administration, research and community engagement.

[4] Though can be, when bargaining strength allows.

B. School Relationship

The school relationship exists to educate students. This is important for both the students and the broader community. As explained by Lord Clyde in *Phelps v Hillingdon London Borough Council*:[5]

> It is not only in the interests of the child and his or her parents that such provision should be made but also in the interest of the country that its citizens should have the knowledge, skill and ability to play their respective parts in society with such degree of competence and qualification as they may be able to develop.

Consequently, all children of a certain age are required by legislation throughout Australia and England and Wales to be educated.[6] This generally means that parents must enrol their child in a school approved by the government,[7] although parents retain a choice as to which school, and what type their child attends. Once at school, students attend classes arranged by the school and receive schooling in accordance with government-set curriculum. The school also makes arrangements for the students to have breaks throughout the day. During this time, students are generally free to engage in whatever activities they like, although any inappropriate behaviour may be restrained and the students must remain within the perimeter of the school.

From this description of the school relationship, it can be seen that a school can direct the activities and behaviour of its students. Schools are vested with authority to direct the behaviour of their students in this way. Such authority is not necessarily derived from parents,[8] but more generally vested by legislation.[9] This legislation first gives schools the authority to require students to attend school. Once a student has been enrolled at a school, the school must monitor attendance[10] and mechanisms are put in place to respond to instances of truancy.[11] Secondly, the legislation gives schools the express authority to maintain discipline within the school.[12]

[5] [2001] 2 AC 619, 668–69.

[6] See, eg, Education Act 1990 (NSW) s 22. See also Education Act 1996 (UK) c 56, s 7.

[7] Although home-schooling is available in limited circumstances. See, eg, Education Act 1990 (NSW), s 25.

[8] *Hole v Williams* (1910) 10 SRNSW 638, 656–57 (Street J): 'but, except in so far as he is restricted, either by agreement with the parent, or by the internal regulations of the department, it appears to me that a public school teacher in teaching or correcting children, in enforcing discipline, in inculcating habits of obedience, or in exercising the various other methods of control and of influence which form part of the child's education, is exercising an authority delegated to him, not by the Government, but by the parent'.

[9] See *Ramsay v Larsen* (1964) 111 CLR 16 (Taylor J): 'I prefer the view that a public schoolteacher in the exercise of his functions as such is exercising an authority delegated to him by the Crown in respect of obligations assumed by the Crown'.

[10] See, eg, Education Act 1990 (NSW) s 24. See also Education Act 1996 (UK) c 56, s 436A.

[11] See, eg, Education Act 1990 (NSW) s 23(5). See also Education Act 1996 (UK) c 56, s 437.

[12] See, eg, Education Act 1990 (NSW) s 35. See also Education and Inspections Act 2006 (UK) c 40, s 88: 'The governing body of a relevant school must ensure that policies designed to promote good behaviour and discipline on the part of its pupils are pursued at the school'.

This means that schools are not only authorised to direct the behaviour of students but to discipline individual students for failing to comply with those directions.

Once again, authority to direct the conduct of a student is an important component of the school relationship. Education is unlikely to happen if students are in an environment where they are not physically safe or where there are numerous disruptions. The success of the school relationship therefore depends on a school being able to exercise authority over the students to ensure that students both attend and have a suitable environment for learning.

C. Agency Relationship

An agency relationship was defined in the previous chapter as a relationship in which one person (the *agent*) was vested with authority to effect legal relations on behalf of another (the *principal*).[13] So defined, agency relationships exist to enable a principal to effect legal relations without being personally involved. To achieve this, a principal will vest an agent with authority to effect legal relations on the principal's behalf. Such authority may be general or specific and can vary considerably in nature. An agent might, for instance, be authorised to enter into any and all legal relations on behalf of a principal or may be authorised only to enter into specific contracts.[14] Alternatively, the authority vested in an agent might be quite limited in that the agent may not enter into legal relations on the principal's behalf at all, but may provide information in respect of such legal relations on behalf of the principal.[15] Provided the authority vested by the principal relates to the process of effecting legal relations in some respect, the person upon whom such authority has been vested can be considered an 'agent'. An agent for these purposes may be an employee, an independent contractor or may also be acting gratuitously.

Where an agent has been appointed, a party wishing to enter into legal relations with the principal (the *transactional party*) will generally do so through the agent, at least initially. A transactional party will receive information about the legal relations from the agent, negotiate the terms of the legal relations with the agent and, depending on the scope of the authority, enter into legal relations with the principal through the agent. This does not mean that the agent is party to such legal relations;[16] an agent instead does all of these acts on the principal's behalf. Consequently, any legal relations effected by an agent are between the principal and the transactional party and the principal will be bound by those legal relations provided the agent has been acting within the scope of their authority.[17]

[13] These definitional difficulties were recently canvassed by the High Court of Australia in *Sweeney v Boylan Nominees Pty Limited* (2006) 226 CLR 161.

[14] eg an enduring power of attorney.

[15] eg a real estate agent.

[16] Except where agency undisclosed. See generally G Dal Pont, *Law of Agency* (2nd ed, Sydney, LexisNexis, 2008) 496–98.

[17] Both actual and apparent. See further ch 6.

As with the employment and school relationships, the feature of authority can once again be seen to be a central component of the agency relationship. It explains both why the relationship exists and how it operates.

II. The Distinguishing Feature of the Cases

That authority is a common feature of the three main types of relationships which give rise to strict liability for the tort of another is not of itself significant. What makes the feature of authority significant is that it can distinguish the cases in which the courts currently impose strict liability for the tort of another from the cases in which the courts currently do not. The explanatory power of the feature of authority will be demonstrated in full in subsequent chapters, but can be highlighted here. As this section examines what the courts currently do, existing labels will once again be used to describe strict liability for the tort of another.

A. Employment Relationship

Consider first the liability imposed by the courts by reason of an employment relationship using the label 'vicarious liability'. Such liability has traditionally been limited to damage tortiously caused by an employee within the course of employment. In accordance with the *Salmond* test, an employee was considered to be acting within the course of her employment when she was acting with the authority of her employer:[18]

> An employee's wrongful conduct is said to fall within the course and scope of his or her employment where it consists of either (1) acts authorised by the employers or (2) unauthorised acts that are so connected with acts that the employer has authorised that they may rightly be regarded as modes – although improper modes – of doing what has been authorised.

The feature of authority has therefore been traditionally used by the courts to determine when strict liability for the tort of another should be imposed by reason of an employment relationship using the label 'vicarious liability'.

There have been recent efforts to expand the concept of 'course of employment' to include conduct 'connected' with employment.[19] The feature of authority is not so relevant under this approach. This expanded concept of 'course of employment' has, however, emerged from cases involving the sexual abuse of children by the employees of schools or similar institutions charged with their care. There is the possibility in these cases that it is not the employment relationship that attracts

[18] RFV Heuston and RA Buckley, *Salmond and Heuston on the Law of Torts* (19th ed, London, Sweet & Maxwell, 1987) 521–22. See further ch 5.

[19] See *Bazley v Curry* (1999) 174 DLR (4th) 45.

the liability, but the co-existing relationship between the school or institution and the child. If this is correct, the proposed 'connection' test does not apply to cases of strict liability for the tort of another imposed by reason of the employment relationship more generally. This possibility will be further explored in chapter 7.

It is less clear whether the feature of authority is relevant when the courts impose strict liability for the tort of another by reason of an employment relationship using the label 'liability for breach of a non-delegable duty of care'. A review of the cases, however, suggests that it is. The most common situation in which such liability is currently imposed on an employer for breach of the so-called 'non-delegable duty of care' is where an employee has been injured as a result of the tort of an independent contractor. The decision of the High Court of Australia in *Kondis v State Transport Authority*[20] provides a good example. Historically, the courts also imposed liability on an employer using the label 'liability for breach of a non-delegable duty of care' where one employee committed a tort in respect of another employee. This was because the doctrine of common employment prevented so-called 'vicarious liability' being imposed on the employer in such circumstances. *Wilsons & Clyde Coal Company Limited v English*[21] is a case in point. Today, such liability is relatively uncommon due to the doctrine of common employment having been abolished and there being no other legal impediment to an employer being held 'vicariously liable' where one employee commits a tort in respect of another.

Two points can be made about the circumstances in which strict liability for the tort of another is imposed by reason of an employment relationship using the label 'liability for breach of a non-delegable duty of care'. First, it is not the case that an employer is held strictly liable in respect of torts committed by *any* person to an employee. For example, an employer will not be held strictly liable to an employee negligently injured by another car driver whilst driving in the course of employment where that car driver is a stranger to the employer. An employer has only ever been held strictly liable to an employee in respect of the torts of an independent contractor or another employee engaged by the employer. This suggests that it is not only the fact that a tort has been committed in respect of the employee with which the law is concerned but the person who commits that tort.

Secondly, it seems that historically an employer was not held strictly liable to an employee for breach of a so-called 'non-delegable duty' for the torts of *all* employees and nor today is an employer held strictly liable to an employee for the torts of *all* independent contractors. Strict liability only seems to arise where the independent contractor or employee had some type of supervisory capacity over and in respect of the injured employee. For example, it has never been suggested that an employer could be held strictly liable to an employee negligently injured by a taxi driver engaged to transport an employee in the course of their employment,

[20] (1984) 154 CLR 672 ('*Kondis*') (discussed more fully in ch 2).
[21] [1938] AC 57 ('*Wilsons*') (discussed more fully in ch 2).

the taxi driver having no supervisory capacity over the employee. More specifically it seems to have been necessary that the person who committed the tort in respect of the employee was someone upon whom authority had been conferred by the employer to direct the behaviour of the injured employee. In *Wilsons*, the person who negligently injured the employee was the mine manager upon whom authority had been conferred to direct the activities of the mine's employees, including the injured employee. In *Kondis*, the negligent crane driver had been charged with dismantling a structure and had been given a gang of men, of which the employee was a member, to assist him in performing that task. The employee was following the directions of the crane driver when he was injured.

It follows that the feature of authority plays an important role in determining whether the courts impose strict liability for the tort of another by reason of an employment relationship using either the label 'vicarious liability' or 'liability for breach of a non-delegable duty of care'.

B. School Relationship

The feature of authority is also relevant in determining whether the courts impose strict liability for the tort of another by reason of a school relationship using the label of 'liability for breach of a non-delegable duty of care'. The most common situation in which a school is held strictly liable for the tort of another person for breach of the so-called 'non-delegable duty of care' owed to a student is where the student has been injured as a result of a tort committed by a teacher against the student. The decision of the High Court in *Ramsay v Larsen*[22] provides a good example. Strict liability for the tort of another can also be imposed on a school, though less commonly, in respect of a tort committed against a student by an independent contractor. This is what occurred in *Commonwealth of Australia v Introvigne*[23] and *Woodland v Essex County Council*.[24]

A review of the circumstances in which strict liability for the tort of another is currently imposed for breach of the so-called 'non-delegable duty of care' owed by a school to a student shows them to be similar to the circumstances in which strict liability for the tort of another is imposed for breach of the so-called 'non-delegable duty of care' owed by an employer to an employee. First, it is not the case that a school is held strictly liable in respect of torts committed by *any* person to a student. For example, a school will not be held strictly liable when one student assaults another student. Liability will only be imposed on a school in such circumstances if it can be shown that the school was personally negligent in failing to adequately supervise the students.[25] As a general rule, schools are only held strictly

[22] (1964) 111 CLR 16 (discussed more fully in ch 2).
[23] (1982) 150 CLR 258 (discussed more fully in ch 2).
[24] [2014] AC 537 (discussed more fully in ch 2).
[25] See *Geyer v Downs* (1977) 138 CLR 91.

liable to a student in respect of torts committed by an employee or an independent contractor[26] engaged by the school. This suggests that once again it is not only the fact that a tort has been committed in respect of the student with which the law is concerned but the person who commits that tort.

Secondly, schools are not held strictly liable for the torts of *all* employees or independent contractors engaged by the school. Strict liability only seems to have arisen where the employee or independent contractor had some type of supervisory capacity over and in respect of the injured student. Consider the child sexual assault cases, assuming for present purposes that it is the school relationship which triggers strict liability for the tort of another in such cases rather than the co-existing employment relationship. In those cases, schools or similar institutions were held strictly liable for sexual assaults committed by teachers and other employees who had been conferred authority to direct the conduct of students,[27] but not for sexual assaults committed by employees who had not been conferred any such authority. In *G(ED) v Hammer*,[28] for instance, the court refused to impose strictly liability on a school for the sexual assault of a student committed by a janitor employed by the school. A janitor, unlike a teacher, is not conferred any authority by a school to direct the conduct of students, such authority not being necessary for a janitor to be able to perform their duties. Similar circumstances arose in *B v Order of the Oblates of Mary Immaculate*.[29] The plaintiff in that case attended a residential school for First Nations children run by the defendant institution. The plaintiff was sexually assaulted on numerous occasions by the school baker. A baker, as with a janitor, is not conferred any authority to direct the conduct of students. Once again, the court refused to hold the institution strictly liable for the sexual assaults.

The feature of authority can be seen, therefore, to not only play an important role in determining whether courts impose strict liability for the tort of another by reason of an employment relationship, but also whether such liability is imposed by reason of a school relationship.

C. Agency Relationship

In the context of the agency relationship, the feature of authority is not only used by the courts to determine when strict liability for the tort of another is imposed using the label 'vicarious liability', but it is also used to determine who is an 'agent' for the purposes of the liability.

In terms of when strict liability for the tort of another is imposed, so-called 'vicarious liability' generally only arises in respect of a tort committed by an

[26] See *Commonwealth of Australia v Introvigne* (1982) 150 CLR 258.
[27] eg a boarding school warden; *Lister v Hesley Hall Ltd* [2002] 1 AC 215.
[28] (2003) 230 DLR (4th) 554.
[29] (2005) 258 DLR (4th) 385.

agent acting within the limits of their authority. As Lord Blackburn explained in *Houldsworth v City of Glasgow Bank*:[30]

> an innocent principal [is] civilly responsible for the fraud of his authorised agent, acting within his authority, to the same extent as if it were his own fraud.

In terms of who is an 'agent', an 'agent' has been traditionally defined as a person who has been vested with authority by a principal to effect legal relations on the principal's behalf. As will be demonstrated in chapter 6, despite efforts to expand the concept of 'agency', it is only when the person who committed the tort is an agent in this narrow, contractual sense that the courts regularly impose strict liability for the tort of another.

As can be seen, authority not only exists in each of the relationships in which strict liability for the tort of another is imposed, but distinguishes the cases in which the courts impose strict liability for the tort of another from the cases in which the courts do not.

III. Why is Authority Significant?

If, as has been suggested, the feature of authority is capable of distinguishing the cases in which the courts impose strict liability for the tort of another from the cases in which the courts do not, the question then is why. Why is this common feature of authority significant? It is submitted that the significance of the authority present in each of the relationships which give rise to strict liability for the tort of another lies in the potential for that authority to be abused.

A. Employment Relationship

There is scope for the authority present in the employment relationship to be abused in two distinct ways. First, the authority vested in an employer can be exercised by the employer for its own benefit. Since an employee faces a risk of immediate disciplinary action should she decide not to follow her employer's directions, there is the potential for an employer to abuse its authority to direct the conduct of an employee by putting an employee in a position that the employee unduly prioritises compliance with the directions of her employer rather than give due weight to any alternate considerations that might reasonably lead the employee to conduct herself differently in the circumstances. Secondly, an employer can confer its authority to direct the conduct of an employee upon another person, who might also abuse that authority.

[30] (1880) 5 App Cas 317, 339 approved in *Lloyd v Grace, Smith & Co* [1912] AC 716, 736 (Lord Macnaghten).

i. Exercise of Authority Interfering with Decision-making Process of Employee

A significant shortcoming of the authority vested in an employer by an employee is the potential for an employer to abuse that authority by putting an employee in a position that the employee unduly prioritises compliance with the directions of her employer rather than give due weight to any alternate considerations that might reasonably lead the employee to conduct herself differently in the circumstances. This potential exists because an employer can exercise that authority for its own benefit and might do so without making adequate allowance for any alternate considerations to which an employee might otherwise have regard when determining how best to act. For instance, an employer may direct an employee not to take reasonable safety precautions which might prolong the length of time it would take the employee to complete a particular task.

It is not that an employer will always put an employee in a position that the employee unduly prioritises compliance with the directions of the employer or that an employee will necessarily have acted any differently in the absence of any such directions. The directions of an employer may indeed align with any alternate considerations to which the employee might have regard when determining how best to act. For example, the content of the performance required of an employee to comply with the term implied into her employment contract that she perform her duties with reasonable care is very similar (if not identical) to the nature of the conduct required of the employee to avoid liability in the tort of negligence for failing to act reasonably.

There is, however, arguably always the potential for an employer to exercise its authority to direct the conduct of an employee in such a way. An employee, for instance, may still be obliged under her employment contract to follow an unreasonable (as opposed to illegal) direction.[31] The decision of the England and Wales Court of Appeal in *Johnston v Bloomsbury Health Authority*[32] provides a good example. In that case, a majority of the court held that an employee doctor might be directed to work 88 hours in one week by a public hospital if the contract of employment stipulated the right of the hospital to make such an order.[33] This was so, even though at some point the doctor became aware of the reasonably foreseeable risks posed by the direction for patients in the doctor's care. It is also possible that an employee's implied duties under her employment contract might be altered by the express terms of that contract.[34]

[31] GJ McCarry, 'The Employee's Duty to Obey Unreasonable Orders' (1984) 58 *Australian Law Journal* 327.

[32] [1991] ICR 269.

[33] This was the finding of a majority of the England and Wales Court of Appeal in *Johnston v Bloomsbury Health Authority* [1991] ICR 269, a case with very similar facts. The capacity of contract to 'trump' general law obligations in terms of directions by an employer was also upheld by the High Court of Australia in *Koehler v Cerebos (Australia) Ltd* (2005) 222 CLR 44.

[34] See *Johnstone v Bloomsbury Health Authority* [1992] QB 333 (Sir Nicolas Browne-Wilkinson VC). See also *Barber v Somerset County Council* [2004] 1 WLR 1089 (Lord Rodger of Earlsferry) and *Koehler v Cerebos (Australia) Ltd* (2005) 222 CLR 44 (McHugh, Gummow, Hayne and Heydon JJ).

By way of contrast, there is not the same potential for an employer to influence the decision-making process of persons in other types of contracts securing the use of human resources (*contractors*).[35] First, such contracts are often not as open-ended as an employment contract as they contain specific parameters for the task to be done with an expectation of contract renegotiation when circumstances change. Secondly, the risks and costs associated with performance of the contract are often broadly capable of being assessed and factored into the terms and price of the contract because the boundaries of the performance have been set. This includes the cost of addressing and/or complying with any alternate considerations that exist outside the contract. As the contract provides the means to identify and provide for the costs of and a mechanism for complying with such alternate considerations, the capacity of an employer to use any authority they might have to influence the decision-making process of the contractor is significantly reduced.

In contrast, it is very difficult for an employee to adequately assess the risks she faces when entering into the employment relationship or take steps to adequately protect herself from those risks when negotiating the terms of the employment contract due to the breadth of the authority vested in an employer by an employee, the long-term nature of the relationship and the common disparity in bargaining power between an employer and an employee. This leaves an employee exposed to the risk that her employer might exercise its authority to direct her conduct by putting the employee in a position that the employee unduly prioritises compliance with the directions of her employer rather than give due weight to any alternate considerations that might reasonably lead the employee to conduct herself differently in the circumstances. For instance, an employee might find herself in the unenviable position of having to weigh the potential risk of harm to a stranger to the employment relationship and the risk of being held legally responsible for that harm, against the risk of immediate disciplinary action for failing to pursue or comply with the directions of their employer. The authority vested in an employer to direct the conduct of an employee is therefore subject to abuse.

ii. Authority Conferred by Employer upon Another Person to Direct Conduct of Employee

An employer creates further potential for the authority present in an employment relationship to be abused when it confers its authority to direct the conduct of an employee upon another person.

[35] This is not to say that there is no scope for an employer to influence the decision-making process of persons in other types of contracts securing the use of human resources other than employment contracts. There are too many different types of contracts utilised by employers with the objective of obtaining flexibility in their work practices to be able to make any such generalisations with certainty. However, it is also not the case that the law can draw a clear line between an employment contract and other types of contracts securing the use of human resources. So in passing, it should be noted that if the analysis in this book proves persuasive, the process for distinguishing an employment contract from other contracts securing the use of human resources may need to be re-evaluated in terms of the potential for such influence to be exerted. This will be discussed further in ch 5.

There is no requirement for an employer to exercise its authority to direct the conduct of an employee personally. Instead, an employer has the capacity to confer that authority upon another person. This capacity exists because the possibility of an employer meeting the commercial objectives which prompted the creation of the employment relationship would be unduly limited if such authority could be exercised by the employer alone.

When an employer confers authority to direct the conduct of an employee upon another person, however, it creates a power relationship which did not previously exist. This power relationship enables the person upon whom authority has been conferred to direct the conduct of an employee and creates an expectation that the employee will obey. The power relationship created by the employer is therefore subject to abuse. The authority conferred by the employer on the crane operator in *Kondis v State Rail Authority*, for instance, enabled the crane operator to negligently direct the employee into a position where he was at risk of harm. The potential for abuse of the authority conferred by an employer upon another person puts the employee over whom authority has been conferred at risk of harm.

As can be seen, there are two very different ways in which the authority present in the employment relationship might be abused. First, since an employee faces a risk of immediate disciplinary action should she decide not to follow the employer's directions, there is the potential for an employer to abuse its authority to direct the conduct of an employee by putting an employee in a position that the employee unduly prioritises compliance with the directions of her employer rather than give due weight to any alternate considerations that might reasonably lead the employee to conduct herself differently in the circumstances, putting both the employee and strangers to the employment relationship at risk of harm. Alternatively, an employer might confer its authority to direct the conduct of an employee upon another person. This conferral of authority creates a power relationship which enables the person upon whom authority has been conferred to direct the conduct of an employee and creates an expectation that the employee will obey, putting the employee at risk of harm.

B. School Relationship

The authority present in the school relationship is very similar to the authority present in the employment relationship, but it is not the same. In the employment relationship, the authority vested in an employer is exercised by the employer for its own benefit, enabling the employer to pursue its commercial objectives. In contrast, the authority vested in a school is exercised primarily for the benefit of the students. The legislation which vests authority in a school to direct the conduct of students does so to enable a school to educate the students. This means that when exercising its authority to direct the conduct of a particular student the school is required to do so in a manner that is consistent with the interests of all other students. For example, when the principal of a school gives a student a direction to sit down on their chair in class, that direction is given in order to protect the particular student from harm and to facilitate the education of all other students in the class. As the direction is consistent with any potential liability the student faces for failing to take reasonable care for her own safety or the safety of others, there is very limited potential for a school to abuse its authority by putting a student in a position that the student unduly prioritises compliance with the directions of the school rather than give due weight to any alternate considerations that might reasonably lead the student to conduct herself differently in the circumstances.

Although there is only very limited potential for a school to influence the decision-making process of a student as the authority vested in the school to direct the conduct of the student has to be exercised in the interests of the student (unlike in the employment relationship where the authority is exercised in the interests of the employer), there is still the potential for the authority present in the school relationship to be abused when that authority is conferred by a school upon another person. A school, as with an employer, is not required to exercise the authority vested in it to direct the conduct of students personally. As a school is not a natural person this would indeed be very difficult.[36] Instead, a school typically confers its authority to direct the conduct of students upon teachers and other educators[37] who then undertake the physical task of educating the students. When a school confers its authority to direct the conduct of students upon a teacher or other educator, however, it creates a power relationship which did not previously exist. This power relationship enables the teacher or other educator to direct the conduct of a student and creates an expectation that the student will obey. The power relationship created by the school is therefore subject to abuse. A teacher, for instance, can use the authority conferred upon them by a school to direct a student into a private room in order to perpetrate a sexual assault. A school consequently puts students at risk of physical harm when it confers authority upon teachers and other educators to direct the conduct of students.

Once again, the authority present in the school relationship is subject to abuse. When a school confers that authority upon a teacher or other educator they create a power relationship which enables the teacher or other educator to direct the conduct of a student and creates an expectation that the student will obey, exposing students to a risk of physical harm. The potential for abuse of the authority present in the school relationship is very similar to that which exists in the employment relationship when an employer confers its authority to direct the conduct of an employee upon another person.

[36] In which case the authority has to be exercised by those in the 'managing mind' of the school, as with corporations.

[37] eg a swimming teacher. See *Woodland v Essex County Council* [2014] AC 537.

C. Agency Relationship

The authority present in the agency relationship is different from the authority present in both the employment and school relationships. It is not an authority to direct the conduct of another person but an authority to effect legal relations on behalf of another person. It follows that the potential for abuse of that authority also differs.

An agency relationship is created when a principal vests authority in an agent to effect legal relations on the principal's behalf. The agent then uses that authority to effect legal relations between the principal and another person (the *transactional party*). As a transactional party is not expected to confirm with the principal the details of those legal relations, the authority vested in an agent by a principal is subject to abuse. An agent, for instance, can use the authority conferred upon them by a principal to misrepresent the nature of property being sold by the principal to a transactional party in order to secure a higher commission. A principal therefore puts a transactional party at risk of harm when she confers authority on an agent to effect legal relations on her behalf.

As with the employment and school relationships, the authority present in the agency relationship is subject to abuse. The vesting of authority by a principal in an agent enables the agent to effect legal relations with a transactional party in circumstances in which the transactional party is not expected to confirm with the principal the details of those legal relations, consequently exposing the transactional party to a risk of harm.

IV. A New Expositive Framework for Strict Liability for the Tort of Another

Although authority is a feature of each of the relationships which give rise to strict liability for the tort of another and such authority determines the cases in which such liability will be imposed, strict liability for the tort of another has never been explained in terms of authority. This book sets out to redress this situation by using this feature of authority to create a new expositive framework within which strict liability for the tort of another can be understood.

The new framework comprises three separate forms of strict liability for the tort of another. Each form of strict liability reflects differences in the nature of the authority present in each of the relationships which give rise to strict liability for the tort of another. The first form of strict liability is *conferred authority strict liability*. This form of strict liability is found in both the employment and school relationships and responds to the potential for abuse of the power relationship created when an employer or school confers authority to direct the conduct of an employee or student upon another person. Conferred authority strict liability will be explained in chapter 4.

The second form of strict liability for the tort of another is *employee strict liability*. This form of strict liability is limited to the employment relationship and responds to the potential for an employer, when exercising its authority to direct the conduct of an employee for its own benefit, to put an employee in a position that the employee unduly prioritises compliance with the directions of the employer rather than give due weight to any alternate considerations that might reasonably lead the employee to conduct herself differently in the circumstances. Employee strict liability will be explained in chapter 5.

The third form of strict liability for the tort of another is *agent strict liability*. This form of strict liability is limited to the agency relationship and responds to the potential for abuse of the authority vested in an agent to effect legal relations on the principal's behalf. Such potential exists because the authority vested in an agent by a principal creates a relationship between the agent and the party wishing to effect legal relations with the principal (the '*transactional party*') which enables the agent to effect legal relations between the principal and the transactional party in circumstances in which the transactional party is not expected to confirm with the principal the details of those legal relations. Agent strict liability will be explained in chapter 6.

Each of the three forms of liability identified above roughly corresponds to an existing form of strict liability for the tort of another. Conferred authority strict liability roughly corresponds to the strict liability currently imposed by the courts using the label of 'liability for breach of a non-delegable duty of care', whilst employee strict liability and agent strict liability roughly correspond to the strict liability currently imposed by the courts using the label 'vicarious liability'. The new expositive framework for strict liability for the tort of another proposed by this book does not seek to change the circumstances in which strict liability for the tort of another currently arises. Instead, it looks to better explain the different forms of strict liability for the tort of another in terms of the authority present in each of the relationships which give rise to such strict liability. To this end, the flawed labels currently used by the courts to describe strict liability for the tort of another will now be abandoned. For the remainder of this book, the different forms of strict liability for the tort of another will be referred to using the terminology proposed by the new expositive framework set out above.

4

Conferred Authority Strict Liability

The first form of strict liability for the tort of another identified by the new expositive framework proposed by this book is *conferred authority strict liability*. As explained in chapter 3, this form of strict liability is found in both the employment and school relationships and responds to the potential of the power relationship created when an employer or school confers its authority to direct the conduct of an employee or student upon another person to be abused.

This chapter will start by examining the basis of conferred authority strict liability. It will then determine the nature of the strict liability, the circumstances in which the strict liability arises, its scope and to whom the strict liability is owed. Finally, the chapter will consider if there are any other relationships in which strict liability might be imposed for the tort of a person upon whom authority has been conferred in relation to another.

I. Basis of the Strict Liability

The authority vested in an employer or school to direct the conduct of an employee or student puts the employer or school in a position of significant power. It also makes an employee or student vulnerable to an abuse of that power. Consequently, restraints are placed on how an employer or school may exercise its authority to direct the conduct of an employee or student. There is an implied term in the employment contract, for instance, that an employer will not use its authority in a manner that is likely to destroy the mutual trust and confidence between an employee and their employer.[1] Legislation also restricts how a school might exercise its authority, for example, schools in a number of jurisdictions are prohibited from using corporal punishment to discipline students.[2]

When an employer or school confers authority to direct the conduct of an employee or student upon another person, the person upon whom that authority is conferred is not necessarily subject to the same restraints in the exercise of that authority as the employer or school. This is because the restraints placed on the

[1] See *Russell v The Trustees of the Roman Catholic Church for the Archdiocese of Sydney* (2008) 72 NSWLR 559. See also C Sappideen, P O'Grady, G Warburton with K Eastman, *Macken's Law of Employment* (6th ed, Sydney, Thomson Reuters, 2009) 171–75.

[2] See, eg, Education Act 1990 (NSW) s 47(h). See also Education Act 1996 (UK) c 56, s 548.

exercise of that authority by an employer or school are generally incorporated into the instruments which create that authority and are not automatically transferred to the person upon whom the authority is conferred. For instance, the obligation of an employer not to use its authority to direct the conduct of an employee in a manner that is likely to destroy the mutual trust and confidence between the employee and the employer is a term implied in the contract of employment and will not transfer to a person upon whom the employer has conferred such authority unless the employer makes such an obligation an express term of the authority being conferred. Similarly, legislative obligations in respect of students are generally placed on schools[3] and do not apply to a person upon whom the school has conferred authority to direct the conduct of students unless the school similarly makes such obligations an express term of the authority being conferred.

Both employers and schools have the capacity to confer authority to direct the conduct of employees and students upon another person. This capacity exists because the possibility of meeting the objectives for which the authority was created would be unduly limited if such authority could be exercised by an employer or school alone. The capacity of an employer or school to confer its authority upon another person, however, is not without its problems. When an employer or school confers authority to direct the conduct of an employee or student upon another person, it creates a power relationship that did not previously exist. This power relationship enables the person upon whom authority has been conferred to direct the conduct of an employee or student and creates an expectation that the employee or student will obey. As the person upon whom authority has been conferred is not necessarily subject to the same restraints in the exercise of that authority as the employer or school, there is significant potential for this power relationship to be abused. A teacher, for instance, may direct a student to perform a scientific experiment, but fail to provide that student with appropriate safety equipment.[4] Employees and students are consequently put at risk of physical harm whenever an employer or school confers authority upon another person to direct the conduct of the employee or student.

It is submitted that it is this potential for a person upon whom authority has been conferred by an employer or school to abuse the power relationship created by the employer or school's conferral of authority that attracts the concern and the intervention of the law. Conferred authority strict liability responds to the potential for abuse of the power relationship created by the employer or school's conferral of authority by holding the employer or school liable for a tort committed against an employee or student by the person upon whom authority has been conferred regardless of the employer or school personally engaging in any conduct to which liability in tort might attach. The liability effectively holds an employer

[3] eg Education Act 1990 (NSW) s 47 requires a school to put in place school policies which do not 'permit corporal punishment of students' but such policies will not necessarily extend to external service providers of activities such as swimming lessons or camps.

[4] *Williams v Eady* (1893) 10 TLR 41.

or school to account for a tort committed against an employee or student by a person upon whom the employer or school has conferred its authority to direct the conduct of the employee or student. In so doing, the liability provides employees and students with a degree of protection from an abuse of the authority conferred by their employer or school upon another person.

It is relatively unusual in tort law for one person to be held strictly liable for the tort of another. As the defendant did not personally engage in any conduct that might attract liability in tort, some other connection between the defendant and the tort needs to be drawn. It has never been sufficient for such purposes that a defendant merely provide an opportunity for another person to commit a tort.[5] When an employer or school confers authority upon another person to direct the conduct of an employee or student, however, they do more than provide a mere opportunity for a tort to be committed.[6] The power relationship created by the conferral of authority can provide the means to commit the tort. A teacher, for instance, can use the authority conferred upon them by a school to direct a student into a private room in order to perpetrate a sexual assault. It is not that an abuse of authority will necessarily occur, but there is always an inherent risk that the authority conferred by the employer or school upon another person to direct the conduct of an employee or student will be abused. As will be seen from the cases, that risk appears sufficient for strict liability for the tort of another to be imposed.

II. Nature of the Strict Liability

Conferred authority strict liability is not an absolute form of liability; it is not imposed in the *absence* of any tort being committed.[7] It still needs to be shown that the person upon whom the employer or school conferred authority to direct the conduct of the employee or student committed a tort against the employee or student. The liability is, however, imposed *regardless* of whether the employer or school engaged in any conduct in respect of the employee or student to which liability in tort might attach.[8] This means that conferred authority strict liability is still imposed even though an employer or school may be able to adduce evidence that the conferral of authority by the employer or school was not a contributing factor in the tort committed against the employee or student by the person upon whom authority was conferred. The liability is also still imposed even though an employer or school may be able to adduce evidence that an abuse of the authority

[5] *Bazley v Curry* (1999) 174 DLR (4th) 45, 63–64.

[6] It being noted by McLachlin CJ in *Bazley v Curry* (1999) 174 DLR (4th) 45 at 63–64 that a mere opportunity for wrongdoing was an insufficient basis upon which to impose strict liability for the tort of another.

[7] P Cane, 'Responsibility and Fault: a Relational and Functional Approach to Responsibility' in P Cane and J Gardner (eds), *Relating to Responsibility* (Oxford, Hart, 2001) 81, 99.

[8] Ibid.

conferred by the employer or school upon the person who committed the tort against the employee or student did not actually take place. This is because conferred authority strict liability responds to a *potential* rather than an *actual* abuse of the authority conferred by the employer or school.

It may seem unfair that an employer or school can be subject to conferred authority strict liability regardless of whether or not the employer or school personally engaged in conduct towards the employee or student to which liability in tort might attach, but an employer or school need not necessarily bear such liability alone. In certain circumstances, an employer or school will be entitled to seek a contribution and/or an indemnity from the person upon whom authority has been conferred in respect of the damages paid by the employer or school to an injured employee or student.[9]

III. In What Circumstances Does the Strict Liability Arise?

Conferred authority strict liability can be imposed on an employer or school whenever an employer or school confers authority upon another person to direct the conduct of an employee or student and that person commits a tort against the employee or student in the course of exercising the conferred authority.[10]

Two points can be made about the general circumstances in which conferred authority strict liability arises. First, conferred authority strict liability is limited to *physical damage*.[11] It is unlikely, for instance, that an employer or school would be held strictly liable to an employee or student defamed by a person upon whom the employer or school had conferred authority to direct the conduct of the employee or student. As the authority conferred by an employer or school is an authority to direct the *physical* conduct of an employee or student, the potential for abuse of the power relationship created by the conferral of that authority is limited to physical harm only.

Secondly, conferred authority strict liability generally only arises in respect of a tort committed by a person upon whom an employer or school has *conferred authority* to direct the conduct of an employee or student. This is because it is only when such authority has been conferred by an employer or school that there is the potential for that authority to be abused by someone other than the employer or school. It does not matter for these purposes whether the person is an employee, an independent contractor or acting gratuitously. What matters is that the person has been conferred authority by an employer or school to direct the conduct of an employee or student. This is borne out by the cases.

[9] Hence an employer's right of indemnity from an employee, for instance. See further ch 5.

[10] What constitutes a tort in the 'course of exercising the conferred authority' will be discussed in the next section.

[11] Including damage consequential upon such physical damage and nervous shock.

A. Employees

As noted in chapter 3, employers are only held strictly liable to employees in respect of torts committed by certain types of people; that is, people who have been conferred authority by an employer to direct the conduct of an employee. Consider *Davie v New Merton Board Mills Ltd.*[12] In that case, the House of Lords held that an employer could not be held strictly liable for the negligence of a tool manufacturer. Although the employee was injured when his employer supplied him with a negligently manufactured tool purchased from the tool manufacturer, the negligence involved in the manufacture of the tool was thought an insufficient basis on which to hold the employer liable. This case has always been thought somewhat anomalous and was ultimately reversed by the Employer's Liability (Defective Equipment) Act 1969 (UK)[13] in order to promote employee safety. The decision of the House of Lords is though explicable on the grounds that the manufacturer had not been conferred any authority to direct the conduct of the injured employee. Arguably, a different conclusion would have been reached on the facts in a case such as *Kondis v State Transport Authority*[14] if the crane driver had given the employee an inappropriate tool to perform a task with the result that the employee was injured. The difference is that in the *Davie* situation no authority over the employee had been conferred upon the tool manufacturer by the employer, whereas in the *Kondis* situation the employee is required by his employer to follow the directions of the independent contractor.[15]

Consider also cases where an employee is sent by her employer to another person's premises and the employee is injured whilst on those premises as a result of that other person not taking reasonable care for the safety of the employee at those premises. Where the other person is a customer, the courts have generally refused to hold the employer strictly liable to the injured employee. The central concern expressed by the courts in such cases has been that the employer had not been to the customer's premises and could not exert any control at the customer's premises.[16] These cases are, however, better explained on the grounds that no authority has been conferred upon the customer by the employer to direct the conduct of the employee. In *Atkinson v Gameco (NSW) Pty Ltd*,[17] for example, the employee had been sent to Thailand with a view to persuading a Thai company to purchase the employer's products. The employee was injured whilst at the premises of the Thai company when inspecting a truck to which it was proposed the

[12] [1959] AC 64 ('*Davie*').

[13] c 37.

[14] (1984) 154 CLR 672 ('*Kondis*').

[15] Similarly, it has not been suggested that an employer is liable to a taxi driver who negligently injures an employee being transported in the course of their employment. Although the taxi driver is an independent contractor, a taxi driver has no supervisory capacity over the employee they are transporting.

[16] See *Pollard v Baulderstone Hornibrook Engineering Pty Ltd* (2008) Aust Torts Reports 81-949.

[17] [2005] NSWCA 338 ('*Atkinson*').

employer's products could be fitted. The employer was not held strictly liable even though the ladder on which the employee was climbing had been inadequately secured by the customer. Similarly, the employer was not held strictly liable in *Estate of the Late M T Mutton by its Executors & R W Mutton trading as Mutton Bros v Howard Haulage Pty Ltd*,[18] where an employee was injured in the process of delivering grain to a customer of the employer as a result of the customer providing unsafe equipment. The key feature in both of these cases is that no authority had been conferred upon either customer by the employer to direct the conduct of the employee.[19] Instead, the employees were making their own decisions as to their conduct at the time they were injured. In *Atkinson*, the employee had requested to inspect the truck and had made his own decision to climb the ladder in order to do so. In *Mutton*, the employee had driven his truck to the position directed by the customer, but had made his own decisions as to when and how the truck was used to unload the grain.

Cases such as *Atkinson* and *Mutton* can be contrasted with those involving a 'borrowed' employee; that is an employee who has been lent by an employer to another business (the '*temporary hirer*').[20] Where the person who commits a tort against an employee is a temporary hirer of that employee, the courts have typically held the employer strictly liable to the employee even though the employee was injured at the premises of the temporary hirer. The decision of the New South Wales Court of Appeal in *English v Rogers*[21] provides a good example. In that case, the employee was a cleaner who had been directed to clean a hotel each night in performance of a contract entered into by his employer and the hotel. Whilst cleaning the hotel one night, the employee was taken hostage by a masked gunman when emptying rubbish at the back of the hotel and suffered psychological trauma as a result. In emptying the rubbish, the employee was following the directions of the hotel owner both as to what to do and how to do it. As the hotel owner had not installed adequate lighting or taken other reasonable security measures, the employee was injured. Although not personally negligent, the employer was held strictly liable to the employee for the negligence of the hotel owner. The decision can be explained in terms of the authority conferred by the employer upon the temporary hirer (in this case, the hotel owner) to direct the conduct of the employee in the course of the temporary hirer's business. Unlike the facts in *Atkinson* and *Mutton*, the employee had been placed under the direction of another person and was injured in the course of complying with those negligent directions.[22]

[18] [2007] NSWCA 340 ('*Mutton*').

[19] For an example from the United Kingdom, see *Cook v Square D Ltd* [1992] ICR 262.

[20] See *Mersey Docks and Harbour Board v Coggins and Griffith (Liverpool) Ltd* [1947] AC 1.

[21] (2005) Aust Torts Reports 81–800.

[22] Ibid 67700 (Mason P): 'the employer submitted that it was not within his power to insist on changes to the physical layout of the hotel premises or the security arrangements that were in place there. I am certainly prepared to accept that the employer was entitled to take these matters into account. But to go further is to argue that the employer's non-delegable duty can be sloughed off by sending the employee to a remote location under another's control. This is not the law.'

Regrettably, courts have not always been alert to the distinction between the two categories of case in which an employee is sent to the workplace of a third party. The resulting confusion can be seen in the decision of the New South Wales Court of Appeal in *Nationwide News Pty Ltd v Naidu*.[23] In that case, the employee was a security guard who was employed by the security firm ISS Security and lent to Nationwide News to provide security services. In lending the employee to Nationwide News, it was agreed that the employee would report directly to the head of security at Nationwide News.[24] Over a period of five years, the head of security repeatedly bullied and abused the employee with the result that the employee suffered a serious psychiatric illness. Two of the judges in the case, Spigelman CJ and Basten JA, held that ISS Security could not be held strictly liable for the various torts[25] committed by the head of security at Nationwide News against the employee because ISS Security had no control over the workplace at Nationwide News. This reasoning is very similar to that used in cases such as *Atkinson* and *Mutton*. In contrast, Beazley JA distinguished cases such as *Atkinson* on the basis that ISS Security had conferred upon the head of security in Nationwide News authority to direct the conduct of the employee.[26] She would have imposed strict liability on ISS Security in much the same way as strict liability was imposed in *English v Rogers*. The reasoning of Beazley JA reflects the broader body of cases and might have been adopted by the other two judges had cases such as *English v Rogers* been brought to their attention.

Cases in which an employee has been injured by a fellow employee in the course of some kind of workplace prank also indicate the significance of an employer having conferred upon another person authority to direct the conduct of an employee before the employer can be held strictly liable for torts committed by that person against the employee. In *Smith v Crossley Bros Ltd*,[27] for instance, an apprentice was severely injured when two fellow apprentices inserted a compressed air pipe into the boy's rectum. In *McCready v Securicor Ltd*[28] an employee's hand was caught in a vault door as the result of the prank of a fellow employee of equal rank. As none of the employees involved in the cases had been conferred any authority over the injured employees, no strict liability was imposed on the employers in respect of the torts committed by the employees which constituted the pranks. In contrast, strict liability *was* imposed on the employer in *Petrou v Hatzigeorgio*[29] in respect of a tort constituting a prank. In that case, an employee

[23] (2007) 71 NSWLR 471.

[24] Ibid 492.

[25] Including assault and battery.

[26] Ibid 515 (Beazley J): 'In ISS Security's case, it had a non-delegable duty to provide him with a safe place and system of work. It breached that duty by having a system of work whereby Mr Naidu was placed under the *supervisory management* of a third party who maltreated him' (emphasis added).

[27] (1951) 95 Sol J 655.

[28] [1991] 81 NI 229. For a more recent example, see *Blake v J R Perry Nominees Pty Ltd* (2010) 195 IR 336, where the Victorian Supreme Court refused to hold an employer liable when one employee hit a fellow employee of equal rank over the back of the legs as a practical joke.

[29] (1991) Aust Torts Reports 81–071.

was injured as a result of the prank of a partner in the business that employed him. The employee was working in a car repair shop when he was covered in paint thinner as a result of horseplay with a fellow employee. The employee then approached the partner complaining that he was wet and asking what he should do to address the situation. The partner lit a cigarette lighter and suggested (in jest) that he could dry himself with that. Unfortunately, the naked flamed got too close to the employee's clothes, causing them to catch alight. The difference between *Petrou* and cases such as *Smith* and *McCready* is that the person responsible for the prank had been conferred authority to direct the conduct of the employee by the employer. The cases therefore confirm the hypothesis that conferred authority strict liability generally only arises by reason of an employment relationship where the person who commits a tort against the employee has been conferred authority by the employer to direct the conduct of the injured employee.

B. Students

As with employers, conferred authority strict liability is generally only imposed on schools where a school has conferred upon another person authority to direct the conduct of a student. This is best seen in the child sexual assault cases where strict liability was imposed on schools or closely analogous institutions for some sexual assaults, but not all.

The first case in which an institution was held strictly liable for the sexual assault of a child within its care was *Bazley v Curry*.[30] In that case, the defendant institution operated 'two residential care facilities for the treatment of emotionally troubled children'.[31] The plaintiff had been placed into full-time care at one of these facilities as a young boy.[32] Whilst at the facility, the plaintiff was sexually assaulted repeatedly by Leslie Curry, an employee of the institution.[33] The Supreme Court of Canada found the institution strictly liable for the sexual assaults.

The circumstances in which strict liability was imposed on the institution in *Bazley v Curry* were as follows. Children were placed in the care of the facilities operated by the defendant institution when those children could no longer be cared for by their parents or foster parents. Whilst at the facility, the institution was solely responsible for the care of the children. It was vested with the same authority to direct the conduct of the children as a parent has to direct the conduct of their own children. This authority was vested in the institution by the government of British Columbia[34] and included the right to discipline the children should they not comply with a direction. Leslie Curry was employed by the institution as a

[30] (1999) 174 DLR (4th) 45.

[31] Ibid 50.

[32] *B(PA) v Curry* (1997) 146 DLR (4th) 72, 76 (Court of Appeal for British Columbia).

[33] Ibid.

[34] Protection of Children Act RSBC 1960, c 303, s 10. This section made the institution the legal guardian of the children in its care.

childcare counsellor.[35] His role was to act a surrogate parent to the children in the facility.[36] This included 'ensuring various house rules were obeyed' and 'ensuring the children got to school on time'.[37] To enable him to perform his duties, the institution conferred its authority to direct the conduct of the children in its care upon Curry. Curry was purporting to exercise that authority immediately prior to committing the assaults.

Similar circumstances existed in *Lister v Hesley Hall Ltd*,[38] the first case in which the House of Lords found an institution strictly liable for the sexual assault of a child within its care by an employee. The defendant institution in that case operated a school and boarding annex for boys. A number of boys were sexually assaulted at the boarding annex by Dennis Grain, who was employed as warden and housemaster of the boarding annex. Boys were sent to the school and boarding annex by local authorities, often because they had 'emotional and behavioural difficulties'.[39] Whilst at the school and boarding annex, the institution was solely responsible for the care of the children. It was vested with the same authority to direct the conduct of the boys as a parent has to direct the conduct of their own children. This authority was vested in the institution by the local authorities[40] and included the right to discipline the children should they not comply with a direction. Dennis Grain's duties as warden and housemaster of the boarding annex included 'making sure the boys went to bed at night, got up in the morning and got to and from school'.[41] It was necessary for the institution to confer its authority to direct the conduct of the boys upon Grain to enable him to perform his duties. Grain was purporting to exercise that authority immediately prior to assaulting the boys.

In *New South Wales v Lepore*[42] and the associated cases, the High Court of Australia considered whether state governments in Australia[43] could be held strictly liable for the sexual assault of children by teachers at government schools. The outcome is of little probative value as the various cases were affected by factual deficiencies and procedural inadequacies which ultimately determined the decisions reached.[44] The factual circumstances of the various cases were not, however, dissimilar to those which were before the courts in *Bazley v Curry* and

[35] (1997) 146 DLR (4th) 72, 76.

[36] Ibid.

[37] Ibid.

[38] [2002] 1 AC 215.

[39] Ibid 220.

[40] Children Act 1975 (UK) c 72, s 60. This section vested in the institution parental rights and duties in respect of the child.

[41] [2002] 1 AC 215, 220.

[42] (2003) 212 CLR 511.

[43] There being a number of cases which were heard together.

[44] In *New South Wales v Lepore* itself, Gleeson CJ, Gaudron, Kirby, Gummow and Hayne JJ ordered a new trial. In *Samin v Queensland* and *Rich v Queensland*, McHugh J allowed the appeal which was dismissed by the remainder of the other judges. As Gleeson CJ noted at 548, however, no evidence as to the nature of the functions and responsibilities of the teachers in these cases had been put before the court.

Lister v Hesley Hall. The various assaults in *New South Wales v Lepore* were alleged to have occurred at schools by teachers in the performance of the teachers' duties. The different schools in those cases, like the residential care facility and boarding annex in the previous cases, were vested with authority to direct the conduct of the children in their care. This authority was similar to that exercised by the parents of the children when they were not at school and was vested in the schools by legislation.[45] That legislation required all children of a certain age to attend school[46] and gave schools the express authority to compel attendance[47] and to maintain discipline within the school.[48] The schools necessarily conferred this authority upon the teachers at the school to enable them to perform their duties. If the teachers were purporting to exercise this authority immediately prior to the assaults in *New South Wales v Lepore* and the associated cases, it is difficult to distinguish the circumstances in *New South Wales v Lepore* and the associated cases from those in *Bazley* v *Curry* and *Lister v Hesley Hall*.[49]

Importantly, schools and closely analogous institutions have not been held strictly liable for all sexual assaults of children within their care. Consider *Jacobi v Griffiths*,[50] a case decided by the Supreme Court of Canada at the same time as *Bazley v Curry*. The defendant institution in that case operated a recreational club for boys and girls held after school and on Saturdays.[51] The plaintiffs, a pair of siblings who regularly attended the club, were sexually assaulted by Harry Griffiths, the club's Programme Director. Although the defendant institution employed Harry Griffiths, it was not held strictly liable for the assaults. An examination of the relationship between the institution and the children who attended the club indicates why. Attendance at the club in *Jacobi v Griffiths* was voluntary and children were free to come and go as they pleased.[52] There was no legislation in place to give the institution authority to direct the conduct of the children at the club or to discipline those children in the event of non-compliance. The children were not engaged in dangerous activities for which disciplinary acts might be justified

[45] *Hole v Williams* (1910) 10 SRNSW 638, 656–57 (Street J): 'but, except in so far as he is restricted, either by agreement with the parent, or by the internal regulations of the department, it appears to me that a public school teacher in teaching or correcting children, in enforcing discipline, in inculcating habits of obedience, or in exercising the various other methods of control and of influence which form part of the child's education, is exercising an authority delegated to him, not by the Government, but by the parent'.

[46] See, eg, Education Act 1990 (NSW) s 22. Education Act 1996 (UK) c 56, s 7 is similar.

[47] Once a student has been enrolled at a school, the school is required to monitor attendance and mechanisms are put in place to respond to instances of truancy. See, eg, Education Act 1990 (NSW) s 24 and s 23(5) respectively.

[48] See, eg, Education Act 1990 (NSW) s 35. See also Education and Inspections Act 2006 (UK) c 40, s 88, which says that 'The governing body of a relevant school must ensure that policies designed to promote good behaviour and discipline on the part of its pupils are pursued at the school'.

[49] Despite its best efforts, the High Court of Australia failed to resolve the uncertainty surrounding *New South Wales v Lepore* in the more recent case of *Prince Alfred College v ADC* (2016) 258 CLR 134. This case is discussed further in ch 7.

[50] (1999) 174 DLR (4th) 71.

[51] Ibid 76–77.

[52] Ibid 83.

on the grounds of keeping the children safe (as with a school bus driver or school-crossing supervisor, for example)[53]. Nor was it apparent that the parents of the children had vested any such authority in the institution. The circumstances of the cases can be distinguished, therefore, from cases such as *Bazley v Curry, Lister v Hesley Hall* and *New South Wales v Lepore* in which the institutions were vested with authority either by legislation or principal carers to direct the conduct of the children in their care and had conferred that authority upon the employee who sexually assaulted the child.[54]

G(ED) v Hammer[55] is another case in which an institution was not held strictly liable for the sexual assault of a child within its care by an employee. The plaintiff in that case attended a government school at which she was sexually assaulted by a janitor employed by the School Board.[56] As in *New South Wales v Lepore*, the School Board was vested with authority to direct the conduct of the children in its care. Unlike in *New South Wales v Lepore*, however, that authority had not been conferred upon the janitor. It was not necessary for the janitor to be conferred any authority to direct the conduct of the children in order for the janitor to perform his duties. As McLachlin CJC commented in delivering the judgment of the Supreme Court of Canada:[57]

> Janitors had no direct duties relating to the care or instruction of students. Nor did they have direct authority over the students – not even the authority to discipline them. If a janitor saw a student misbehaving, the most he could do was report the behaviour to the principal, who would then discipline the child herself.

Similar circumstances arose in *B v Order of the Oblates of Mary Immaculate*.[58] The plaintiff in that case attended a residential school for First Nations children run by the defendant institution. The plaintiff was sexually assaulted on numerous occasions by Martin Saxey, the school baker.[59] The baker, like the janitor in *G(ED) v Hammer*, did not need to be able to direct the conduct of children at the school to perform his duties. As no such authority had been conferred upon Martin Saxey, the institution was not held strictly liable for the sexual assaults.

The conferral of authority can be seen, therefore, to be as significant in the school relationship, as it is in the employment relationship. The cases concerning the school relationship confirm the hypothesis that conferred authority strict

[53] F Trindade, P Cane and M Lunney, *The Law of Torts in Australia* (4th ed, Melbourne, OUP, 2007) 100.

[54] Even if some type of authority could be found to have been vested in the club in certain limited circumstances (either because dangerous activities were being engaged in or because parents had conferred specific authority upon the club), most of the assaults in *Jacobi v Griffiths* occurred at Harry Griffiths' home so that it could not have been said that he was exercising any authority to direct the conduct of the children that had been conferred upon him at the time the assaults occurred.

[55] (2003) 230 DLR (4th) 554.

[56] See also *Alma W v Oakland Unified School District* (1981) 123 Cal App 3d 133.

[57] Ibid 557–58.

[58] (2005) 258 DLR (4th) 385.

[59] Ibid 389.

liability generally only arises where the person who commits a tort against a student has been conferred authority by a school or closely analogous institution to direct the conduct of the student.

IV. Scope of the Strict Liability

Employers and schools are not held strictly liable whenever a person upon whom authority has been conferred to direct the conduct of an employee or student commits a tort against the employee or student. Conferred authority strict liability is generally limited to circumstances in which the person upon whom authority has been conferred by an employer or school commits a tort against the employee or student *in the course of exercising the conferred authority*. The reason is that unless the authority conferred by an employer or school is first being exercised, the power relationship created by the conferral of authority is not in a position to be abused. Without the potential for the power relationship created by the conferral of authority to be abused, there is no basis upon which conferred authority strict liability can be imposed.

Importantly, whether a person upon whom authority has been conferred by an employer or school to direct the conduct of an employee or student commits a tort against the employee or student in the course of exercising the conferred authority is to be determined by reference to the terms of the *apparent* authority conferred by the employer or school, as opposed to the terms of the actual authority conferred by the employer or school. Provided an employee or student reasonably believes that the person upon whom authority has been conferred by the employer or school is purporting to exercise the conferred authority immediately prior to any tort being committed by that person against the employee or student, the tort will be viewed as having occurred in the course of exercising the conferred authority. It follows that conferred authority strict liability can still be imposed even when the person who commits a tort against an employee or student is acting outside the terms of the actual authority conferred by the employer or school. This is best demonstrated by the child sexual assault cases.

In the child sexual assault cases, conferred authority strict liability could not have been imposed if the terms of the actual authority conferred by the schools or closely analogous institutions upon their employees determined the scope of the liability. The employees who committed the assaults in those cases would have known that it was not within the terms of their actual authority to sexually assault a child in their care or to engage in conduct with the purpose of sexually assaulting the child.[60] Immediately prior to the assaults occurring, however, the employees

[60] It was acknowledged by the Supreme Court of New Zealand in *Dollars & Sense Finance Ltd v Rerekohu Nathan* [2008] 2 NZLR 557 (at 576) that acts knowingly done for the purpose of enabling wrongdoing to occur could not be considered to have been done within the actual authority of the wrongdoer.

were engaged in activities such as putting the child within their care to bed[61] or disciplining the child.[62] Consequently, the employees were acting within the terms of the apparent authority which had been conferred upon them by the schools or closely analogous institutions. As the employees were acting within the terms of the apparent authority conferred upon them by the schools or closely analogous institutions, there was the potential for the conferred authority to be abused. It follows that the assaults occurred in the course of exercising the conferred authority so that conferred authority strict liability could be imposed.

The reason the scope of conferred authority strict liability is determined by reference to the terms of the apparent (as opposed to the actual) authority conferred by an employer or school upon another person is because the employee or student over whom authority has been conferred will interact with the person upon whom authority has been conferred on the basis of the terms of the apparent authority conferred by the employer or school. One reason a student will go with a teacher into a storeroom, for instance, is because the teacher has the apparent authority to direct the student to do so.[63] The power relationship between the person upon whom authority has been conferred and the employee or student over whom authority has been conferred is therefore shaped by the terms of the apparent authority conferred by the employer or school upon that person and not by the terms of the actual authority that has been conferred. It is the potential for this power relationship to be abused which puts employees and students at risk of physical harm.

The terms of the apparent (as opposed to the actual) authority conferred by an employer or school upon another person are also used in the employment context to determine the scope of conferred authority strict liability. Consider *Petrou v Hatzigeorgio*[64] which was mentioned above. The partner in that case would have known that he did not have actual authority to physically threaten the employee or set the employee on fire. Despite this, the partnership was still held strictly liable to the employee. The decision can be explained on the basis that, immediately prior to the tort being committed, the partner was acting within the terms of the apparent authority conferred by the partnership by directing the employee as how best to deal with the problem of the spilt paint thinner. As the employee in such circumstances would have been expected to stand and listen to the partner's response, limiting the options the employee might have had in responding to the impending danger, there was the potential for the power relationship created by the conferral of authority to be abused. This is subsequently what happened when the partner struck the match. It follows that the tort was committed by the partner in the course of exercising the conferred authority and conferred authority strict liability could be imposed.

[61] See, eg, *Lister v Hesley Hall Ltd* [2002] 1 AC 215.
[62] See, eg, *New South Wales v Lepore* (2003) 212 CLR 511.
[63] See, eg, ibid.
[64] (1991) Aust Torts Reports 81–071.

The facts of the Scottish case of *MacMillan v Wimpey Offshore Engineers and Constructors Ltd*[65] provide another example, even though the case was decided under statute. In that case, the pursuer was employed on an oil rig. He was standing outside his employer's office on the oil rig discussing with his foreman and another employee a job he was required to do in the course of his employment when the foreman grabbed the pursuer and 'battered his head against a metal skip'.[66] The employer was held liable under the statute for this battery,[67] but arguably could also have been held strictly liable at common law. Once again, although neither the battery nor the acts leading up to the battery were within the terms of the actual authority conferred upon the foreman by the employer to direct the conduct of the pursuer, the foreman was acting within the terms of the apparent authority that had been conferred upon him by the employer immediately prior to committing the battery by directing the pursuer as to the work he was required to do on the rig. As the pursuer was expected to stand and listen to those directions, there was the potential for the foreman to abuse the power relationship created by the employer's conferral of authority. This is subsequently what happened when the foreman thrust the pursuer's head into the metal skip.

Critically, it does not appear necessary for the authority conferred by the employer to direct the conduct of the employee to be being exercised within the workplace at the time the tort is committed for conferred authority strict liability to be imposed. As determined by the England and Wales Court of Appeal in *Bellman v Northampton Recruitment Limited*,[68] the relevant factor is the apparent exercise of the authority conferred in respect of the employee, not the location where the authority is being exercised. In that case, the managing director of Northampton Recruitment punched the claimant sales manager at a hotel following a Christmas party, causing catastrophic injuries. Lady Justice Asplin described the circumstances of the punch as follows:[69]

> At around 2am, the conversation amongst the remaining employees turned to work, including NR's plans for the following year. In fact, at all times after 2am the conversation was focussed on NR's business. At around 2.45am, a group of six including Mr Major and Mr Bellman went outside. They stood together and continued to discuss NR's business. Mr Bellman mentioned a Mr Steven Kelly, a new NR employee. Mr Kelly had been the subject of conversation in the office and it was understood that he was being paid substantially more than anyone else. Mr Major became annoyed at being questioned about Mr Kelly's appointment and pointedly returned to the hotel lobby.

[65] [1991] SLT 515 ('*MacMillan*').

[66] Ibid 516.

[67] Offshore Installations (Operational Safety, Health and Welfare) Regulations 1976 (UK) No 1672, reg 32(3) enacted under the Mineral Workings (Offshore Installations) Act 1971 (UK) c 61 stated that every person on the oil rig had a duty 'not to do anything likely to endanger the safety or health of himself or any other person on or near the installation' and reg 32(2) made it the duty of the employer to ensure that every employee complied with reg 32(3). The liability of the employer under these regulations was described as a 'direct' liability rather than a vicarious liability by the court.

[68] (2018) EWCA Civ 2214.

[69] Ibid [6].

> Once inside, he 'summoned' the remaining company employees and began to lecture them on how he owned the company, that he was in charge and that he would do what he wanted to do; that the decisions were his to take and that he paid their wages.

Once again, although the battery was not within the terms of the actual authority conferred upon the managing director by the employer to direct the conduct of the employee, the managing director was acting within the terms of the apparent authority that had been conferred upon him by the employer immediately prior to committing the battery. The employee had been 'summoned' to attend the lecture and was expected to stand and listen to that lecture. It follows that there was the potential for the managing director to abuse the power relationship created by the employer's conferral of authority which eventually occurred when the managing director punched the employee. The importance of the managing director purporting to exercise the authority conferred upon him by the employer to direct the conduct of the employee was highlighted by Asplin LJ:[70]

> It seems to me that despite the time and the place, Mr Major was purporting to act as managing director of NR. He was exercising the very wide remit which had been granted to him by NR. His managerial decision making having been challenged, he took it upon himself to seek to exercise authority over his subordinate employees. The lecture itself was concerned with the nature and extent of his authority in relation to NR's business and the exercise of that authority over his fellow employees. He chose to wear his metaphorical managing director's hat and to deliver a lecture to his subordinates. He was purporting to use his position and drove home his managerial authority, with which he had been entrusted, with the use of blows. Looked at objectively, he was purporting to exercise his authority over his subordinates and was not merely one of a group of drunken revellers whose conversation had turned to work. It seems to me that the attack arose out of a misuse of the position entrusted to Mr Major as managing director. He asserted his authority in the presence of around 50% of NR's staff and misused that authority. It was not merely a discussion leading to an altercation between hotel guests and visitors, as the Judge described them.

The facts of *Petrou*, *MacMillan* and *Bellman* are indistinguishable from cases such as *Kondis*. Yet contrast those facts with a situation where two employees of equal rank fight in the staff room.[71] It is generally recognised that no strict liability for the tort of another can be imposed on an employer in such circumstances.[72] The reason is that neither employee has been conferred authority to direct the conduct of the other by the employer. It follows that each employee is in a position to take steps for their own protection and there is no power relationship created by the conferral of authority that has the potential to be abused.

Consider further cases in which an employee has been sexually assaulted in the workplace. In *Reilly v Devereux*,[73] a gunner in the army was sexually assaulted

[70] Ibid [25].
[71] An example used in *Bazley v Curry* (1999) 174 DLR (4th) 45, 65.
[72] Ibid. Cf *Mohamud v WM Morrison Supermarkets plc* [2016] AC 677, discussed further in ch 7.
[73] [2009] IESC 22.

by his sergeant. Despite the Supreme Court of Ireland refusing to hold the army strictly liable for the sexual assault, the facts are indistinguishable from those in *MacMillan*. The assaults took place in the sergeant's office and the sergeant was acting within the terms of the apparent authority conferred upon him by the army to direct the conduct of the gunner immediately prior to the assaults occurring. *Reilly v Devereux* can be contrasted with *Antoniak v Commonwealth*[74] in which the Commonwealth government was not held strictly liable for a sexual assault committed by one soldier against another of equal rank.

As the scope of conferred authority strict liability is not limited by the terms of the actual authority conferred by an employer or school upon the person who commits a tort against the employee or student, the scope of the strict liability is broader than it otherwise would be. It is not, however, unlimited. It is still possible to envisage situations in which an employer or school will not be held strictly liable for a tort committed by a person upon whom authority has been conferred to direct the conduct of an employee or student.

It is unlikely, for instance, that an employer would be held strictly liable if a foreman upon whom authority had been conferred in relation to another employee walked into the staff room and shot that employee whilst the employee was at lunch.[75] As the employee in such circumstances is on a break and not dealing with the foreman in any official capacity, the apparent authority conferred by the employer upon the foreman to direct the conduct of the employee is not being exercised. As the foreman is not exercising the conferred authority, the power relationship created by the conferral of authority is not in a position to be abused and there is no basis upon which conferred authority strict liability can be imposed. At best, the employer provided an opportunity for the tort to be committed by giving the employees access to the staff room and it has long been recognised that providing a mere opportunity for a tort to be committed is an insufficient basis upon which strict liability for the tort of another can be imposed.

Nor is it likely that a school would be held strictly liable to a student sexually assaulted by a teacher at the teacher's home on the weekend.[76] The authority conferred upon a teacher by a school is limited to the school relationship so that the teacher cannot reasonably be considered to be exercising that authority outside the school relationship.[77] Once again, if the teacher is not exercising the conferred authority, the power relationship created by the conferral of authority is not in a position to be abused and there is no basis upon which conferred authority strict liability can be imposed.

[74] (1962) 4 FLR 454.

[75] For a similar factual scenario, where one employee shot another outside the work premises, see *Gittani Stone Pty Limited v Pavkovic* (2007) Aust Torts Reports 81–924.

[76] As occurred in *Jacobi v Griffiths* (1999) 174 DLR (4th) 71.

[77] The school relationship extends to school excursions; cf *ST v North Yorkshire County Council* [1999] LGR 584, which was overruled by *Lister v Hesley Hall Ltd* [2002] 1 AC 215.

Any concern that conferred authority strict liability is still too broad[78] needs to be considered in light of the principal requirement that needs to be satisfied for the strict liability to be imposed. The key feature of conferred authority strict liability is that it only arises where the person who commits a tort against an employee or student has been conferred authority by an employer or school to direct the conduct of an employee or student. This narrows considerably the scope of conferred authority strict liability.

V. To Whom is the Strict Liability Owed?

As conferred authority strict liability arises by reason of both the employment and school relationships, the strict liability is owed to both employees and students.

A. Employees

Determining who is an employee for the purposes of tort law is not necessarily a straightforward exercise. Currently, a range of indicia are used to determine whether a contract securing the use of human resources is an employment contract. Those indicia include:[79]

> the right to have a particular person do the work, the right to suspend or dismiss the person engaged, the right to the exclusive services of the person engaged and the right to dictate the place of work, hours of work and the like.

They also include control.[80] Control has often been criticised as an indicium of employment on the basis that it is very difficult to say that an employer can control how a skilled employee does their work.[81] Despite such criticisms, 'control' continues to be used as an indicia of employment, although in the more refined sense of an employer having the authority to direct the behaviour of an employee. As the High Court of Australia explained in *Zuijis v Wirth Brothers Pty Ltd*:[82]

> The duties to be performed may depend so much on special skill or knowledge or they may be so clearly identified or the necessity of the employee acting on his [sic] own responsibility may be so evident, that little room for direction or command in detail may exist. But this is not the point. What matters is lawful authority to command so far as there is scope for it. And there must always be room for it, if only in incidental or collateral matters.

[78] See, eg, *New South Wales v Lepore* (2003) 212 CLR 511, 601–03 (Gummow and Hayne JJ). See also *Reilly v Devereux* [2009] IESC 22 (Kearns J): 'To hold otherwise would be to extend to the Defence Forces a virtual new species of liability where the defendants would be liable for virtually every act or omission of an employee'.

[79] *Stevens v Brodribb Sawmilling Company Pty Ltd* (1986) 160 CLR 16, 36 (Wilson and Dawson JJ).

[80] Ibid 24.

[81] PS Atiyah, *Vicarious Liability in the Law of Torts* (London, Butterworths, 1967) 46–49.

[82] (1955) 93 CLR 561, 571.

This more modern sense of 'control' reflects the notion of authority which is at the centre of conferred authority strict liability. It follows that for conferred authority strict liability to be imposed, a person needs at the very least to have been engaged under a contract which vests an employer with general authority to direct the conduct of the person in the course of the employer's enterprise.[83] Such authority is broad in scope and has the potential, when conferred upon another person, to be abused. This can be contrasted with any of the other types of contracts that might be entered into by an employer in order to secure the use of human resources. For example, an employer may engage a person to do a particular thing, such as write a report or build a structure. Under such contracts, although some type of authority may be vested in the employer, it will necessarily be limited by reference to the task and its duration. The narrow nature of such authority and its limited duration is therefore generally insufficient to attract conferred authority strict liability as there is only limited capacity for such authority to be abused.

B. Students

It is less difficult to identify who is a student for the purposes of conferred authority strict liability. A student is any child enrolled at a private or public institution regulated as a school by legislation in the jurisdiction in which it is situated. Schools, however, are not the only institutions which care for children and the child sexual assault cases show that institutions other than schools might be subject conferred authority strict liability. The question then is what other child care institutions are sufficiently analogous to a school that conferred authority strict liability can be imposed in respect of children attending those institutions.

It is very difficult to make generalisations as to what types of child care organisations other than schools might be subject to conferred authority strict liability. Ideally, each child care organisation would have to be individually assessed to see whether the organisation was vested with sufficient authority to direct the conduct of the children in its care. Although such an analysis is beyond the scope of this book, over time what could foreseeably emerge is a scale of child care organisations with child care organisations at one end of the scale that are analogous to schools so that they are subject to conferred authority strict liability, and child care organisations at the other end of the scale that are not subject to conferred authority strict liability. Where a child care organisation sat on this scale would depend on the degree of authority vested in the child care organisation to direct the conduct of the children in its care.

[83] That enterprise may be not-for-profit. See, eg, *Cox v Ministry of Justice* [2016] AC 660. In that case, Lord Reed noted that although 'control' could not be the sole indicator of an employment relationship, 'the absence of even that vestigial degree of control would be liable to negative the imposition of vicarious liability' (669).

For instance, it is possible to analyse the relationship between long-day child care centres and the children in their care in very similar terms to the relationship between a school and a student. A long-day child care centre, for example, will organise certain activities throughout the day, will arrange for children to eat and take naps and will even, where necessary, take steps to discipline children. The centre is essentially appointed to act as a surrogate parent of a child whilst the child is in its care. The centre is authorised to do this by way of the contractual relationship between the centre and the parent of the child. In this sense, a long-day child care centre is quite like the care facility upon which conferred authority strict liability was imposed in *Bazley v Curry*.[84] There is also an increasing amount of government regulation of such centres.[85] Governments in a number of jurisdictions have advocated the use of the centres so as to encourage women with children into the workplace.[86] Consequently, it might be possible in future to say that the authority to direct the conduct of children is derived from legislation, as has since become the case with schools.[87]

In contrast, it is difficult to analyse the relationship between children and organisations which provide a range of recreational activities in similar terms. It is not clear what authority can be exercised by these organisations over the children in their care. For instance, does an organisation like the Scouts have the authority to discipline a child? If not, it might be seen as analogous to the recreational child care provider in *Jacobi v Griffiths*[88] such that conferred authority strict liability cannot be imposed.[89]

VI. Other Relationships

Are there relationships other than the employment and school relationships by reason of which conferred authority strict liability might be imposed? Possibly; but it would need to be shown that one of the parties in the relationship was vested with authority to direct the conduct of the other party and that such authority could be conferred upon another person.

A. Police

One such relationship which gives rise to conferred authority strict liability is the relationship between a state and its citizens in respect of a tort committed against

[84] (1999) 174 DLR (4th) 45.

[85] See, eg, Children and Young Persons (Care and Protection) Act 1998 (NSW).

[86] By way of childcare subsidies, child benefits and family taxation. F Jaumotte, 'Female Labour Force Participation: Past Trends and Main Determinants in OECD Countries' OECD Economics Department Working Papers, No 376, (2003).

[87] See *Ramsay v Larsen* (1964) 111 CLR 16; cf *Hole v Williams* (1910) 10 SRNSW 638.

[88] (1999) 174 DLR (4th) 71.

[89] cf *Fitzgerald v Hill* (2008) 51 MVR 55 which involved a Tae Kwon Do academy.

a citizen by a member of the police force. A state is vested with coercive authority to direct the conduct of its citizens which is then conferred upon members of the police force to uphold the laws of the state. This authority is closely analogous to that found in the employment and school relationships.

Consider the decision of the Supreme Court of California in *Mary M v City of Los Angeles*.[90] In that case, a police officer, whilst in uniform and driving a marked police vehicle, pulled over a female driver and subjected her to a sobriety test. When she failed the test, the police officer drove her home and raped her. Her efforts to resist the attack were rebuffed with threats that the police officer would take her to jail.[91] The female driver successfully sued the governmental authority that employed the police officer for the injuries she sustained as a result of the rape. In holding the City of Los Angeles strictly liable for the rape, the court focused on the coercive authority conferred upon the police officer by the City:[92]

> Police officers occupy a unique position of trust in our society. They are responsible for enforcing the law and protecting society from criminal acts. They are given the authority to detain and to arrest and, when necessary, to use deadly force. As visible symbols of that formidable power, an officer is furnished a distinctively marked car, a uniform, a badge, and a gun. Those who challenge an officer's actions do so at their peril; anyone who resists an officer's proper exercise of authority or who obstructs the performance of an officer's duties is subject to criminal prosecution.

Immediately prior to the assault in *Mary M*, the police officer was exercising the authority which had been conferred upon him by the city of Los Angeles. It is unlikely, for instance, that the female driver would have allowed herself to be pulled over or gone with the police officer other than for the reason that he was a police officer who had been conferred authority to direct her conduct. In such circumstances, there was the potential for the police officer to abuse the conferred authority. This is subsequently what happened when the police officer raped her. It follows that, in the circumstances of the case, conferred authority strict liability could be imposed.

The Privy Council reached a similar decision in *Bernard v Attorney General of Jamaica*.[93] In that case a uniformed police officer had jumped in at the front of a queue waiting to use a telephone at the Central Sorting Office in Kingston. The plaintiff, who was next in line, refused to let go of the phone, even after the police officer asserted that the telephone was needed for police business. In response, the police officer shot him in the head at point-blank range. It was later established that there was no emergency for which the police officer needed the phone. The plaintiff succeeded in suing the governmental authority responsible for employing the police officer in respect of the injuries he sustained as a result of the shooting. The basis of the judgment was the fact that the police officer 'had purported to act

[90] (1991) Cal 3d 202 ('*Mary M*').
[91] Ibid 219.
[92] Ibid 206 (Kennard J).
[93] [2005] IRLR 398.

as a policeman immediately before he shot the plaintiff'.[94] Once again, as the police officer was exercising the apparent authority conferred upon him by the governmental authority immediately before the shooting, there was the potential for the police officer to abuse the conferred authority. This is subsequently what happened when the police officer shot the plaintiff. It follows that, in the circumstances of the case, there was a sufficient basis for conferred authority strict liability to be imposed.

Before conferred authority strict liability can be imposed on a state in respect of a tort committed by a police officer, it first needs to be shown that the tort occurred in the course of the police officer exercising the apparent authority conferred upon the police officer by the state. This is because it is only in such circumstances that there is the potential for the power relationship created by the conferral of authority to be abused. This requirement was satisfied in both of the above cases as the police officers were both in uniform and acting within the terms of the apparent authority conferred upon the police officers immediately prior to the tort being committed. By way of contrast, consider the decision of the Privy Council in *Attorney-General of the British Virgin Islands v Hartwell*.[95] The police officer in that case was based in the British Virgin Islands. Whilst on duty, he abandoned his post and went to look for his life partner who he suspected of having an affair. He took a gun with him from a cabinet at the police station, but was not wearing his police uniform at the time.[96] When the police officer found the bar at which his life partner was having dinner with another man, he fired four shots without warning, one of which struck the plaintiff causing him serious injuries. At no time in the lead up to the shooting did the police officer identify himself as a police officer. The plaintiff failed in his attempt to hold the governmental authority which employed the police officer liable for the shooting. The court found that the shooting 'had nothing whatever to do with any police duties, either actually or ostensibly'.[97] As the police officer did not shoot the plaintiff in the course of exercising the authority conferred upon him by the state, the power relationship created by the conferral of authority was not in a position to be abused. Consequently, there was no basis upon which conferred authority strict liability could be imposed.

Unfortunately, it is not always easy to determine whether or not a police officer commits a tort in the course of exercising the authority conferred upon them by the state. It can be quite difficult, as seen in the English decision of *N v Chief Constable of Merseyside Police*.[98] The police officer in this case had gone off duty at about 2am in the morning. Whilst remaining in uniform, he got into his car and parked outside a night club. He was still there at 4am in the morning when a woman left the club to run across the road to get a kebab. The woman was under

[94] Ibid [26].
[95] [2004] 1 WLR 1273.
[96] Ibid 1276.
[97] Ibid 1278.
[98] [2006] 1 Pol LR 160.

the influence of both drugs and alcohol and the first aid officer at the club was trying to encourage her to get in a cab and go home. The police officer had the window of his vehicle down and asked the first aid officer if everything was ok. The first aid officer explained what he was trying to do and the police officer said he would 'sort it'. He told the women that he was the police and that he would drive her to the police station. Instead of driving her to the police station, however, the police officer drove her to his own home and raped her. Justice Nelson in the High Court found that the governmental authority which employed the police officer could not be held strictly liable for the rape. The basis of his judgment appears to be the judge's view that the police officer was 'on the prowl' for a victim at the time he came across the plaintiff, which was why he was sitting in his car outside the night club at 4am in the morning. The judge was therefore concerned that the police officer was out on a 'frolic of his own'.[99] This might be true, but given that the police officer was exercising his apparent authority as a member of the police force immediately prior to the woman getting into his car,[100] it is very difficult to say that the potential for the police officer to abuse the conferred authority did not exist. It is very unlikely that the woman would have got in the car, or the first aid officer would have allowed her to get in the car, but for the fact that it was driven by a police officer who said he was going to take her to the police station. On this basis, it is very difficult to distinguish *N v Chief Constable of Merseyside Police* from a case such as *Mary M*.

It follows that conferred authority strict liability can be imposed on a state in respect of a tort committed by a police officer when the police officer commits that tort against another person in the course of exercising the authority conferred upon the police officer over that person by the state.[101] Such liability arguably also extends to the torts of prison officers who are conferred similar authority in respect of prison inmates.[102]

B. Churches

With the recent publicity surrounding the abuse of children in churches and church-run organisations throughout the world,[103] there has been speculation as to whether conferred authority strict liability might be imposed on a church in respect of a tort committed by a priest. It is not clear, however, whether the

[99] See *Bugge v Brown* (1919) 26 CLR 110.

[100] [2006] 1 Pol LR 160, [33].

[101] Previous restrictions on the capacity of the Crown to be sued in respect of the wrongdoing of police officers have been removed by legislation in most Australian states and territories. See RP Balkin and JLR Davis, *Law of Torts* (4th ed, Sydney, LexisNexis, 2009) 754, fn 283. See also Police Act 1996 (UK) c 16, s 88.

[102] See *Racz v Home Office* [1994] 2 AC 45. See also *British Columbia v Zastowny* (2008) 290 DLR (4th) 219.

[103] See, eg, Commission to Inquire into Child Abuse, Parliament of Ireland, *Report* (2009). See also S Lunn, 'Sexual abuse apology welcomed', *The Australian*, 21 July 2008.

relationship between a church and its parishioners is sufficiently analogous to either the employment and school relationships for such liability to be imposed.

Courts have traditionally been very reluctant to impose strict liability on a church in respect of a tort committed by a priest. In *Rita M v Roman Catholic Archbishop of Los Angeles*,[104] for instance, the Californian Court of Appeal refused to hold the Roman Catholic Church strictly liable when six parish priests conspired to use their position to have regular sexual intercourse with a 16-year-old girl in the parish. The girl fell pregnant, was sent by the priests to the Philippines to have her baby and subsequently abandoned. The Californian Court of Appeal also refused to hold the Baptist Church strictly liable in *Jeffrey E v Central Baptist Church*[105] for a series of sexual assaults committed by a Sunday school teacher of a six-year-old boy.

Part of the reason why courts have been reluctant in the past to impose strict liability on a church in respect of a tort committed by a priest was that the nature of the torts committed went so far beyond the ideology of the church that it was difficult to make a connection between the church and the tort. As Sonenshine J commented in *Jeffrey E*, 'the acts were independent, self-serving pursuits unrelated to church activities'.[106] There have also been difficulties assessing whether a priest is an employee in the traditional sense and if so, whether there is a single entity that can be identified as their employer.[107]

More recently, however, courts have started to impose strict liability on churches in respect of torts committed by priests. In *John Doe v Bennett*,[108] for instance, the Supreme Court of Canada held the Roman Catholic Church strictly liable when a priest sexually assaulted a number of choir boys in his parish over a period of almost two decades. In *Maga v The Trustees of the Birmingham Archdiocese of the Roman Catholic Church*,[109] the England and Wales Court of Appeal held the Roman Catholic Church liable for the sexual assault of a 12-year-old boy who had come into contact with the priest in a shopping centre carpark, although the boy was not actually a parishioner of the church.

This shift towards imposing strict liability on a church in respect of a tort committed by a priest has been prompted by the recent cases in which schools have been held strictly liable in respect of torts committed by teachers, including sexual assaults. The courts have reasoned that just as a school puts a teacher into a position of intimacy with respect to students, a church puts a priest into a position of psychological intimacy with respect to the children of the parish.[110]

[104] (1986) 187 Cal App 3d 1453.

[105] (1988) 197 Cal App 3d 718 ('*Jeffrey E*').

[106] Ibid (5b).

[107] Such issues are canvassed in IR Stauffer and CB Hyde, 'The Sins of the Fathers: Vicarious Liability of Churches' (1993) 25 *Ottawa Law Review* 561. They were also recently considered by the New South Wales Court of Appeal in *Trustees of the Roman Catholic Church v Ellis* (2007) 70 NSWLR 565.

[108] (2004) 236 DLR (4th) 577.

[109] [2010] 1 WLR 1441.

[110] *John Doe v Bennett* (2004) 236 DLR (4th) 577, 588.

This analogy, however, is not precise. Schools are vested with legally recognised authority to direct the conduct of students and confer that authority on a teacher to enable students to be educated. Churches might be intimate with their parishioners but they are not vested with any formal authority to direct the conduct of the parishioners.

Whether conferred authority strict liability can be imposed on a church in respect of a tort committed by a priest is a difficult question. It might be possible to develop an authority-based analogy which relates more closely to the strict liability imposed on schools than the current analogy based on intimacy. It could be argued, for instance, that although a church is not vested with formal authority to direct the conduct of its parishioners, it is vested with a different type of authority in respect of the spiritual behaviour of its parishioners. Such authority is not dissimilar in nature to the authority vested in a school or an employer as a failure to obey directions may be perceived as having disciplinary consequences (though perhaps not immediate). The strength of such authority will also tend to increase the more 'immature and inexperienced' members of the congregation are, as is the case with children. The danger with this kind of analogy, however, is that the concept of 'authority' is weakened to the point that it can be found in any relationship in which an opportunity for a tort to be committed is provided. This is not what the cases suggest conferred authority strict liability is about. It has been said time and time again that something more is needed to impose strict liability on one person for the tort of another than a defendant simply providing the opportunity for a tort to be committed.[111] Hospitals, for instance, are not generally held strictly liable when a doctor sexually assaults a patient.[112] Although a hospital provides an opportunity for a sexual assault to occur, doctors are not conferred any authority to direct the conduct of the patient by the hospital.[113] Consequently, there is an insufficient connection between the hospital and the tort for strict liability to be imposed. Instead tort law responds to the vulnerability of the patient in such circumstances by extending liability in negligence to cover omissions, as well as acts (as it does in similar professional relationships characterised by an information deficit between the lay person and the professional).[114]

The dangers of extending conferred authority strict liability to churches in respect of torts committed by priests can be seen in *Maga v The Trustees of the*

[111] *Bazley v Curry* (1999) 174 DLR (4th) 45, 63–64.

[112] See *Lisa M v Henry Mayo Newhall Memorial Hospital* (1995) 12 Cal 4th 291 (in respect of a radiologist) and *Brayshaw v Aspley Surgery* [2018] EWHC 3286 (QB) (in respect of a locum GP). Cf *Barclays Bank v Various Claimants* [2018] EWCA Civ 1670, a case which involved sexual assaults by a doctor commissioned by a bank to conduct employee checks (rather than being engaged by a hospital). Case discussed further in ch 9.

[113] Ibid 304 (Werdegar J): 'Hospital did not give Tripoli any power to exercise general control over plaintiff's liberty. He was not vested with any coercive authority, and the trust plaintiff was asked to place in him was limited to conduct of an ultrasound examination'.

[114] See further C Beuermann, 'Do Hospitals Owe a so-called "Non-Delegable" Duty of Care to their Patients?' (2018) 26 *Medical Law Review* 1.

Birmingham Archdiocese of the Roman Catholic Church.[115] The church was held strictly liable for the assault of the boy in that case even though the church 'did not seek to engage with [the boy] on any religious level'.[116] Various reasons were given for the strict liability, including the 'degree of general moral authority'[117] vested in the priest by the church. It is very difficult, however, to say that the church in that case was vested with any authority over the boy given that the boy was not a parishioner and did not engage with the priest on a religious level (if indeed he had any faith at all). It is therefore unclear how the church might have created a power relationship between the priest and the boy which the priest had the potential to abuse.

C. Parents and Foster Parents

Another relationship within which authority is present is the relationship between a parent and child. In much the same way as an employer or school is vested with authority to direct the conduct of an employee or student, a parent is able to direct the conduct of their child. Such authority, however, typically arises without the intervention of the state.[118] It is an authority which typically arises naturally by virtue of established non-legal social practice as opposed to being created and enforced by the law.[119]

Although a parent is able to direct the conduct of their child, courts have not been very willing to impose liability on parents in respect of the exercise of that authority. Parents, for instance, have long been thought not to be liable in negligence to a child unless the harm to the child results from some type of action by the parent that places the child in danger.[120] In contrast, schools are subject to a positive duty to take reasonable steps for the safety of the children in their care.[121] Compare the following cases. In *Arnold v Teno*,[122] the Supreme Court of Canada found that a mother was not liable to her daughter who had been struck by a car on a busy road after purchasing an ice-cream at an ice-cream van after the mother had given her daughter money for that purpose and sent her off alone. In contrast, the House of Lords in *Barnes v Hampshire County Council*[123] found a school liable to a

[115] [2010] 1 WLR 1441.

[116] Ibid 1447.

[117] Ibid 1455.

[118] The authority is not created by legislation and cannot be upheld by the courts by way of a civil action. In contrast, an employer can approach the courts to enforce their authority over an employee through an action for breach of contract.

[119] Cf some cases of adoption.

[120] eg the parent of a child hit by a car was held liable to the child in *McCallion v Dodd* [1966] NZLR 710 because the parent had required the child to walk on the side of the road at night.

[121] See, eg, *Geyer v Downs* (1977) 138 CLR 91.

[122] (1978) 83 DLR (3rd) 609.

[123] [1969] 1 WLR 1563.

student that was injured by a truck on her way home from school after the children were released from school five minutes before the official closing time.

Various reasons have been given for the reluctance of the courts to impose liability on a parent in respect of harm to their children, including: difficulties in setting the standard of care;[124] a concern not to interfere in family relationships;[125] and a concern that if liability were imposed no one would be prepared to assist parents in looking after their children.[126] The 24/7 nature of the parent/child relationship and the general inability of a parent to surrender parental responsibility in respect of their child are also likely to be relevant factors.[127] Whatever the reason, there do not appear to be any cases in which conferred authority strict liability has been imposed on a parent; for instance, in respect of a tort committed by a babysitter engaged by a parent who has injured a child.[128] In fact, it would be quite odd if the courts did impose such liability given that the courts rarely impose liability when the authority is exercised by parents themselves.

Notwithstanding the position taken in respect of parents, the Supreme Court of the United Kingdom recently held in *Armes v Nottinghamshire County Council*[129] that a local authority could be held strictly liable for the sexual assault of a foster child placed by the local authority in the care of a foster parent. How might this result be explained in light of the reluctance to impose similar strict liability for the tort of another on a parent?

The roles of both parents and foster parents are similar. Like parents, a foster parent has day-to-day responsibility for the care of a foster child. Typically, a foster parent has no parental responsibility for a foster child before that child is placed in the foster parent's care by a local authority. A local authority may, however, under current regulations, place a foster child in the care of their legal parent if it is in

[124] See *Surtees v The Royal Borough of Kingston Upon Thames* [1992] PIQR 101, 123–24 (Vice-Chancellor): 'The studied calm of the Royal Courts of Justice, concentrating on one point at a time, is light years away from the circumstances prevailing in the average home. The mother is looking after a fast moving toddler at the same time as cooking the meal, doing the housework, answering the telephone, looking after the other children and doing all the other things that the average mother has to cope with simultaneously or in quick succession in the normal household. We should be slow to characterize as negligent the care which ordinary loving and careful mothers are able to give to individual children, given the rough and tumble of home life'.

[125] *Posthuma v Campbell* (1984) 37 SASR 321, 329 (Jacobs J): 'to assert that the duty is absolute an unqualified, and that only the breach of that duty, as distinct from the existence of the duty, is to be determined by what is reasonable in the circumstances, represents to my mind a wholly unacceptable intrusion of the law of negligence into family and domestic relationships. It would impose a fetter on parental judgment and discretion, presumably by reference to some imaginary norm'.

[126] *Robertson v Swincer* (1989) 52 SASR 356, 361–62 (King CJ): 'The threat to the financial security of parents and families is by no means the only adverse social consequences to be feared. Parents and children in our society are very depending upon the support and assistance of benefactors. Children are cared for frequently by supportive relatives and friends and by kindly neighbours. What would be the effect upon such supportive arrangements of the knowledge that a failure of care in supervision might expose the benefactor to being stripped of his assets in consequence of an action for damages?'.

[127] Children Act 1989 (UK) c 41, s 2(9). See more generally *Surtees v Royal Borough of Kingston upon Thames* [1992] PIQR 101, 123–24.

[128] Though see *Horejsi v Anderson* (1984) 353 N W 2d 316 (Supreme Court of North Dakota).

[129] [2018] AC 355.

the best interests of the child.[130] Where the foster parent is not the foster child's legal parent, the local authority confers authority on the foster parent to direct the conduct of the foster child as if the foster child was a child of their own. Where the foster parent is the legal parent of the foster child, there is no need for such authority to be conferred as the legal parent is already vested with authority to direct the conduct of the child. In both situations, the local authority has extensive regulatory obligations to supervise and monitor the placement.[131]

What makes the position of a foster parent relatively unusual is that, unlike most parents, a foster parent is simultaneously acting as both a parent and a service provider. These dual aspects of the foster parent's role are legally problematic in that the standard of care expected of a parent and a service provider with responsibility for the care of children can differ. As noted above, a school may be held liable to a child who, as a result of poor supervision, runs onto a busy road and is injured, but the courts have resisted imposing such liability on a parent.

The Supreme Court was not unaware of the potential incongruity in the treatment of a local authority and a parent when conferring authority to direct the conduct of a child upon a third party in deciding to impose strict liability on the local authority in *Armes* in respect of the sexual assault committed by a foster parent of a foster child placed in their care by the local authority. The particular concern was how a local authority could be held strictly liable for the abuse of a foster child by a foster parent but a parent would not be held so liable if they were to leave their child in the care of a friend or family member who abused the child. It is possible, however, to explain the different treatment with a close examination of the particular features of the relationship between a local authority and a foster child compared with the particular features of the relationship between a parent and child.

The position of a local authority and a parent conferring authority to direct the conduct of a child upon a third party is undoubtedly similar; both are vested with authority to direct the conduct of the child and both may confer that authority upon a third party, creating a power relationship that did not previously exist and is at risk of abuse (where the foster carer was not also the child's legal parent). There is, however, an important difference. This difference arises not from the nature of the act of conferring authority, but in the nature of the legal responsibility of a local authority and a parent for the care of the child. As previously noted, the courts have long been reluctant to impose liability on a parent in respect of their children. Whatever the reason for this reluctance, there is a risk in imposing strict liability on a parent that the parent would be subject to greater liability for a tort committed by a person conferred authority by the parent to direct the conduct of the child than the parent would otherwise be subject to in respect of the care of their own child. Given the practical need during the life of a child for a parent to

[130] Child Care Act 1980 (UK) c 5, s 21(2).
[131] See description of statutory framework by Lord Reed; [2018] AC 355, 363–65.

arrange for at least some aspects of their parental responsibility to be performed by another person, this is a significant risk.

It follows that there is good reason not to impose strict liability on a parent who confers authority on another person to care for their child and commits a tort against the child in the process. The same cannot be said for local authorities. The standard of care owed by a foster parent to a foster child is typically less onerous than that owed by the local authority itself.[132]

The risk of a parent being subjected to greater liability for a tort committed by a person upon whom they have conferred authority to direct the conduct of their child than they would otherwise be subjected to in respect of their own actions or inactions does not, of course, arise in respect of all torts. In cases of battery, for instance, the prospective liability of a parent in respect of their own tort would be the same as that which would be imposed on the parent for a battery committed by another person who engaged in similar conduct. The prospect of holding a parent liable for a tort committed by a person upon whom they have conferred authority to direct the conduct of their child is not, however, restricted to instances of child sexual abuse. As there is a risk of greater liability being imposed on a parent in other cases, such as those involving negligence, the risk of higher liability remains a valid concern and can explain the general position that parents are not held strictly liable for a tort committed by a person upon whom the parent has conferred authority to direct the conduct of their child. In contrast, as recognised by the Supreme Court in *Armes*, the relationship between a local authority and a foster child can give rise to conferred authority strict liability. Although the majority of judges used the term 'vicarious liability' to describe the strict liability for the tort of another imposed on the local authority in *Armes*, the reasoning of the majority confirms that the basis of the liability was the conferral of authority by the local authority to the foster parent to direct the conduct of the foster child. As Lord Reed explained:[133]

> the local authority's placement of children in their care with foster parents creates a relationship of authority and trust between the foster parents and the children, in circumstances where close control cannot be exercised by the local authority, and so renders the children particular vulnerable to abuse. Although it is generally considered to be in the best interests of children in care that they should be placed in foster care, since most children benefit greatly from the experience of family life, it is relevant to the imposition of vicarious liability that a particular risk of abuse is inherent in that choice. That is because, if the public bodies responsible for decision-making in relation to children in care consider it advantageous to place them in foster care, notwithstanding the inherent risk that some children may be abused, it may be considered fair that they should compensate the unfortunate children for whom that risk materialises, particularly bearing in mind that the children are under the protection of the local authority and have no control over the decision regarding their placement.

[132] *Surtees v Royal Borough of Kingston Upon Thames* [1992] PIQR 101.
[133] [2018] AC 355, 379.

VII. Conclusion

Conferred authority strict liability was previously imposed under the label 'liability for breach of a non-delegable duty of care'. Such a label gave few clues as to basis of the liability or its limits. By focusing on the one feature which the various relationships in which the courts impose strict liability for the tort of another have in common, it can now be seen that conferred authority strict liability responds to the potential for abuse of the power relationship created by the conferral of authority by an employer or school by holding the employer or school strictly liable for a tort committed by a person upon whom authority has been conferred. Unlike previous explanations, the conferral of authority to the person who commits a tort against the employee or student is both necessary and sufficient for conferred authority strict liability to be imposed.

5

Employee Strict Liability

The second form of strict liability for the tort of another identified by the new expositive framework proposed by this book is *employee strict liability*. As explained in chapter 3, this form of strict liability is limited to the employment relationship and responds to the potential for an employer, when exercising its authority to direct the conduct of an employee for its own benefit, to put an employee in a position that the employee unduly prioritises compliance with the directions of the employer rather than give due weight to any alternate considerations that might reasonably lead the employee to conduct herself differently in the circumstances.

This chapter will start by examining the basis of employee strict liability. It will then determine the nature of the strict liability, the circumstances in which the strict liability arises, its scope and who is an employee for the purposes of the strict liability. Finally, the chapter will consider the associated 'both ways test' and whether it is appropriate to describe employee strict liability as either liability for a master's or a servant's tort.

I. Basis of the Strict Liability

The authority vested in an employer to direct the conduct of an employee is unique, for it is an authority that can be exercised by an employer for its own benefit. This enables an employer to use the authority to further its business objectives.[1] It can, however, also put strangers to the employment relationship at risk of harm.

Consider a scenario where an employee is allocated a number of tasks to complete by her employer on a particular day. The tasks are at different locations so that, in order to complete the tasks, the employee needs to travel by car. Her employer, however, has made inadequate allowance for travel times when allocating the employee her tasks. This means that to get her tasks done, the employee will have to rush whilst travelling between tasks. Alternatively, she might drive with reasonable care and risk failing to complete her allocated tasks. The employee is therefore faced with a choice. She must either prioritise compliance with

[1] Subject to the terms of the employment contract.

the directions of her employer and risk harming strangers to the employment relationship and being held legally responsible for that harm, or prioritise taking reasonable care for the safety of strangers to the employment relationship and risk the immediate threat or fear of disciplinary action for failing to pursue or comply with the directions of her employer.

As this scenario demonstrates, the problem with an employer being able to exercise its authority to direct the conduct of an employee for its own benefit is that the employer might do so without making adequate allowance for alternate considerations that might reasonably lead an employee to conduct herself differently in the circumstances. Due to the potential threat of immediate disciplinary action by an employer, an employee may unduly prioritise compliance with the employer's directions rather than give due weight to those alternate considerations. It follows that the exercise of authority by an employer over an employee is subject to abuse. Strangers to the employment relationship are consequently put at risk because an employer can exercise its authority to direct the conduct of an employee for its own benefit.

It is submitted that it is the potential for an employer to abuse the authority to direct the conduct of an employee by putting an employee in a position that the employee unduly prioritises compliance with the directions of the employer rather than give due weight to alternate considerations that might lead an employee to conduct herself differently in the circumstances that attracts the concern and the intervention of the law. Employee strict liability responds to the potential for abuse of the authority vested in an employer to direct the conduct of an employee by holding an employer strictly liable (regardless of the employer personally engaging in any conduct to which liability in tort might attach) whenever an employee commits a tort against a stranger to the employment relationship within the course of her employment. In so doing, employee strict lability provides strangers to the employment relationship with a degree of protection from an abuse of the authority vested in an employer to direct the conduct of an employee for its own benefit.

As noted in the previous chapter, it is relatively unusual in tort law for one person to be held strictly liable for the tort of another, and a defendant has to do more than merely provide an opportunity for a tort to be committed for such liability to be imposed. Because an employer can exercise its authority to direct the conduct of an employee for its own benefit, an employer does do more than merely provide an employee with an opportunity to commit a tort. An employer can encourage, motivate or even induce an employee to commit a tort by putting pressure on the employee to follow the employer's directions rather than give due weight to any alternate considerations that might reasonably lead the employee to conduct herself differently in the circumstances. It is not that an employer will necessarily abuse its power to direct the conduct of an employee, but there is always an inherent risk that an employer will do so. As will be seen from the cases, this risk appears sufficient for employee strict liability to be imposed.

II. Nature of the Strict Liability

As with conferred authority strict liability, employee strict liability is not an absolute form of liability; it is not imposed in the *absence* of any tort being committed.[2] It still needs to be shown that the employee committed a tort against a stranger to the employment relationship. The liability is, however, imposed *regardless* of whether the employer personally engaged in conduct towards the stranger to the employment relationship to which liability in tort might attach. This means that employee strict liability is still imposed even though an employer may be able to adduce evidence that the directions given by the employer were not a contributing factor in the tort committed by the employee against the stranger to the employment relationship. It is also not possible for an employer to escape employee strict liability by adducing evidence that the employer did not abuse the authority to direct the conduct of the employee. This is because employee strict liability responds to a *potential* rather than an *actual* abuse of the authority vested in an employer to direct the conduct of the employee.

It may seem unfair that an employer can be subject to employee strict liability regardless of whether the employer personally engaged in conduct to which liability in tort might attach, but an employer need not necessarily bear such strict liability alone. In certain circumstances, an employer will be entitled to seek an indemnity from the employee.[3]

It has not always been clear why an employer should have the right to be indemnified by an employee against any loss sustained by the employer in meeting a claim brought by a stranger to the employment relationship for employee strict liability. Indeed, the right of indemnity has been removed by statute in a number of jurisdictions.[4] The indemnity does, however, play an important role in employee strict liability. It enables an employer to recover the loss sustained in meeting a claim brought by a stranger to the employment relationship where the employer's exercise of authority was not a contributing factor in the tort committed by the employee against the stranger to the employment relationship.[5] This does not mean that an employer will necessarily call on the indemnity.[6] There are a number of reasons why an employer might choose not to do so.[7] What is important is that the indemnity exists and may be called upon by an employer.[8]

[2] P Cane, 'Responsibility and Fault: a Relational and Functional Approach to Responsibility' in P Cane and J Gardner (eds), *Relating to Responsibility* (Oxford, Hart, 2001) 81, 99.

[3] *Lister v Romford Ice and Cold Storage Co Ltd* [1957] AC 555.

[4] See, eg, Employees Liability Act 1991 (NSW), s 3.

[5] Although it is a right rarely exercised by employers, it is a right which exists should they choose to exercise it.

[6] See references to the 'gentleman's agreement' entered into by insurers not to enforce the indemnity in *Morris v Ford Motor Co Ltd* [1973] 1 QB 792, 799.

[7] eg to maintain good workplace relations.

[8] The consequence being that the employer, rather than an injured claimant, bears the risk of an employee's impecunity.

This will generally be in those circumstances in which an employer did not actually abuse its authority to direct the conduct of an employee by putting the employee in a position that the employee unduly prioritised compliance with the directions of the employer rather than give due weight to alternate considerations that might reasonably have led the employee to conduct herself differently in the circumstances.[9]

Should an employer choose to call on the indemnity, the extent to which the employer might have contributed to the tort committed by the employee's will need to be assessed. It follows that the employer's indemnity from an employee is not absolute. An employer should only have a right to be indemnified up to the point at which it can be shown that the exercise of the employer's authority to direct the conduct of the employee was not a contributing factor in the tort committed by the employee against the stranger to the employment relationship. Were the indemnity to go further than this it would remove the basis for imposing employee strict liability in the first place; it would effectively shift the risk that an employer might abuse its authority to direct the conduct of an employee away from the employer and onto the employee. That there are limitations on the capacity of an employer to call on the indemnity was acknowledged by Singleton LJ in *Jones v Manchester Corporation*:[10]

> It may well be that in the ordinary simple case a servant must indemnify his master against his wrongful acts for which the master is made liable. A chauffeur who, through negligence, causes damage for which his employer is held responsible, may well be liable to his master. On the other hand, if the chauffeur is young and inexperienced, and is suddenly told to drive another and bigger car, or lorry, which he does not understand, and an accident follows, it is by no means certain that the employer would be entitled to an indemnity.

The existence of such limitations can also be seen in those jurisdictions where steps have been taken to remove the indemnity.[11] In those jurisdictions, an employer can still resort to the indemnity where the employee has engaged in 'serious or wilful misconduct'.[12] This qualification can be seen as an attempt to enunciate those circumstances in which it is unlikely that the directions given by the employer were a contributing factor in the tort committed by the employee against the stranger to the employment relationship.

[9] eg where one employee shoots another outside the workplace; *Gittani Stone Pty Limited v Pavkovic* (2007) Aust Torts Reports 81–924. To prevent an employer's hand being forced into taking such a decision, some jurisdictions have now removed the right of insurers to be subrogated to an employer's right of indemnity. See, eg, Insurance Contracts Act 1984 (Cth), s 66.

[10] [1952] 2 QB 852, 865. Although this decision predated *Lister v Romford Ice and Cold Storage Co Ltd* [1957] AC 555, Singleton LJ was prepared to acknowledge the existence of an employer's right of indemnity against their employee in accordance with the suggestion made in the 10th edition of *Salmond on the Law of Torts* (London, Sweet & Maxwell, 1945).

[11] See, eg, Employees Liability Act 1991 (NSW), s 3.

[12] See, eg, Employees Liability Act 1991 (NSW), s 5.

III. In What Circumstances Does the Strict Liability Arise?

Employee strict liability can be imposed on an employer whenever an employee commits a tort against a stranger to the employment relationship whilst acting within the course of their employment.

Three points can be made about the general circumstances in which employee strict liability arises. First, unlike conferred authority strict liability, employee strict liability is not restricted to physical damage. Although the authority vested in an employer is an authority to direct the physical conduct of an employee, it is not the fact that an employer can direct the conduct of an employee for its own benefit which gives rise to a risk of harm to strangers to the employment relationship per se, but the fact that an employer may potentially abuse that authority by putting an employee in a position that she unduly prioritises compliance with her employer's directions rather than giving due weight to any alternate considerations that might reasonably lead the employee to conduct herself differently in the circumstances. As this potential abuse of authority (where it eventuates) may impact strangers to the employment relationship in different ways, there is no reason to limit employee strict liability to physical damage. Employers have consequently been held strictly liable for types of damages other than just physical damage. For instance, employers have been held strictly liable for damage caused by defamatory comments made by their employees.[13] Employers have also been held strictly liable for economic loss caused by an employee, such as when an employee tortiously procures a breach of contract.[14]

Second, unlike conferred authority strict liability, employee strict liability only arises in respect of a tort committed by an employee; it does not generally arise in respect of a tort committed by an independent contractor. As explained in chapter 3, this is because an employer does not have the general authority to direct the conduct of an independent contractor. As an employer does not have such authority, there is only limited potential for an employer to unduly influence the decision-making process of an independent contractor in a way that might lead the independent contractor to commit a tort against a stranger to the relationship between the employer and the independent contractor. Even in those relatively unusual circumstances where there may be a risk of some limited form of authority vested in the employer to direct the conduct of the independent contractor being abused, such a risk can be anticipated and addressed by the independent contractor's contractual terms of engagement.

Finally, unlike conferred authority strict liability, there is no restriction on the type of person to whom employee strict liability is owed. As demonstrated in the previous chapter, conferred authority strict liability is owed only to persons

[13] See *Bonette v Woolworths Ltd* (1937) 37 SRNSW 142, where an employee at Woolworths wrongfully accused the plaintiff of shoplifting.

[14] See *Hamlyn v John Houston & Co* [1903] 1 KB 81.

over whom authority has been conferred. In contrast, any person against whom an employee commits a tort in the course of employment can seek to impose employee strict liability on an employer. This is because the authority in question arises in respect of the relationship between the employer and the employee and not the relationship between the employer and the stranger to the employer relationship against whom the employee commits a tort.

IV. Scope of the Strict Liability

Before employee strict liability can be imposed, it needs to be shown that an employee was acting within the *course of employment* immediately prior to the tort being committed. This is because it is only where an employee is acting within the course of employment that there is the potential for an employer to abuse its authority to direct the conduct of an employee by putting the employee in a position that she unduly prioritises compliance with her employer's directions rather than give due weight to any alternate considerations that might reasonably lead the employee to conduct herself differently in the circumstances. Where an employee is acting outside the course of employment, the employee is no longer subject to the employer's authority and is free to make her own decisions about her conduct without risk of influence from the employer's exercise of authority. As there is very little potential, in such circumstances, for the employer to abuse its authority to direct the conduct of an employee by putting the employee in a position that the employee unduly prioritises compliance with her employer's directions rather than give due weight to any alternate considerations that might reasonably lead the employee to conduct herself differently in the circumstances, there is no basis upon which employee strict liability can be imposed. It is submitted that whether or not an employee is acting within the course of employment is to be determined by reference to what it is an employee is *actually* (as opposed to *apparently*) directed by her employer to do.

Whether or not an employee is acting within the course of employment has traditionally been determined by reference to the *Salmond* test:[15]

> An employee's wrongful conduct is said to fall within the course and scope of his or her employment where it consists of either (1) acts authorised by the employers or (2) unauthorised acts that are so connected with acts that the employer has authorised that they may rightly be regarded as modes – although improper modes – of doing what has been authorised.

As can be seen, the *Salmond* test focuses on what an employee is authorised, or to save confusion with how the term 'authority' is used in this book, directed to do.[16]

[15] RFV Heuston and RA Buckley, *Salmond and Heuston on the Law of Torts* (19th ed, London, Sweet & Maxwell, 1987) 521–22.

[16] The distinction is discussed further in C Beuermann, 'Vicarious Liability: A Case Study in the Failure of General Principles' (2017) 33 *Journal of Professional Negligence* 197.

This is consistent with the general basis of employee strict liability proposed by this book. If an employee is following her employer's directions, there is the potential for the employer to abuse its authority to direct the conduct of the employee by putting the employee in a position that she unduly prioritises compliance with her employer's directions rather than give due weight to any alternate considerations that might reasonably lead the employee to conduct herself differently in the circumstances. If an employee is not following her employer's directions, she is not subject to her employer's authority and is free to make her own decisions about her conduct without risk of influence from the employer's exercise of authority.

The first limb of the *Salmond* test essentially refers to conduct which an employer has *expressly* directed an employee to engage in. It is not the tort itself that the employer must have directed the employee to commit for these purposes,[17] but the conduct that the employee was engaged in immediately prior to committing the tort against the stranger to the employment relationship. For example, an employer will be viewed as having expressly directed the negligent driving of an employee under the first limb of the *Salmond* test if the employer has directed the employee to drive from A to B and the negligent driving occurs in the course of that journey. An employer may issue an employee with express directions personally, or such directions may be set out in the express or implied terms of the employment contract.[18]

Conduct which an employer has expressly directed an employee to engage in is not the only type of conduct which has been found to fall within the course of employment. The second limb of the *Salmond* test provides that improper modes of performing an act which the employer has expressly directed an employer to engage in can also fall within the course of employment. This has been found, in certain circumstances, to extend to conduct which an employer may even have expressly prohibited.[19] This broad approach to determining the course of employment can be difficult to explain when just focusing on the express directions issued by an employer in respect of the specific conduct engaged in by an employee immediately prior to the employee committing a tort against a stranger to the employment relationship. More sense of the approach can be made by examining the directions issued by an employer to an employee as a whole. The reason is that although an employer might expressly prohibit certain conduct or modes of performance, if the employer issues other directions[20] that can be construed as promoting the conduct, there is still the potential for the employer to abuse its authority to direct the conduct of an employee by putting the employee

[17] Where an employer directly instructs an employee to commit a tort, the employer will be viewed as having committed the tort personally; see, eg, PS Atiyah, *Vicarious Liability in the Law of Torts* (London, Butterworths, 1967) 4.

[18] Ibid 178–79.

[19] See *Limpus v London General Omnibus Co.* (1862) 1 HC & C 526; 158 ER 993. Discussed below.

[20] Defined broadly as including express directions given by an employer as well as any other policies, incentives or penalties instituted by an employer to shape how an employee performs their tasks. See further ch 3.

in a position that the employee unduly prioritises compliance with her employer's directions rather than give due weight to any alternate considerations that might reasonably lead the employee to conduct herself differently in the circumstances. In such circumstances, although the employer did not expressly direct the employee to engage in the conduct which occurred immediately prior to the tort being committed, such conduct can still be seen to fall within the employer's *implied* directions and therefore within the course of employment.

Consider the decision of the High Court of Australia in *Bugge v Brown*.[21] In that case, an employee was sent to clear thistles from a field on the employer's property. He was provided with a lunch of raw meat and potatoes and told to take it to a nearby house to be cooked. As the house was a considerable distance from the field, the employee decided to cook his lunch in an old chimney near the field in order to save time. The employee subsequently lost control of the fire and the employer was found strictly liable for the damage it caused to a neighbouring property. At first glance, it is difficult to explain how the employee's conduct can be construed as having been within the course of his employment when the fire would not have been lit if the employer's express directions about cooking the lunch had been followed. The reason becomes apparent, however, when the employer's directions are examined as a whole. Although the employer had told the employee to go to the house to have his lunch cooked, the employer had also provided the employee with a lunch which needed cooking and had set the employee a time-sensitive task. These other directions could be construed as actually promoting the employee's conduct. Consequently, when the employer's directions were viewed as a whole, there was still the potential for the employer to have abused his authority to direct the conduct of the employee by putting the employee in a position that the employee unduly prioritised compliance with his employer's directions rather than give due weight to any alternate considerations that might reasonably have led the employee to conduct himself differently in the circumstances. It followed that the employer had impliedly directed the employee to engage in the conduct which occurred immediately prior to the tort being committed so that the employee's conduct could be construed as falling within the course of employment.

Consider also the English case of *Limpus v London General Omnibus Co*.[22] The employee in that case was a bus driver who had been expressly directed by his employer not to drive in such a way as to obstruct the buses of a rival company. Despite the direction, the employee drove in front of a rival company's bus when it attempted to overtake him, causing an accident. The employee's conduct was found to be within the course of employment. Once again, an examination of the employer's directions as a whole may explain why. Although the employer had prohibited the employee from obstructing the buses of the rival company, the employer had directed the employee to drive the bus on the bus route and may have issued any one of a number of other directions that might have encouraged the employee's

[21] (1919) 26 CLR 110. ('*Bugge*').
[22] (1862) 1 HC & C 526; 158 ER 993 ('*Limpus*')

behaviour; for example, offering the bus driver a bonus for completing his route ahead of the bus of the rival company. The possibility that such directions might have been issued by the employer was expressly acknowledged by Willes J:[23]

> The law is not so futile as to allow a master, by giving secret instructions to his servant, to discharge himself from liability.

It was not too difficult, therefore, for the judges to see the potential in the circumstances for the employer to abuse its authority to direct the conduct of the employee by issuing directions in addition to the direction not to obstruct the buses of the rival company and putting the employee in a position that the employee unduly prioritised compliance with his employer's directions rather than give due weight to any alternate considerations that might reasonably have led the employee to conduct himself differently in the circumstances. This could explain why the judges found the employee to have been acting within the course of employment immediately prior to the accident, even though the employer had expressly prohibited the specific conduct engaged in by the employee.

As can be seen, in determining whether an employee's conduct falls within the course of employment, the *Salmond* test focuses on what it is that an employee is *actually* directed by her employer to do (either expressly or impliedly). To this extent, the test reflects the basis of employee strict liability put forward by this book. Where an employee is following her employer's actual directions, there is the potential for an employer to abuse its authority to direct the conduct of an employee by putting the employee in a position that she unduly prioritises compliance with her employer's directions rather than give due weight to any alternate considerations that might reasonably lead the employee to conduct herself differently in the circumstances. Where an employee is acting outside the course of her employment, the employee is no longer subject to her employer's authority and is free to make her own decisions about her conduct without risk of influence from the employer's exercise of authority. As this rationale is supported by a broader analysis of the relationships within which strict liability for the tort of another arises, there is no reason to think that the *Salmond* test, which has been in use for the best part of a century,[24] should not continue to be used as the test for determining whether an employee's conduct falls within the course of employment.[25] Concerns have, however, recently been raised as to whether the *Salmond* test accurately captures all the circumstances in which a tort committed by an employee has been found by the courts to fall within the course of employment.[26] Specifically, it has now been suggested that employee strict liability can be imposed on an

[23] Ibid 998.

[24] First reference was in JW Salmond, *The Law of Torts* (1907) 83. See generally C Beuermann, 'The abstraction of form and the associated dangers for the English courts: the case study of vicarious liability', paper presented at Obligations IX Melbourne, 18 July 2018.

[25] This being the current view of the High Court of Australia; *Prince Alfred College Inc. v ADC* (2016) 258 CLR 134.

[26] See *Bazley v Curry* (1999) 174 DLR (4th) 45.

employer in circumstances in which an employee was not following her employer's actual directions (express or implied) immediately prior to the employee committing the tort against the stranger to the employment relationship provided the tort committed was sufficiently connected with 'field of activities' engaged in by an employee.[27] Such concerns reflect the confused state of the cases, but do not necessarily suggest that the *Salmond* test is out of date.

The cases show that there are two broad categories of case in which an employer typically escapes employee strict liability because the employee was not following the employer's actual directions (express or implied) immediately prior to committing the tort against the stranger to the employment relationship with the result that the tort is viewed as falling outside the course of employment. The first are cases in which the conduct engaged in by the employee immediately prior to the tort being committed was not just an 'improper' or prohibited mode of doing something the employee had actually been directed to do but was conduct which the employer had no reason to believe that the employee would be engaged in at all. For example, where a bus conductor decides to drive the bus[28] or a miner fires a shot 'instead of leaving it to the shotfirer'.[29] In such cases, even when viewing an employer's directions as a whole, it is unlikely that an employer would have been minded to exercise its authority to direct the conduct of the employee in such a way as to put the employee in a position that she unduly prioritises compliance with her employer's directions rather than give due weight to any alternate considerations that might have reasonably led the employee to conduct herself differently because the employer had no reason to suspect that the employee was engaging in such activities in the first place. Without the potential in such circumstances for an employer to abuse its authority to direct the conduct of an employee, there is no basis upon which employee strict liability can be imposed. It follows that such conduct is generally viewed as falling outside the course of employment.

Included in this category is conduct which a stranger to the employment relationship might view as being within the *apparent* scope of employment, but which was engaged in contrary to the *actual* directions (express or implied) issued by an employer.[30] Paula Giliker provides an account of a French case, the facts of which provide a useful example.[31] The employee in the case was an '*aide-chauffeur*'

[27] The best example being the sexual assault of a child. See more generally *Mohamud v WM Morrisons Supermarkets plc* [2016] AC 677.

[28] See *Iqbal v London Transport Executive* (1973) 16 KIR 329.

[29] See *Kerr v James Dunlop & Co Ltd* [1926] AC 377 cited by Atiyah, *Vicarious Liability in the Law of Torts* (n 17) 195.

[30] As will be explored further in ch 7, although conferred authority strict liability extends to circumstances in which the person upon whom authority has been conferred is acting within the terms of the apparent authority that has been conferred upon that person, employee strict liability is limited to circumstances in which the employee is acting within the actual directions (express or implied) issued by the employer.

[31] Although not the result, as the French court imposed liability on the employer. P Giliker, *Vicarious Liability in Tort: A Comparative Perspective* (Cambridge, CUP, 2010) 182.

employed at a garage. He had been directed by his employer to drive a truck to a mechanic for repairs and was given the keys to the garage for this purpose. Rather than returning the truck to the garage straight away, the employee decided to make some money and use the truck to drive a group of people to a local dance. Due to the negligence of the employee, the truck crashed and one of the passengers was killed. On these facts, even when viewing the employer's directions as a whole, it is very difficult to view the employee's conduct immediately prior to the accident as falling within the course of his employment. The employer had no reason to believe that the employee would be engaged in the activity of carrying people in the truck, even though the employee worked at the garage and the passengers might have presumed he had such authority.[32] It is therefore unlikely in such circumstances that the employer would have been minded to exercise his authority to direct the conduct of the employee in such a way as to put the employee in a position that he unduly prioritised compliance with his employer's directions rather than give due weight to any alternate considerations that might reasonably have led the employee to conduct himself differently.[33] There was consequently very little potential for the employer to abuse his authority to direct the conduct of the employee, and no basis upon which employee strict liability could be imposed.

Similar facts were considered by the Privy Council in an appeal from the Supreme Court of New South Wales in *Kooragang Investments Pty Ltd v Richardson & Wrench Ltd*.[34] In that case, the employee valuer had been carrying out valuations on behalf of his employer's former client after being given explicit instructions not to do so. Although the valuations were on the employer's letterhead and within the apparent scope of the employee's authority, the Privy Council found the employee's conduct to fall outside the scope of employment. Once again, as the employer had no reason to believe that the employee would be engaged in preparing such valuations, it is unlikely that the employer would have been minded to exercise its authority to direct the conduct of the employee in such a way as to put the employee in a position that he unduly prioritised compliance with his employer's directions rather than give due weight to any alternate considerations that might reasonably have led the employee to conduct himself differently in the circumstances. Without the potential for the employer to abuse its authority to direct the conduct of the employee, there was no basis upon which employee strict liability could be imposed.

The second broad category of case in which an employee's conduct is typically found to fall outside the course of employment are cases in which the conduct engaged in by the employee immediately prior to the tort being committed against the stranger to the employment relationship was intentional or wilful. For example,

[32] Cf *Limpus v London General Omnibus Co* (1862) 1 HC & C 526; 158 ER 993 where the employer knew the bus driver would be driving on the bus route with passengers in the bus.

[33] The decision of the England and Wales Court of Appeal in *Twine v Bean's Express Ltd* [1946] 1 All ER 202 can be explained on similar grounds.

[34] [1982] AC 462.

where a barmaid glasses an abusive customer,[35] a security guard sets fire to a customer's property,[36] a cleaner decides to use a customer's phone to make £1,400 worth of calls[37] or a service station attendant racially assaults a customer who is leaving the service station.[38] Once again, even when viewing the employer's directions as a whole, there is very limited potential in such cases for an employer to abuse its authority to direct the conduct of an employee by putting the employee in a position that she unduly prioritises compliance with her employer's directions rather than give due weight to any alternate considerations that might reasonably lead the employee to conduct herself differently in the circumstances because the employer has no reason to expect that the employee would be engaged in such activities in the first place. To the extent that the employee is driven by her own motivations when engaging in such conduct, it is unlikely that the employee is at risk of being influenced by an exercise of her employer's authority which, even were it to be exercised by an employer, would most likely be done in a manner to discourage the employee from engaging in such conduct given the broader ramifications of such conduct for the employer's business.[39] Without the potential in such circumstances for an employer to abuse its authority to direct the conduct of an employee, there is no basis upon which employee strict liability can be imposed. It follows that such conduct is generally viewed as falling outside the course of employment.

Exceptions to these two general categories of case do exist. There are a number of cases which notionally fit within one or the other of the above categories of case in which the courts have imposed employee strict liability. Most of those cases, however, can be explained by alternate means. For instance, a large number of such cases involve property. The classic example of intentional misconduct found to be within the course of employment is *Morris v C W Martins & Sons Ltd*.[40] In that case the employee of a furrier ran off with a mink stole owned by a customer which had been given to the employee for the purposes of cleaning. The employer was held strictly liable to the customer for the theft. It does not necessarily follow, however, that just because the tort against a stranger to the employment relationship is committed by an employee, that the liability imposed on an employer is employee strict liability. *Morris v C W Martins & Sons Ltd* can alternatively be explained on the basis that the employer was a bailee and had conferred authority upon the employee to deal with the bailor's mink stole.[41] This form of liability is closer in nature to conferred authority strict liability and is discussed in chapter 8.

Other cases of intentional misconduct involve employees who have been vested with authority by their employer to effect legal relations on the employer's

[35] *Deatons Pty Ltd v Flew* (1949) 79 CLR 370.

[36] *Pains Engineering v Barnes Security* (1987) 43 CCLT 129.

[37] *Heasmans v Clarity Cleaning Co. Ltd* [1987] ICR 949.

[38] *Mohamud v VM Morrisons Supermarkets plc* [2016] AC 677.

[39] In *Mohamud*, for instance, the employee's supervisor physically tried to restrain the employee from committing the assault.

[40] [1966] 1 QB 716.

[41] Atiyah (n 17) 200.

behalf; that is, they were agents. In *Barwick v English Joint Stock Bank*,[42] a bank was held strictly liable when a bank manager gave a fraudulent guarantee to the plaintiff that the bank would honour a cheque written by a customer of the bank in favour of the plaintiff even though the bank manager was aware that the customer was heavily indebted to the bank. As bank manager, the employee in that case had been vested with authority to issue guarantees on behalf of the bank and was acting within the terms of that apparent authority immediately prior to the fraud. *Armagas Ltd v Mundogas SA*[43] concerned the vice-president of a company who had been vested with authority to negotiate and enter the sale and charter of a ship on behalf of the company. The House of Lords held that the company would have been strictly liable for the fraudulent conduct of the vice-president in negotiating the transaction had the vice-president been acting within the terms of his apparent authority. Once again, it does not necessarily follow that just because the tort against a stranger to the employment relationship is committed by an employee, that the strict liability imposed on an employer is employee strict liability. Cases such as these can alternatively be explained on that the basis that the employees were agents who had been vested with authority to effect legal relations on behalf of their employers. Agent strict liability is discussed in chapter 6.

The most recent cases in which intentional misconduct has been found to fall within the course of employment are the child sexual assault cases. Quite remarkably, courts have been prepared to find that such a self-serving act as sexually assaulting a child can fall within the course of employment.[44] As outlined in the previous chapter, however, these cases can alternatively be explained on the basis that the employee had been conferred authority by their employer to direct the conduct of the child who was abused. Such liability might therefore be better described as conferred authority strict liability rather than employee strict liability.[45]

A similar approach can be taken to explain the increasing willingness of courts to impose strict liability on the employers of security guards who physically assault patrons at pubs and clubs.[46] The decision of the Queensland Court of Appeal in *Ryan v Ann St Holdings Pty Ltd*[47] provides a good example. The patron in that case had left a nightclub and was talking on the street outside where he was being 'quiet and well-behaved'.[48] One of the security guards then asked the patron to return to the club where he was assaulted. It is very difficult to see the conduct of the security guard in this case as within the course of his employment given that the patron had left the club prior to the assault. The decision might be explained, however, on the

[42] (1867) II LR Exch 259.

[43] [1986] 1 AC 717.

[44] See *Bazley v Curry* (1999) 174 DLR (4th) 45.

[45] This issue will be discussed further in ch 7.

[46] See *Starks v RSM Security Pty Ltd* (2004) Aust Torts Reports 81–763. See also *Mattis v Pollock* [2003] 1 WLR 2158 and *Zorom Enterprises Pty Ltd v Zabow* (2007) 71 NSWLR 354.

[47] [2006] 2 Qd R 486.

[48] Ibid 487–88 (Williams JA).

basis that the employer had conferred authority upon the security guard to direct the conduct of the patron and the security guard was acting within the terms of that apparent authority immediately prior to the assault.[49] In such circumstances, the assault can be seen as an abuse of the authority conferred by the employer upon the security guard so that the strict liability imposed on the employer can be better described as conferred authority strict liability rather than employee strict liability.

Historically, it has not been easy to make sense of the cases concerning the course of employment for the purposes of employee strict liability. A lack of understanding as to the basis of the liability[50] has left the cases in a considerable state of confusion. The *Salmond* test does, however, suggest a basis for employee strict liability which can provide a way through the maze. In accordance with the test, a tort committed by an employee against a stranger to the employment relationship does not fall within the course of her employment unless the conduct engaged in by the employee immediately prior to the tort being committed was actually directed (either expressly or impliedly) by the employer. This is because where conduct is actually directed (either expressly or implied) by an employer, there is the potential for an employer to abuse its authority to direct the conduct of an employee by putting the employee in a position that she unduly prioritises compliance with her employer's directions rather than give due weight to any alternate considerations that might reasonably lead the employee to conduct herself differently in the circumstances. Without the potential for an employer to abuse its authority to direct the conduct of an employee, it is difficult to make a connection between the tort committed by the employee and the employer which is sufficient for employee strict liability to be imposed. Once it is recognised that not all strict liability imposed on an employer in respect of torts committed by an employee is employee strict liability, but may instead be conferred authority strict liability or agent strict liability, the *Salmond* test can be seen to accurately explain the cases in which employee strict liability has been imposed.

Furthermore, accepting the basis of employee strict liability suggested by the *Salmond* test can promote greater consistency in the application of the *Salmond* test into the future. Consider one of the more difficult types of situations to determine whether a tort committed by an employee against a stranger to the employment relationship occurs within the course of employment; the situation where an employee has been skylarking. It was noted in the previous chapter that employers are generally not held strictly liable when one employee plays a prank on a fellow employee of equal rank, causing that employee harm. Such conduct can be seen as self-serving and ill-thought out. The act of lighting a cigarette whilst delivering petrol can be similarly described. Unlike the prank cases, however, the employer in *Century Insurance Co Ltd v Northern Ireland RTB*[51] was held strictly

[49] In the same way that cases involving errant police officers can be explained. See further ch 4.
[50] See further ch 1.
[51] [1942] AC 509.

liable for the damage caused by the foolishness of its employee. When faced with facts such as these, how is a judge to determine whether the tort committed by the employee falls within the course of employment? If the basis for employee strict liability suggested by the *Salmond* test is accepted, one approach will be to consider whether the employer had the potential to abuse its authority to direct the conduct of an employee by putting the employee in a position that she unduly prioritises compliance with her employer's directions rather than give due weight to any alternate considerations that might reasonably lead the employee to conduct herself differently in the circumstances. From this perspective, it can be seen that the two factual scenarios are quite different. In the cigarette case there was potential for the employer to abuse its authority because the time at which the employee decided to have a cigarette could have been affected by how many breaks the employee had been allowed by his employer to take. In contrast, it is very difficult to see how an employer could have abused its authority in the prank cases as the employees were at no time meant to be engaging in pranks, so the employers would not have been minded to exercise any authority to direct the conduct of the employees in such a way as to put the employees in a position that they unduly prioritised compliance with their employer's directions rather than give due weight to any alternate considerations that might reasonably have led the employees to conduct themselves differently in the circumstances.

V. Who is an Employee?

Chapter 4 canvassed the difficulties associated with determining who is an employee for the purposes of tort law. It also noted that, for a person to be considered an employee for the purposes of conferred authority strict liability, it was necessary for that person to have been engaged under a contract which vested the employer with general authority to direct the conduct of that person in the course of the employer's business.[52] The analysis in this chapter elaborates on the nature of the authority which needs to be vested in an employer for a person to be considered an employee. It can now be seen that an employer must not only have authority to direct the conduct of a person, but that such authority must be broad enough for there to be the potential when exercising that authority for an employer to put the person in a position that she unduly prioritises compliance with the employer's directions rather than give due weight to any alternate considerations that might reasonably lead the person to conduct herself differently in the circumstances.

Consider the example of a contractor engaged to work on a construction site. The contractor might agree that the employer can direct her conduct whilst on the

[52] Note that although conferred authority strict liability is a different form of strict liability from employee strict liability, the definition of who is an employee is the same for both forms of strict liability.

construction site for safety reasons. The granting of such authority, however, does not necessarily turn the contractor into an employee. The contractor might retain sufficient discretion under the contract of engagement to regulate her own behaviour so that there is very limited potential for the employer to put the contractor in a position that she unduly prioritises compliance with the employer's directions rather than give due weight to any alternate considerations that might reasonably lead the contractor to conduct herself differently in the circumstances. Alternatively, a mechanism for allocating the risks and costs of complying with alternate considerations outside the contract may be included which could prevent a potential abuse of any authority vested in the employer over the contractor from arising.[53] In neither of these situations can the contractor be considered an employee. It is necessary therefore to examine carefully the nature of the authority vested in an employer under a contract securing the use of human resources, as well as the terms of that contract, to determine the status of the person engaged under that contract. Without the potential for an employer to put the person in a position that she unduly prioritises compliance with the employer's directions rather than give due weight to any alternate considerations that might reasonably lead the person to conduct herself differently in the circumstances, it is very difficult to say that the person engaged under the contract is an employee.

An employee for the purposes of employee strict liability includes not only an employee who works under the direction of her employer but an employee who has been hired out by her employer (the *hired employee*) to another business (the *temporary hirer*). The House of Lords confirmed in *Mersey Docks and Harbour Board v Coggins & Griffith (Liverpool) Limited*[54] that an employer may still be held strictly liable for torts committed against a stranger to the employment relationship by a hired employee even though the hired employee was working for the temporary hirer when the tort was committed. The reason is that, although a hired employee works for the temporary hirer, the hired employee's contract of employment remains with her employer.[55] Consequently, the employer still has the right to discipline the hired employee in accordance with the employment contract and may retain sufficient authority to direct the conduct of the hired employee under the arrangements with the temporary hirer for there to be the potential for the employer to abuse its authority to direct the conduct of the hired employee by putting the hired employee in a position that she unduly prioritises compliance with her employer's directions rather than give due weight to any alternate considerations that might reasonably lead the hired employee to conduct herself differently in the circumstances. Two questions generally arise with respect to the potential liability of an employer for a tort committed against a stranger to the employment relationship by a hired employee. First, will an employer always be held strictly liable for a tort committed by a hired employee? Second, if a

[53] See further ch 3.

[54] [1947] 1 AC 1 ('*Mersey Docks*').

[55] Despite anything the contract between the general employer and the temporary employer might say to the contrary; see *Mersey Docks* ibid.

temporary hirer can be held strictly liable for a tort committed by a hired employee, can the employer be held strictly liable at the same time?

In respect of the first question, an employer will not always be held strictly liable for a tort committed against a stranger to the employment relationship by a hired employee.[56] Whether an employer is held strictly liable for a tort committed by a hired employee will depend upon the facts of the case. In *Mersey Docks*, for instance, the hired employee was a crane operator who had been hired out by the harbour authority along with a crane to a firm of stevedores for the purposes of unloading ships. In imposing strict liability on the employer harbour authority for the negligence of the crane operator, the House of Lords thought it important that, although the stevedores could direct the crane operator where to move things on the dock, they could not direct what the crane operator did with the crane as it remained the property of the employer harbour authority.[57] In contrast, the courts have been much more prepared to impose strict liability on a temporary hirer rather than the employer for a tort committed by a hired employee where the hired employee was operating equipment owned by the temporary hirer. At the turn of the twentieth century, for instance, it was relatively common for a temporary hirer to be held strictly liable for a tort committed by a hired employee engaged to drive the temporary hirer's horse and carriage.[58] A temporary hirer might also be held strictly liable for a tort committed by a hired employee who has been engaged to provide more general labour as opposed to operating specific equipment. The circumstances giving rise to such liability are, however, considered quite limited; for instance, where the hired employee is 'seconded for a substantial period of time to the [temporary hirer], to perform a role embedded in [the temporary hirer's] organisation'.[59]

There is no settled test for distinguishing the circumstances in which the employer or temporary hirer will be held strictly liable for a tort committed against a stranger to the employment relationship by a hired employee.[60] The cases set out above suggest that the more authority a temporary hirer has been conferred by an employer to direct the conduct of a hired employee, the more likely it is that the temporary hirer will be held strictly liable for the tort. A temporary hirer, for instance, will generally be conferred greater authority to direct the conduct of a hired employee where the hired employee is operating equipment owned by the temporary hirer than where the hired employee is providing general labour for a short period of time. A temporary hirer will usually seek such authority in order to protect the equipment the hired employee is using. Similarly, a temporary hirer will generally be conferred greater authority to direct the conduct of a hired employee

[56] See generally Atiyah (n 17) 158–68.

[57] *Mersey Docks* [1947] 1 AC 1, 13 (Lord Macmillan): 'The stevedores were entitled to tell him where to go, what parcels to lift and where to take them, that is to say, they could direct him as to what they wanted him to do; but they had no authority to tell him how he was to handle the crane in doing his work'.

[58] Atiyah (n 17) 165–66.

[59] *Viasystems (Tyneside) Ltd v Thermal Transfer (Northern) Ltd* [2006] QB 510, 536 (Rix LJ).

[60] Atiyah (n 17) 158.

who is performing a role 'embedded in that [temporary hirer's] organisation'[61] for a considerable period of time than where the hired employee is providing general labour for a short period of time only. It is submitted, therefore, that for a temporary hirer to be held strictly liable for a tort committed against a stranger to the employment relationship by a hired employee, the temporary hirer must have been conferred sufficient authority to direct the conduct of a hired employee by the employer so that it is the temporary hirer, rather than the employer, who has the greater potential to abuse its authority to direct the conduct of the hired employee by putting the hired employee in a position that she unduly prioritises compliance with the directions of the temporary hirer rather than give due weight to any alternate considerations that might reasonably lead the employee to conduct herself differently in the circumstances. Admittedly, such circumstances will be quite rare; but as the horse and carriage cases suggest, it is possible.[62] Note that as the temporary hirer is not party to the employment contract, for the temporary hirer to be in a position to abuse its authority to direct the conduct of the hired employee, the temporary hirer will also need to have been conferred some rights to discipline the hired employee; at the very least, the right to return the hired employee to the employer if the hired employee's work proves unsatisfactory.[63] Without this capacity, a temporary hirer is in much the same position as any other stranger to the employment relationship.

That a temporary hirer can be held strictly liable for a tort committed against a stranger to the employment relationship by a hired employee does not mean that the temporary hirer and the hired employee are in an employment relationship. A hired employee remains in the employ of her employer. It follows that the imposition of employee strict liability on a temporary hirer is an exception to the general rule that employee strict liability only arises in respect of a tort committed against a stranger to the employment relationship by an employee. The exception is allowed because a temporary hirer who has been conferred sufficient authority to direct the conduct of a hired employee for its own benefit puts strangers to the relationship between the temporary hirer and the hired employee at risk of harm in much the same way as an employer puts strangers to the employment relationship at risk of harm because the employer can exercise its authority to direct the conduct of an employee for its own benefit. In both situations, there is the potential for the employer or temporary hirer to abuse its authority to direct the conduct of the hired employee by putting the hired employee in a position that she unduly prioritises compliance with the directions of either the employer or temporary hirer rather than give due weight to any alternate considerations that

[61] *Viasystems (Tyneside) Ltd v Thermal Transfer (Northern) Ltd* [2006] QB 510, 536 (Rix LJ).

[62] *Mersey Docks* [1947] 1 AC 1, 10 (Viscount Simon).

[63] eg although a building contractor might be given the right to return an electrician hired from a labour firm to provide electrical services on site, the building contractor will have very limited rights to insist on a change of staff where the provision of electrical services on site has been subcontracted to an independent firm. In the latter situation, the building contractor will have bargained for the provision of the services and not necessarily for the right to control who the subcontractor uses to provide such services.

might reasonably lead the employee to conduct herself differently in the circumstances. As the risks created by the potential for the abuse of the employer's or temporary hirer's authority to direct the conduct of the hired employee are closely analogous, employee strict liability can be imposed on the temporary hirer even though the temporary hirer and the hired employee are not strictly in an employment relationship.

The second question in respect of the imposition of strict liability on an employer for a tort committed against a stranger to the employer relationship by a hired employee is that, once it has been shown that a temporary hirer can be held strictly liable for the tort committed by a hired employee, is it possible for both the employer and the temporary hirer to be held strictly liable in respect of the same tort committed by the hired employee? Historically, it seems to have been assumed that only one person could be held strictly liable for a tort committed by a hired employee; that is either the employer *or* the temporary hirer.[64] The basis of this assumption appears to have been a concern that the hired employee could not be transferred from one employer to another without their consent.[65] As has already been pointed out, however, it is not necessary for the employment of the hired employee to have been transferred to the temporary hirer for the temporary hirer to be held strictly liable for a tort committed against a stranger to the employment relationship by the hired employee. Once this is acknowledged, there does not seem to be any obvious reason why both the employer and the temporary hirer could not both be held strictly liable in respect of the same tort committed by a hired employee[66] where both the employer and the temporary hirer had sufficient authority to direct the conduct of the hired employee so that there was the potential for both the employer and the temporary hirer to abuse that authority by putting the hired employee in a position that she unduly prioritises compliance with the directions of both the employer and the temporary hirer rather than give due weight to any alternate considerations that might reasonably lead the employee to conduct herself differently in the circumstances.

Courts have recently considered the possibility of imposing employee strict liability on both an employer and a temporary hirer. This can be seen in the England and Wales Court of Appeal decision in *Viasystems (Tyneside) Ltd v Thermal Transfer (Northern) Ltd.*[67] In that case, a labour hire company lent a fitter and his young mate to a subcontractor charged with installing air conditioning in a factory. The fitter's young mate accidentally set off the factory's fire protection sprinkler system when he selected an inappropriate route to return to the fitter after he had been sent to retrieve some fittings. Both the labour hire company and the subcontractor were held strictly liable for the damage caused by the sprinkler system. The reason appears to be that the fitter's young mate was not only under the supervision of the fitter supplied by the labour hire company at the time he engaged in the negligent

[64] Atiyah (n 17) 156–58.
[65] *Mersey Docks* [1947] 1 AC 1, 14 (Lord Macmillan).
[66] Atiyah (n 17) 156–58.
[67] [2006] QB 510.

conduct, but was also answerable to another fitter engaged by the subcontractor who was coordinating the air conditioning work.[68] Whether *Viasystems* was an appropriate case for employee strict liability to be imposed on both the employer and the hirer is not entirely clear on the facts. The capacity of the subcontractor to discipline the fitter's young mate, for instance, was not considered. Nor was the duration of the contract between the labour hire company and the subcontractor. What is evident from *Viasystems* is that the circumstances in which employee strict liability can be imposed on both an employer and a temporary hirer will be relatively rare.[69] This is confirmed by subsequent cases which have so far refused to impose such strict liability in respect of a tort committed against a stranger to the employment relationship by a hired employee.[70]

VI. The 'Both Ways' Test

A tort committed by an employee is not only relevant where a stranger to the employment relationship seeks to hold the employer strictly liable for the tort of an employee, but can also be relevant where an employer is seeking to hold a stranger to the employment relationship liable in respect of a tort committed by the stranger to the employment relationship. Under the 'both ways' test,[71] an employer's claim in tort against a stranger to the employment relationship will be reduced to the extent that an employee's tortious conduct may have contributed to any loss suffered by the employer. A common example of the 'both ways' test being applied is where an employer brings a claim in respect of damage to a motor vehicle involved in a road traffic accident where the accident was partly caused by the negligence of the employee driving the vehicle and partly by the negligence of a stranger to the employment relationship. The employer's claim against the stranger to the employment relationship in such circumstances will be reduced to the extent to which the negligence of the employee contributed to the employer's loss. The New South Wales Court of Appeal also applied the 'both-ways' test in a claim brought by a company against its auditors for negligence in *Daniels v Anderson*.[72] The damages payable by the negligent auditors to the company were reduced because the management of the company had also been 'grossly negligent'.[73]

The 'both ways' test only applies to the contributory negligence of an employee. It does not apply to the contributory negligence of an independent contractor engaged by the employer. The negligence of a taxi driver, for instance, is not imputed to a passenger injured in a road traffic accident which was partly caused

[68] *Viasystems (Tyneside) Ltd v Thermal Transfer (Northern) Ltd* [2006] QB 510, 518–19 (May LJ).
[69] Ibid 537 (Rix LJ).
[70] See *Biffa Waste Services Ltd v Maschinenfabrik Ernst Hese Bmbh* [2009] QB 725.
[71] JG Fleming, *The Law of Torts* (9th ed, Sydney, Law Book Company, 1998) 323.
[72] (1995) 37 NSWLR 438.
[73] Ibid 576.

by the negligence of the taxi driver and partly by the negligence of another driver. It is more than likely, therefore, that the basis for the 'both ways' test is the same as the basis for imposing employee strict liability itself. The potential for an employer to abuse its authority to direct the conduct of an employee by putting the employee in a position that she unduly prioritises compliance with her employer's directions rather than give due weight to any alternate considerations that might reasonably lead the employee to conduct herself differently in the circumstances, not only creates a risk in respect of strangers to the employment relationship but also a risk in respect of the employer's own property (although in an admittedly much narrower range of circumstances as the employer should have considered such a risk when giving the employee directions). The 'both ways' test responds to this risk by reducing an employer's claim for damages against a stranger to the employment relationship by the extent to which a tort committed by the employee contributed to the employer's loss.

VII. Master's Tort or Servant's Tort

It has long been debated whether the liability imposed on an employer by employee strict liability is best viewed as liability for the master's tort or liability for the servant's tort.[74] Under the master's tort theory, the tort committed by an employee is attributed to an employer so that any liability imposed on the employer is considered personal. Alternatively, under the servant's tort theory, it is accepted that the tort committed was that of the employee so that the liability imposed on the employer can only be a form of strict liability for the tort of another.

Over time, most courts and academics have accepted the servant's tort theory as the basis of employee strict liability.[75] This has come from a concern with the fictitious nature of attributing or identifying the acts of one person with that of another. Some academics, however, have preferred to hold on to the master's tort theory[76] and the ease with which it can explain some of the more difficult cases, such as where an employee enjoys some type of immunity from suit in respect of the tort committed by the employee. In *Broom v Morgan*,[77] for instance, the employer of a husband and wife team argued in accordance with the servant's tort theory that the employer could not be held strictly liable for the negligence of the husband in leaving open a trapdoor in which his wife fell. As the wife was prohibited from suing the husband by legislation at the time of the accident, it was submitted that there was no liability which could be passed on to the employer.

[74] R Stevens, 'Vicarious Liability or Vicarious Action' (2007) 123 *Law Quarterly Review* 30.

[75] Atiyah (n 17) 6.

[76] See G Williams, 'Vicarious Liability: Tort of the Master or of the Servant' (1956) 72 *Law Quarterly Review* 522 and, more recently Stevens, 'Vicarious Liability or Vicarious Action' (n 74).

[77] [1952] 2 QB 1007.

The court, however, utilised the master's tort theory in order to impose liability on the employer. Lord Goddard CJ explained:

> although it is common to speak of the master's liability as vicarious, it is none the less regarded as the liability of a principal. The master is just as much liable as though he commits the tort himself because the servant's act is his act.[78]

Although much energy has been poured into the debate as to whether employee strict liability is best described as liability for the master's tort or liability for the servant's tort, it is not clear whether the question underlying the debate is either useful or appropriate. When employee strict liability is seen in terms of the risk of harm to strangers to the employment relationship that exists because an employer may potentially abuse its authority to direct the conduct of an employee by putting the employee in a position that she unduly prioritises compliance with her employer's directions rather than give due weight to any alternate considerations that might reasonably lead the employee to conduct herself differently in the circumstances, the trigger for the liability is necessarily viewed as the tort committed by the employee because it is only when the employer's potential to abuse its authority to direct the conduct of an employee for its own benefit converts to the commission of an actual tort by the employee that the strict liability arises. The extent of the strict liability is also quantified by reference to the damage that the employee causes in the process of committing the tort. At the same time, the employer is held strictly liable because of the potential for the employer to itself abuse its authority to direct by the conduct of an employee for its own benefit. Employee strict liability can therefore be seen to reflect different aspects of both the master's and the servant's tort theories. Labelling the strict liability one or the other, does not seem particularly helpful in the circumstances.

It is also possible to deal with cases such as *Broom v Morgan* without having to resort to the master's tort theory. It did not matter in that case that the employee could not be held personally liable to his wife because of spousal immunity. The trigger for employee strict liability is not whether the employee could be held liable to the claimant but the fact that the employee had committed a tort against the claimant, regardless of whether or not the claimant might sue the employee in respect of that tort. Provided such a tort occurred in the course of employment, there was a risk that the employer might have abused its authority to direct the conduct of an employee by putting the employee in a position that she unduly prioritised compliance with her employer's directions rather than give due weight to any alternate considerations that might reasonably have led the employee to conduct herself differently in the circumstances. The employer is held liable for creating that risk and it is therefore irrelevant that the employee herself could not be held personally liable to the claimant by virtue of some form of immunity.

[78] Ibid 1009. Similar sentiments were expressed on appeal which upheld Lord Goddard CJ's decision, [1953] 1 QB 597.

VIII. Conclusion

Employee strict liability was previously imposed under the label 'vicarious liability'. Such a label gave few clues as to the basis of the strict liability or its limits. By focusing on the one feature which the various relationships in which the courts impose strict liability for the tort of another have in common, it can now be seen that employee strict liability responds to the potential for an employer, when exercising its authority to direct the conduct of an employee for its own benefit, to abuse that authority by putting the employee in a position that she unduly prioritises compliance with her employer's directions rather than give due weight to any alternate considerations that might reasonably lead the employee to conduct herself differently in the circumstances. Unlike previous explanations, the potential for an employer to abuse its authority to direct the conduct of an employee for its own benefit is both necessary and sufficient for employee strict liability to be imposed. It also explains why employers are not held strictly liable for all damage caused by employees whilst carrying out the employer's business. The law is not concerned with the possibility that an employee might cause damage of itself, but the possibility that such damage might be brought about by an employer abusing their authority to direct the conduct of an employee for its own benefit.

6

Agent Strict Liability

The third and final form of strict liability for the tort of another identified by the new expositive framework proposed by this book is *agent strict liability*. As explained in chapter 3, this form of strict liability is limited to the agency relationship and responds to the potential for an agent to abuse the authority vested in her by a principal to effect legal relations on the principal's behalf.

This chapter will start by examining who is an agent for the purposes of agent strict liability. It will then determine the basis of the strict liability, its nature, the circumstances in which the strict liability arises and its scope. Finally, the chapter will explore whether it is possible to combine the conduct of a principal and an agent in order to establish a single tort, examine the strict liability imposed on a solicitor for the tort of an employee who has been vested with authority to effect legal relations on behalf of the solicitor's clients and consider whether the basis of agent strict liability lies in contract or tort.

I. Who is an Agent?

To understand agent strict liability, it is first necessary to define who is an 'agent' for the purposes of the strict liability. This is no easy task given Lord Herschell's comment in *Kennedy v de Trafford* that '[n]o word is more commonly and constantly abused than the word "agent"'.[1] It is appropriate then that this chapter starts by tracing the historical use of the term to see how the definition has developed.

One of the first cases to impose strict liability on a principal for the tort of an agent was *Hern v Nichols*.[2] The case involved the sale of silk, the quality of which had been misrepresented. The misrepresentation had been made by a factor[3] who had been entrusted with the silk by the vendor for the purposes of arranging a sale. Similar facts arose in *Udell v Atherton*,[4] except that rather than selling silk, the vendor was selling a mahogany log. Once again, there had been a

[1] [1897] AC 180, 188.
[2] (1708) 1 Salk 289 [91 ER 256] ('*Hern*').
[3] For an explanation of factors, see GE Dal Pont, *Law of Agency* (2nd ed, Sydney, LexisNexis, 2008) 21–22.
[4] (1861) 7H & N 172 ('*Udell*').

misrepresentation as to the quality of the log made by an agent appointed by the vendor to sell timber on a commission basis. The vendor was held strictly liable for the agent's misrepresentation by two of the four judges, the views of whom are now generally considered to be correct.[5] In both these cases, the agents had been vested with authority to effect legal relations on behalf of the vendors. The term 'agent' was therefore being used in the narrow, contractual sense of the word. It follows, that an 'agent' for the purposes of agent strict liability was originally quite limited.[6]

Confusion as to the meaning of the term 'agent' seems to have started with its use in cases concerning employee strict liability, specifically those in which an employee had engaged in some type of intentional misconduct. By using the term 'agent' the courts tried to take advantage of cases such as *Hern* and *Udell* to smooth over difficulties in finding that the tort committed by the employee could occur within the course of employment. The decision of the Court of the Exchequer Chamber in *Barwick v English Joint Stock Bank*[7] provides a good example. The question in that case was whether a bank could be held strictly liable for a bank manager who had fraudulently issued a guarantee on behalf of the bank in order to encourage the plaintiff to continue dealing with a customer of the bank. When explaining the general rule as to when an employer could be held strictly liable for a tort committed by an employee, Willes J applied the rule to agents also:[8]

> The general rule is, that the master is answerable for every wrong of the servant *or agent* as is committed in the course of the service and for the master's benefit, though no express command or privity of the master be proved.

When it came to explaining why the bank should be held strictly liable for the manager's fraud on the facts of the case, Willes J dropped the reference to 'employee' altogether:[9]

> It is true, he has not authorised the particular act, but he has put the agent in his place to do that class of acts, and he must be answerable for the manner in which the agent has conducted himself in doing the business which it was the act of his master to place him in.

Throughout his judgment, Willes J can be seen to use the terms 'employee' and 'agent' interchangeably. It was this interchangeable use of the terms which first suggested that the term 'agent' might not be restricted to a person who had been vested with authority by a principal to effect legal relations on the principal's behalf.[10]

One type of case to make particular use of this technique of describing employees as agents was cases involving the employees of solicitors who defrauded clients,

[5] PS Atiyah, *Vicarious Liability in the Law of Torts* (London, Butterworths, 1967) 111–12.

[6] The award in both cases was for damages rather than rescission of the contract.

[7] (1867) II LR Exch 259.

[8] Ibid 265 (emphasis added).

[9] Ibid 266.

[10] Although in *Barwick v English Joint Stock Bank* the employee had been given such authority. See below.

the most well-known being the decision of the House of Lords in *Lloyd v Grace Smith & Co.*[11] The employee in that case was engaged by a solicitor as a conveyancing manager and had been vested with authority by the solicitor 'to arrange and negotiate sales of real property and to carry them out, and also to receive deeds for safe custody'.[12] A client of the solicitor gave the conveyancing manager the title deeds to a property so that he could arrange a sale. Instead of arranging the sale, the conveyancing manager tricked the client into signing a transfer document in his favour and used the deeds to mortgage the property and misappropriate the proceeds. In holding the solicitor liable for the fraud of the conveyancing manager, the House of Lords relied heavily on the earlier decision of *Barwick*. Lord Macnaghten said of that decision:[13]

> And I think it follows from the decision, and the ground on which it was based, that in the opinion of the Court a principal must be liable for the fraud of his agent committed in the course of his agent's employment and not beyond the scope of his agency, whether the fraud be committed for the principal's benefit of not.

Once again, although the conveyancing manager was an employee, the concepts of employment and agency were being used interchangeably.

Further confusion as to the meaning of the term 'agent' arose with its use in a series of cases in which the owners of motor vehicles were held strictly liable for a tort committed by a person who was driving the vehicle on the owner's behalf.[14] Earlier cases involving a horse and carriage had identified the driver with the owner, essentially treating the driver and the owner as one and the same for the purposes of tort law.[15] Such reasoning lost favour with the rise of the fault-based tort of negligence towards the end of the nineteenth century[16] and it became necessary to find an alternate ground upon which to base such liability. In the motor vehicle cases, the courts took the lead of Willes J in *Barwick* and chose to describe the driver of a motor vehicle who was driving the vehicle on the owner's behalf as the owner's 'agent'. The basis of the motor vehicle owner's liability was explained by du Parcq LJ in *Hewitt v Bonvin* in the following terms:[17]

> The driver of a car may not be the owner's servant, and the owner will be nevertheless liable for his negligent driving if it be proved that at the material time he had authority, express or implied, to drive on the owner's behalf. Such liability depends not on ownership, but on the delegation of a task or duty.

This was a much broader use of the concept of 'agency' in that it was not limited to a person who had been vested with authority by a principal to effect legal relations

[11] [1912] AC 716.
[12] Ibid 717.
[13] Ibid 731.
[14] Culminating with the House of Lords decision in *Morgans v Launchbury* [1973] AC 127.
[15] See, eg, *Wheatley v Patrick* (1837) 6 LJ Ex 193.
[16] JG Fleming, *The Law of Torts* (9th ed, Sydney, Law Book Company, 1998) 367–68.
[17] [1940] 1 KB 188, 194–95.

on the principal's behalf, but extended to include a person who had been asked to drive a motor vehicle on the motor vehicle owner's behalf.

The varied senses in which the term 'agent' was being used meant that the courts had to try and rationalise the meaning of the term 'agent' for the purposes of agent strict liability. This can be seen in the decision of the High Court of Australia in *Colonial Mutual Life Assurance Society Limited v The Producers and Citizens Cooperative Assurance Company of Australia Limited*.[18] The case concerned a life insurance agent who had been appointed to canvass members of the public for life insurance proposals. In explaining why the life insurance company could be held strictly liable for torts committed by the life insurance agent but not for other independent contractors engaged by the life insurance company, Dixon J said:[19]

> The independent contractor carries out his work, not as a representative but as a principal. But a difficulty arises when the function entrusted is that of representing the person who requests its performance in a transaction with others, so that the very service to be performed consists in standing in his place and assuming to act in his right and not in an independent capacity.

On the facts of *CML*, there was very little doubt that the life insurance agent was an agent; he had been vested with authority to obtain proposals and collect premiums on behalf of the life insurance company[20] and was therefore an agent in the narrow, contractual sense of the word.[21] The decision has been significant, however, because in distinguishing an agent from an independent contractor Dixon J drew on the 'representative' capacity of an agent. Subsequent judges have taken Dixon J's use of the term 'representative' to mean that an agent is not just a person who has been vested with authority by a principal to effect legal relations on the principal's behalf, but can include a person engaged to do any other number of things on behalf of another. In this way, *CML* has provided a means by which the definition of 'agent' might be expanded.

The judge most well-known for using *CML* to expand the definition of the term 'agent' is Justice McHugh. His first attempt came in the decision of the High Court of Australia in *Scott v Davis*,[22] a case involving a plane accident in which the pilot was killed and a young boy severely injured. In determining whether the parents of the young boy could hold the owner of the plane strictly liable for the pilot's negligence, McHugh J looked to the ratio decidendi of *CML* which he described as follows:[23]

> a principal is liable for the wrongful act of an agent causing damage to a third party when that act occurred while the agent was carrying out some activity as the principal's authorised representative in a dealing with a third party.

[18] (1931) 46 CLR 41 ('*CML*').
[19] Ibid 48–49.
[20] But not to issue policies.
[21] See further ch 3.
[22] (2000) 204 CLR 333.
[23] Ibid 357.

As the owner of the plane had asked the pilot to take the young boy up on a joyride, McHugh J was of the view that the pilot was acting as the owner's authorised representative and was therefore an 'agent'. It followed that the owner could be held strictly liable for the pilot's negligence. He was supported in this conclusion by the motor vehicle cases mentioned above.[24] The remainder of the High Court,[25] however, were not convinced that the pilot could be considered an 'agent' on the facts of the case. The following statement by Gummow J is typical:[26]

> It may be conceded … that the activities of an agent with authority to bring about a contractual or other legal relationship between the principal and third parties may have legal consequences in tort for which the principal is responsible. But the pilot was not an agent in this sense.

Nor could the remaining members of the High Court find any other basis upon which to hold the owner of the plane liable for the pilot's negligence.

Justice McHugh had a further opportunity to try and expand the definition of the term 'agent' (and attendant legal consequences) in *Hollis v Vabu Pty Ltd*.[27] The case involved the liability of a courier company for a bicycle courier who had struck a pedestrian whilst delivering packages in Sydney. The bicycle courier had not been identified, but was wearing the defendant courier company's uniform at the time. The central issue in the case was whether a bicycle courier engaged by the courier company was an employee or an independent contractor. After much discussion, a majority of the High Court found the bicycle courier to be an employee.[28] It followed that employee strict liability could be imposed on the courier company for the bicycle courier's negligence. Justice McHugh, however, was concerned that the majority's decision might unduly extend the 'classical tests' of employment.[29] He consequently decided to take a different route. Rather than find that the bicycle courier was an employee, he instead found the bicycle courier to be an 'agent':[30]

> Rather than expanding the definition of employee or accepting the employee/independent contractor dichotomy, the preferable course is to hold that employers can be vicariously liable for the tortious conduct of agents who are neither employees nor independent contractors … To hold an employer vicariously liable for the conduct of a worker who is not an employee or independent contractor does not affect their relationship in other areas of the law or their freedom to contract between themselves or to arrange their business affairs. And it has the great advantage of ensuring that the doctrine of vicarious liability remains relevant in a world of rapidly changing working practices.

[24] Ibid 359–69.
[25] Gleeson CJ, Gummow, Hayne and Callinan JJ.
[26] *Scott v Davis* (2000) 204 CLR 333, 423.
[27] (2001) 207 CLR 21.
[28] Gleeson CJ, Gaudron, Gummow, Kirby, Hayne and Callinan JJ.
[29] *Hollis v Vabu Pty Ltd* (2001) 207 CLR 21, 49.
[30] Ibid 57.

In finding the bicycle courier to be an 'agent,' McHugh J again relied on the earlier decision of the High Court in *CML*.[31]

Another judge to have used *CML* to expand the definition of the term 'agent' is Justice Kirby. In *Sweeney v Boylan Nominees Pty Limited*,[32] the High Court of Australia had to decide whether a fridge owner who had leased a fridge to a service station could be held liable for the negligence of a refrigeration mechanic sent to repair the fridge under the terms of the lease. Justice Kirby was of the view that the fridge owner could be held so liable on the basis that the refrigeration mechanic was an agent of the fridge owner. The basis of his reasoning was once again the decision in *CML*:

> Whilst the rule in *CML* remains, it should be applied by this Court in accordance with its terms. It is part of Australian law. Its terms apply in the present case. The [refrigeration mechanic] was the representative of [the fridge owner] which afforded him the means to persuade others that he should be admitted to their premises, permitted to repair a refrigerator placed there for which [the fridge owner] was responsible by lease and even allowed to receive [the fridge owner's] money and to give a receipt for what he received.

As with McHugh J's previous efforts to expand the definition of the term 'agent', however, the majority of the High Court disagreed. The majority noted that McHugh J's views in both *Scott* and *Hollis* had been a minority position and returned to a more traditional definition of the 'term' agency:[33]

> But neither in *Scott* nor in *Hollis*, nor earlier in *CML*, was there established the principle that A is vicariously liable for the conduct of B if B 'represents' A (in the sense of B acting for the benefit or advantage of A). On the contrary, *Scott* rejected contentions that, at their roots, were no different from those advanced in this case under the rubric of 'representation' rather than, as in *Scott*, under the rubric 'agency'. As was said in *Scott* of the word 'agent', to use the word 'representative' is to begin but not to end the inquiry.

In reviewing the historical use of the term 'agent', it is not difficult to see why Lord Herschell said that '[n]o word is more commonly and constantly abused than the word "agent"'.[34] Ever since agent strict liability was first recognised, there seems to have been constant pressure to expand the meaning of the term 'agent'. Constant pressure, however, does not equate to success. There are actually very few higher court cases in either Australia or England and Wales in which a person has been held strictly liable for a tort committed by an agent where that agent was not an agent in the narrow, contractual sense of the term. As noted by a majority of the High Court of Australia in *Sweeney*, support for expanding the meaning of the term 'agent' in *Scott*, *Hollis* and indeed *Sweeney* was a minority position.

[31] Ibid 58–60.
[32] (2006) 226 CLR 161 ('*Sweeney*').
[33] Ibid 172.
[34] [1897] AC 180, 188.

The majority instead endorsed the traditional, narrow definition. In *CML*, despite the use of the word 'representative', the life insurance agent had been vested with authority to effect legal relations on behalf of the life insurance company.[35] Similarly, in *Barwick*, although the term 'agent' was used interchangeably with the term 'employee', the employee in that case was an agent because, as bank manager, he had been vested with authority to execute guarantees on behalf of the bank.

This just leaves the cases involving the employee of a solicitor who has defrauded the solicitor's clients (the *solicitor's employee* cases) and the motor vehicle cases. With respect to the solicitor's employee cases, although the employees in those cases had not been vested with authority to effect legal relations on behalf of the solicitor, they had been vested with authority to effect legal relations on behalf of the solicitor's clients. This authority had been vested in the employee by the solicitor who was ultimately held strictly liable for the fraud. This is a very similar notion to agency in its narrow, contractual sense, although the notion has been modified for the particular role played by members of the legal profession in arranging legal transactions on behalf of their clients. Indeed the similarities are so great, that the reasons for imposing strict liability in both situations appear to be the same (see section VII below). It can be argued, therefore, that the solicitor's employee cases are an exception to the general rule that an 'agent' is a person who has been vested with authority by a principal to effect legal relations on the principal's behalf. The exception is confined to very specific facts and the general principles of agent strict liability apply.

With respect to the motor vehicle cases, to the extent that drivers in the motor vehicle cases have been described as 'agents' it might be argued that the term 'agent' for the purposes of agent strict liability means more than someone who has been vested authority by a principal to effect legal relations on the principal's behalf. The concept of 'agency' used in the motor vehicle cases was, however, restricted to cases involving motor vehicles by a majority of the High Court of Australia in *Scott v Davis*.[36] This means that whatever the basis of the strict liability in those cases, it is a basis which cannot be applied more generally. Furthermore, it will be shown in chapter 8 that the courts are no longer as willing as they once were to impose such strict liability. It follows that there is no longer any reason to treat the motor vehicle cases as instances of 'agency' and the cases can be left to one side.

Although there are numerous cases which have purported to impose agent strict liability, once the solicitor's employee cases and the motor vehicles cases are addressed, it can be seen that who is an 'agent' for the purposes of agent strict liability has been drawn quite narrowly. The cases show that it is only when an 'agent' has been vested with authority by a principal to effect legal relations on the principal's behalf that agent strict liability is consistently imposed.

[35] Although such authority did not extend to issuing policies.
[36] See, eg, (2000) 204 CLR 333, 419–20 (Gummow J).

II. Basis of the Strict Liability

Traditionally, the basis of agent strict liability was thought to be very similar to the basis of employee strict liability. As both a principal and an employer received the benefit of an agent or an employee's work, it was thought appropriate that they should both also bear the burden of any torts committed by an employee or agent in obtaining that benefit.[37]

The new expositive framework for strict liability for the tort of another proposed by this book has suggested an alternative basis for employee strict liability. In chapter 5 it was argued that employee strict liability responds to the potential for an employer, when exercising its authority to direct the conduct of an employee for its own benefit, to abuse that authority by putting the employee in a position that she unduly prioritises compliance with her employer's directions rather than give due weight to any alternate considerations that might reasonably lead the employee to conduct herself differently in the circumstances. When viewed in such terms, the basis of agent strict liability cannot be the same as that of employee strict liability. This is because an agent may be an employee, an independent contractor or may even be acting gratuitously. Consequently, not all principals are vested with authority to direct the conduct of an agent so that not all principals have the potential to abuse that authority by putting the agent in a position that she unduly prioritises compliance with directions issued in an exercise of that authority.

Rather than being similar to employee strict liability, it now appears that the basis of agent strict liability is more closely aligned with that of conferred authority strict liability. As explained in chapter 4, conferred authority strict liability responds to the potential for abuse of the power relationship created when an employer or school confers its authority to direct the conduct of an employee or student upon another person. In much the same way, agent strict liability can be seen to respond to the potential for abuse of the authority vested in an agent by a principal. Such potential exists because the authority vested in an agent by a principal creates a relationship between the agent and the party wishing to effect legal relations with the principal (the *transactional party*) that enables the agent to effect legal relations between the principal and the transactional party in circumstances in which the transactional party is not expected to confirm with the principal the details of those legal relations.

Consider a scenario where a vendor is selling a property through a real estate agent. The vendor vests the real estate agent with authority to negotiate the sale of the property on the vendor's behalf. The real estate agent then provides prospective purchasers with information about the property on the vendor's behalf. In such circumstances, a prospective purchaser is not expected to confirm with the principal the information provided by the real estate agent. Were a prospective purchaser to take such steps they would effectively negate the advantages of using

[37] The flaws associated with this approach were demonstrated in ch 1.

a real estate agent in the first place. Instead, a prospective purchaser is entitled to rely on the information provided by the agent.

As this scenario demonstrates, the problem with a principal vesting authority in an agent to effect legal relations on the principal's behalf is that because a transactional party is not expected to confirm with the principal the details of those legal relations, the authority vested in the agent by the principal is subject to abuse. An agent, for instance, can use the authority vested in her by a principal to misrepresent the nature of property being sold by the principal to a prospective purchaser. A principal consequently puts a transactional party at risk of harm whenever the principal vests authority in an agent to effect legal relations on the principal's behalf. It is submitted that it is this potential for an agent to abuse the authority vested by the principal in the agent that attracts the concern and the intervention of the law. Agent strict liability responds to the potential for an agent to abuse the authority vested in her by a principal to effect legal relations on the principal's behalf by holding the principal liable, regardless of whether the principal also personally engaged in any conduct in respect of the transactional party to which liability in tort might attach, for any tort committed by the agent in respect of the transactional party in the course of effecting legal relations on the principal's behalf. The liability effectively holds a principal to account for a tort committed by an agent in the course of effecting those legal relations. In so doing, the liability provides transactional parties with a degree of protection from an abuse of the authority vested in the agent by the principal. This is important given that any restraints placed on how an agent exercises the authority vested in her by a principal typically protect the principal rather than a transactional party. For instance, although an agent owes a fiduciary duty to the principal, an agent owes no equivalent duty to a transactional party.

As noted in the previous chapters, it is relatively unusual in tort law for one person to be held strictly liable for the tort of another, and a defendant has to do more than merely provide an opportunity for a tort to occur for such liability to be imposed. When a principal vests an agent with authority to effect legal relations on the principal's behalf, a principal does do more than merely provide the agent with an opportunity to commit a tort. A modification to the above real estate scenario demonstrates the point. If a vendor not only appoints a real estate agent, but engages an electrician to repair a faulty stove to be sold with the property, the vendor will provide the electrician with an opportunity to commit a tort which might harm a prospective purchaser. The vendor, however, does no more than that. There is nothing the vendor does that can be seen to assist or enable the electrician to commit a tort in respect of a prospective purchaser. Consequently, the vendor will not be held strictly liable for a tort committed by the electrician.[38] In contrast, where a vendor appoints a real estate agent, the authority vested in the real estate agent by the vendor can provide the means by which the agent might commit a tort in respect of a prospective purchaser. A real estate agent, for instance, can use the

[38] *Northern Sandblasting Pty Ltd v Harris* (1997) 188 CLR 313.

authority vested in her by a vendor to obtain money from a prospective purchaser (perhaps in the form of a deposit) and then appropriate that money for their own purposes.[39] It is not that an abuse of authority will necessarily occur, but there is always an inherent risk that the authority vested by the principal in the agent to effect legal relations on the principal's behalf will be abused. As will be seen from the cases, that risk appears sufficient for strict liability for the tort of another to be imposed.

III. Nature of the Strict Liability

As with the other forms of strict liability for the tort of another outlined in this book, agent strict liability is not an absolute form of liability; it is not imposed in the *absence* of any tort being committed.[40] It still needs to be shown that an agent committed a tort in respect a transactional party in the course of effecting legal relations between the transactional party and the principal. The liability is, however, imposed *regardless* of whether the principal engaged in any conduct in respect of the transactional party to which liability in tort might attach. This means that agent strict liability can be imposed even though a principal may be able to adduce evidence that the vesting of authority in the agent was not a contributing factor in the tort committed by the agent in respect of the transactional party. The liability can also be imposed even though a principal may be able to adduce evidence that an abuse of the authority vested in the agent did not actually take place. This is because agent strict liability responds to the *potential* rather than an *actual* abuse of the authority vested in an agent by the principal.

It may seem unfair that a principal can be subject to agent strict liability regardless of engaging in any conduct to which liability in tort might attach, but a principal need not necessarily bear such liability alone. In certain circumstances, a principal will be entitled to seek an indemnity from the agent in respect of the damages paid to the transactional party in respect of whom the agent committed the tort.[41]

IV. In What Circumstances Does the Strict Liability Arise?

Agent strict liability can be imposed on a principal whenever an agent commits a tort in respect of a transactional party in the course of effecting legal relations between the principal and a transactional party.

[39] As occurred in *Lloyd v Grace, Smith & Co* [1912] AC 716.

[40] P Cane, 'Responsibility and Fault: a Relational and Functional Approach to Responsibility' in P Cane and J Gardner (eds), *Relating to Responsibility* (Oxford, Hart, 2001) 81, 99.

[41] FMB Reynolds, *Bowstead and Reynolds on Agency* (18th ed, London, Sweet & Maxwell, 2006) 165.

Three points can be made about the general circumstances in which agent strict liability arises. First, agent strict liability is generally limited to economic loss. The reason is that the authority vested in an agent by the principal is an authority to effect legal relations on the principal's behalf. The potential for that authority to be abused is therefore typically limited to circumstances involving the contractual expectancies of a transactional party. The damage suffered in such circumstances generally materialises in the form of economic loss. Agent strict liability may also extend to property loss, given that a transactional party may hand over property to an agent in the course of effecting legal relations with the principal with which the agent may subsequently abscond. What agent strict liability does *not* extend to is personal injury or damage to other personal interests. As the authority vested by a principal in an agent does not include authority to direct the conduct of a transactional party, there is very limited potential for any abuse of that authority to result in physical harm. Consequently, whilst a vendor might be held strictly liable to a prospective purchaser induced to buy a property as a result of a negligent misrepresentation made by a real estate agent or to part with a deposit with which the real estate agent absconds, a vendor will not be held strictly liable to a prospective purchaser injured in a car accident negligently caused by a real estate agent whilst driving the purchaser to view the property.[42]

There is *one* case in which the High Court of Australia has imposed strict liability on a principal for something other than economic loss or property loss, but it is the *only* higher court case in either Australia or England and Wales to do so. In *CML*, which was discussed above, the life insurance company was held strictly liable for defamatory statements made by its agent about a rival life insurance company whilst the agent was canvassing members of the public for life insurance proposals. A defamatory statement, however, is not like a negligent misrepresentation; the authority vested in an agent by the principal does not provide the means by which an agent might make a defamatory statement. A defamatory statement is more like the negligent driving of the real estate agent in that, at best, the life insurance company created an opportunity for the defamatory statement to be made. On this basis, it is submitted that the decision of the High Court in *CML* is incorrect.[43] Although *CML* has been referred to by Australian courts on numerous occasions, the possibility that the decision is incorrect is plausible because the references to *CML* have been to Dixon J's emphasis on the need for an agent to be acting in a 'representative' capacity rather than to the actual decision that a principal can be held strictly liable for defamatory statements made by an agent.

A second and closely associated point that can be made about the general circumstances in which agent strict liability arises is that the strict liability is owed *only* to transactional parties. A principal will not be held strictly liable to any

[42] See, eg, the South African case of *Colonial Mutual Life Assurance Society Ltd v McDonald* 1931 AD 412, cited by Atiyah, *Vicarious Liability in the Law of Torts* (n 5) 109 and 113–14.

[43] Note that it was a 4 (Gavan Duffy CJ, Rich, Starke and Dixon JJ)/2 (Evatt and McTiernan JJ) decision.

person in respect of whom an agent commits a tort, only a transactional party in respect of whom an agent commits a tort in the course of effecting legal relations with the principal. This is because the vesting of authority by a principal in an agent creates a relationship between the agent and a transactional party and it is only within that relationship that there is the potential for the authority vested in the agent by the principal to be abused.

A final point that can be made about the general circumstances in which agent strict liability arises is that there are not any restrictions on who can be an agent for the purposes of the strict liability. An agent for these purposes may be an employee, an independent contractor or may even be acting gratuitously. What is important is not who the agent is or how they were appointed, but that they have been vested with authority by the principal to effect legal relations on the principal's behalf. In cases such as *Hern v Nichol*, for instance, the agent for whom the principal was held strictly liable was an independent contractor. In other cases, such as *Barwick v English Joint Stock Bank*, the agent for whom the principal was held strictly liable was an employee.

V. Scope of the Strict Liability

Agent strict liability is generally limited to circumstances in which an agent commits a tort in respect of a transactional party *in the course of effecting legal relations between the principal and the transactional party.* This is because the liability responds to the potential for the authority vested in an agent by a principal to be abused and such potential generally only exists where the agent is using that authority to effect legal relations with a transactional party on the principal's behalf.

Importantly, whether an agent commits a tort in respect of a transactional party in the course of effecting legal relations between the principal and the transactional party is determined by reference to the terms of the *apparent* authority vested in the agent by the principal, as opposed to the terms of the actual authority vested in the agent by the principal. Provided the transactional party reasonably believes that the agent is purporting to exercise the authority vested in the agent by the principal immediately prior to the tort being committed, any tort committed by the agent will be taken to have occurred in the course of effecting legal relations between the principal and the transactional party. This is best demonstrated by the fraud cases referred to above.[44] In those cases, agent strict liability could not have been imposed if the terms of the actual authority vested in the agent by the principal determined the scope of the liability. This is because each of the agents involved in those cases would have known they had no actual authority to commit fraud or engage in conduct with the purpose of committing a fraud. Immediately prior to

[44] See, eg, *Hern v Nichol* (1708) 1 Salk 289; 91 ER 256.

the frauds occurring, however, the agents in those cases were engaged in conduct within the terms of the apparent authority that had been vested in them by a principal, conduct such as negotiating the sale of a log or negotiating the issue of a guarantee. As the agents were acting within the terms of the apparent authority vested in them by their principals, there was the potential for the authority to be abused. It follows that the frauds occurred in the course of effecting legal relations between the principal and the transactional party and agent strict liability could be imposed.

The reason the scope of agent strict liability is determined by reference to the terms of the apparent (as opposed to the actual) authority vested in an agent by a principal is because a transactional party will interact with an agent on the basis of the terms of the apparent authority vested in the agent by the principal. One reason a transactional party will hand over money to an agent, for instance, is because the agent has the apparent authority to collect that money on the principal's behalf. The relationship between the agent and the transactional party is therefore shaped by the terms of the apparent authority vested in the agent by the principal and not by the terms of the actual authority that has been so vested. It is the potential for this authority to be abused which puts transactional parties at risk of harm.

Arguably, it is this potential for agent strict liability to extend beyond the terms of the actual authority vested in an agent by a principal which has made it an attractive, alternative form of strict liability in cases involving torts committed by employees. Chapter 5 showed that a tort committed by an employee does not fall within the course of employment for the purposes of employee strict liability unless the conduct engaged in by the employee immediately prior to the tort being committed was *actually* directed (either expressly or impliedly) by the employer. This is because it is only where conduct is actually directed by an employer that there is the potential for the employer to abuse its authority to direct the conduct of an employee by putting the employee in a position that she unduly prioritises compliance with her employer's directions rather than give due weight to any alternate considerations that might reasonably lead the employee to conduct herself differently in the circumstances. Agent strict liability is therefore potentially much broader in scope than employee strict liability. It follows that there might be circumstances in which agent strict liability can be imposed but employee strict liability cannot.

Consider *Barwick v English Joint Stock Bank*.[45] If the bank manager in that case had been working for his own benefit when issuing the fraudulent guarantees, employee strict liability could not have been imposed on the bank because, immediately prior to the tort being committed, the bank manager would have been acting pursuant to his own motivations and not in accordance with any actual directions (express or implied) issued by the bank. It follows that there would have been very little risk of the bank manager being influenced by an exercise of his

[45] (1867) II LR Exch 259.

employer's authority which, even were it to be exercised by the bank, would most likely be done in a manner to discourage the bank manager from engaging in such conduct given the broader ramifications of such conduct for the bank's business.[46] On the facts of *Barwick*, however, the bank manager's conduct appeared to have been engaged in for the benefit of the employer so that there was scope to argue that the tort was committed in accordance with the implied directions of the employer. In this respect, the case is not dissimilar to *Limpus v London General Omnibus Co.*[47] It would appear, therefore, that the House of Lords may have been a little hasty in de-emphasising the significance of whether the employee had been acting in the employer's benefit in the subsequent case of *Lloyd v Grace Smith & Co*[48] (discussed above).

Determining the scope of agent strict liability by reference to the terms of the apparent authority vested in an agent by a principal does not mean that a principal will be held strictly liable for all torts committed by an agent in respect of a transactional party. It still has to be shown that the agent was acting within the terms of the apparent authority vested in the agent by the principal immediately prior to the tort being committed, for it is only then that the authority vested in the agent is in a position to be abused. The decision of the House of Lords in *Armagas Ltd v Mundogas SA*[49] provides a good example. The case involved the sale and charter-back of a ship owned by Mundogas. The deal was negotiated on Mundogas' behalf by the company's vice-president (transportation) who had been vested with authority by Mundogas to effect legal transactions on its behalf, making him also an agent. In the course of the negotiations with Armagas, the vice-president fraudulently misrepresented to Armagas that he was authorised to charter-back the ship for a period of three years. Armagas knew that a person in the position of the vice-president was generally only authorised to enter into charterparties of up to 12 months and the terms of the actual authority vested in the vice-president was limited to entering into charterparties of 12 months. As Armagas was aware that the vice-president was acting outside the terms of his apparent authority, it could not hold Mundogas strictly liable for the vice-president's deceit. As Lord Keith of Kinkel explained, Mundogas had not done anything to induce Armagas' belief as to the authority of the vice-president:[50]

> At the end of the day the question is whether the circumstances under which a servant has made the fraudulent misrepresentation which has caused loss to an innocent party contracting with him are such as to make it just for the employer to bear the loss. Such circumstances exist where the employer by words or conduct has induced the injured party to believe that the servant was acting in the lawful course of the employer's business. They do not exist where such belief, although it is present, has been brought about

[46] In *Mohamud v VM Morrison Supermarkets plc* [2016] AC 677, for instance, the employee's supervisor physically tried to restrain the employee from committing the assault.

[47] (1862) 1 HC & C 526; 158 ER 993.

[48] [1912] AC 716.

[49] [1986] 1 AC 717.

[50] Ibid 782–83.

> through misguided reliance on the servant himself, when the servant is not authorised to do what he is purporting to do, when what he is purporting to do is not within the class of acts that an employee in his position is usually authorised to do, and when the employer has done nothing to represent that he is authorised to do it.

It follows that the fraudulent misrepresentation made by the vice-president could not be considered an abuse of the authority vested in the vice-president by Mundogas because Armagas did not reasonably believe that the vice-president was purporting to exercise that authority immediately prior to making the fraudulent misrepresentation. In explaining what would have been necessary to impose strict liability on Mundogas for the fraudulent misrepresentation of the vice-president, Lord Keith of Kinkel said:[51]

> The essential feature for creating liability in the employer is that the party contracting with the fraudulent servant should have altered his position to his detriment in reliance on the belief that the servant's activities were within his authority, or, to put it another way, were part of his job, this belief having been induced by the master's representations by way of words or conduct.

Such reasoning reinforces the reasons given above as to why agent strict liability is imposed. It is imposed because a principal vests authority in an agent to effect legal relations on the principal's behalf and there is an expectation that a transactional party will enter into those legal relations without confirming any of the details with the principal. A transactional party is therefore entitled to rely on an agent in the course of entering into legal relations with the principal. Such reasoning also provides further support for the view that *CML* was incorrectly decided. The plaintiff in *CML* cannot be said to have 'altered his position to his detriment in reliance' on the agent's defamatory statement. Note that as the vice-president's fraudulent misrepresentation in *Armagas v Mundogas* was intentional and outside the actual directions issued by Mundogas, there was not any possibility of imposing employee strict liability on the facts of the case.

The reasoning in *Armagas v Mundogas* also explains the unusual series of cases involving companies who have not been held strictly liable for the fraudulent misconduct of company secretaries. Typical of those cases is the decision of the House of Lords in *Ruben v Great Fingall Consolidated*.[52] That case involved a company secretary who fraudulently issued a share certificate in his own favour which he then used to secure a loan from Rubens. Although the company secretary had been vested with authority to record transfers of shares and to keep the share register, the company secretary had not been vested with actual or apparent authority to issue shares. It was therefore not open to Rubens to argue that the company secretary had been acting within the terms of his apparent authority when he issued the share certificate. Once again, as the fraudulent misconduct of the company secretary was intentional and outside the actual directions issued by the company, employee strict liability could not be imposed.

[51] Ibid 781.
[52] [1906] AC 439.

VI. Composite Torts

Can the conduct of both an agent and a principal be combined so that agent strict liability can be imposed even though the conduct of the agent does not itself amount to the commission of a completed tort? This is the question which arose in *Armstrong v Strain*.[53] In that case, the purchaser of a bungalow tried to hold a vendor strictly liable for a misrepresentation made by the vendor's real estate agent in the course of the sale. This would have been a straightforward case of agent strict liability except that, although the vendor knew the misrepresentation to be false, the real estate agent thought the misrepresentation to be true. The real estate agent had therefore not actually made a fraudulent misrepresentation for which the principal could be held strictly liable.

In most situations the idea of a composite tort would not even be raised. As a general rule, a person either commits a tort or they do not.[54] The reason it arises in the context of agent strict liability is the same reason why debates still occur as to whether employee strict liability is liability for the master's tort or liability for the servant's tort.[55] The issue is whether agent strict liability attributes an agent's *conduct* to a principal so that the principal is held personally liable or attributes *liability* for the conduct to the principal so that the principal is held strictly liable for the agent's tort. If agent strict liability attributes an agent's conduct to the principal, perhaps it is possible for there to be a composite tort. If only liability is being attributed, there is no basis upon which the conduct of two separate individuals can be combined.

In terms of what is being attributed to a principal for the purposes of agent strict liability, the same response can be given as that provided in the previous chapter in respect of employee strict liability; what is being attributed to the principal is liability for the tort committed by the agent in respect of the transactional party rather than the conduct constituting the tort. As agent strict liability responds to the potential for abuse of the authority vested in an agent by a principal to effect legal relations on the principal's behalf, the liability can be seen to be triggered by the commission of the tort by the agent. The extent of the strict liability is also quantified by reference to the damage that the agent causes in the commission of the tort. It follows that agent strict liability cannot be imposed unless an agent has themselves committed a tort. This does not mean that agent strict liability is imposed solely because the agent committed a tort. The principal is held strictly liable because the principal created a risk that a transactional party might be harmed by vesting authority in the agent to effect legal relations on the principal's behalf. Despite the principal's conduct, however, there is no reason for agent

53 [1952] 1 KB 232.

54 Though see Fleming's comment on *Anderson v Rhodes* [1967] 2 All ER 850; Fleming, *The Law of Torts* (n 16) 700.

55 See further ch 5.

strict liability to be imposed on a principal unless an agent actually commits a tort. It follows that there is no such thing as a composite tort for the purposes of agent strict liability.[56] This was confirmed by the England and Wales Court of Appeal in *Armstrong v Strain*.[57]

VII. Solicitor's Employee

It was suggested in section I of this chapter, in the discussion of who is an 'agent' for the purposes of agent strict liability, that there is an exception to the general rule that an 'agent' is a person vested with authority by a principal to effect legal relations on the principal's behalf. That exception is a solicitor's employee where that employee has been vested with authority by the solicitor to effect legal relations on behalf of the solicitor's clients. In such circumstances a solicitor, just like a principal, will be held strictly liable for a tort committed by such an employee in the course of effecting legal relations between the solicitor's clients and a transactional party. In order for the exception to be considered sound, however, it first needs to be shown that the basis for holding a solicitor strictly liable for the tort of an employee who has been vested with authority by a solicitor to effect legal relations on behalf of the solicitor's clients is similar to the basis for imposing agent strict liability.

Looking first at the cases. Most cases in which solicitors have been held strictly liable for the tort of an employee who has been vested with authority to effect legal relations on behalf of the solicitor's clients are cases in which the employee has defrauded a client. The classic case is *Lloyd v Grace Smith & Co*,[58] mentioned above, which concerned a solicitor's conveyancing manager who tricked a client into transferring property to him, enabling him to mortgage the property and misappropriate the proceeds.

Defrauded clients are not, however, the only people to whom a solicitor has been held strictly liable for the tort of an employee vested with authority by the solicitor to effect legal relations on behalf of the solicitor's clients. Solicitors have also been held strictly liable to third parties looking to enter into legal relations with the solicitor's clients. The decision of the England and Wales Court of Appeal in *Uxbridge Permanent Benefit Building Society v Pickard*[59] provides a good example. The solicitor in that case carried on business in London, but had a branch office at Slough. As the solicitor was not permanently based at Slough, he appointed a managing clerk to run the branch office. The managing clerk was vested with

[56] Although this does not stop the principal being personally liable in such situations, eg where the principal authorises the wrongdoing or uses an ignorant agent to deliberately deceive the claimant of the truth. See Fleming (n 16).

[57] [1952] 1 KB 232.

[58] [1912] AC 716.

[59] [1939] 2 KB 248.

'full authority to conduct the business of a solicitor's office'[60] by the solicitor. That authority included:[61]

> not merely acting for clients, but the carrying through of all transactions which would normally be carried through by a solicitor – namely, completion of conveyancing business with third parties having dealings with clients and the obtaining from such third parties upon completion of the transaction sums of money and giving receipts therefor.

One of the third parties from whom the managing clerk had regularly obtained sums of money for and on behalf of the solicitor's clients was the plaintiff building society. The managing clerk took advantage of the regular dealings with the plaintiff building society by forging documents and securing loans on behalf of clients who did not exist. The solicitor was held strictly liable for the managing clerk's fraud.

On what basis might a solicitor be held strictly liable for the tort of an employee in such cases? The problem seems to be that, when a solicitor vests an employee with authority to effect legal relations on behalf of the solicitor's clients, the solicitor creates a relationship between the employee and the solicitor's client or the employee and a third party wishing to enter into legal relations with the solicitor's client. This relationship enables the employee to effect legal relations on behalf of the solicitor's client in circumstances in which the neither the solicitor's client nor any third party wishing to enter into legal relations with the solicitor's client is expected to confirm with the principal the details of those legal relations. In *Lloyd v Grace Smith & Co*, for instance, the client relied on the solicitor's employee to prepare appropriate documentation for her to sign. In *Uxbridge Permanent Benefit Building Society v Pickard*, the building society relied on the representation of the solicitor's employee that he was acting for genuine clients. It follows that the authority vested by a solicitor in an employee to effect legal relations on behalf of the solicitor's clients is subject to abuse. A solicitor consequently puts both the solicitor's clients and third parties wishing to enter into legal relations with the solicitor's clients at risk of harm when they vest authority in an employee to effect legal relations on behalf of the solicitor's clients.

Although a solicitor's employee is not an 'agent' in the narrow, contractual sense of the term, the vesting of authority in an employee by a solicitor to effect legal relations on behalf of the solicitor's clients is closely analogous and creates the same risk of harm that exists when a principal vests authority in an agent to effect legal relations on the principal's behalf. The only difference is that in the solicitor's employee cases, the risk of harm is borne by both the solicitor's clients and third parties wishing to enter into legal relations with those clients. In contrast, where a principal vests an agent with authority to effect legal relations on the principal's behalf, the only risk created by the principal is a risk to transactional parties wishing to enter into legal relations with the principal. It follows, that the basis of agent

[60] Ibid 253.
[61] Ibid.

strict liability is very similar to the basis for holding a solicitor strictly liable for the tort of an employee who has been vested with authority by the solicitor to effect legal relations on behalf of the solicitor's clients. There is no reason, therefore, why solicitor's employees should not be seen as a valid exception to the general rule that an 'agent' is a person in whom a principal has vested authority to effect legal relations on the principal's behalf so that the general principles governing agent strict liability can consequently be applied as if the solicitor's employee was an agent.[62] The need for the exception reflects the particular role played by members of the legal profession in arranging legal transactions on behalf of others.

VIII. Contract or Tort?

So far it has been argued that an 'agent' for the purposes of agent strict liability is restricted to an agent in the narrow, contractual sense of the term. If this is the case, it might be asked whether there is a valid role for tort law in regulating the liability of a principal for the tort of an agent. This is an appropriate question; however, to the extent that there are some circumstances in which liability can arise in tort but not in contract, it is submitted that there remains a valid role for tort law even though an 'agent' for the purposes of agent strict liability is so narrowly defined.

The boundaries between liability in contract and tort in respect of an agent have never been particularly clear, but they are bound to intersect where an 'agent' is defined in the same narrow, contractual sense for the purposes of both forms of liability. For the purposes of contract law, where a disclosed agent validly enters into a contract on behalf of a principal, the parties to the contract are taken to be the principal and the contracting party rather than the agent and the contracting party.[63] It follows that the acts of an agent in entering into a contract on a principal's behalf are attributed to the principal for the purposes of contract law.[64] This includes any tort committed by the agent in the course of negotiating the contract. For example, where an agent makes a fraudulent representation which becomes a term of the contract, the principal will be held liable for that fraudulent misrepresentation in contract law as if the principally personally made the fraudulent misrepresentation. Liability in contract, however, is not the only type of liability which might arise in such circumstances. On the principles outlined in this chapter, agent strict liability might also arise, though any such liability is treated as strict liability for the tort of another and not personal liability.

If agent strict liability was restricted to circumstances in which liability also arose in contract, tort law would not be adding much and any liability imposed in such circumstances could be construed as contractual liability. There are, however,

[62] An exception which might also extend to other professionals who confer authority on their employees to effect legal relations on behalf of clients, eg a broker.

[63] Dal Pont, *Law of Agency* (n 3) 478.

[64] Ibid 595.

circumstances, in which agent strict liability can be imposed even though no liability in contract might arise. The clearest example is where no contract comes into existence. As has already been noted, there are agents who have authority to effect legal relations on behalf of a principal but who did not necessarily have authority to enter into legal relations on behalf of a principal. Take, for example, a real estate agent. A real estate agent does not generally have authority to enter into legal relations on behalf of a vendor, but will have authority to provide information about the property and to negotiate the terms of the sale. If the real estate agent made a fraudulent misrepresentation which did not become a term of the contract, no liability in contract can arise. Liability can be imposed in tort law though, provided the fraudulent misrepresentation was made within the apparent scope of the real estate agent's authority. Similarly, a life insurance agent such as the one in *CML* does not have authority to enter into legal relations on behalf of a life insurance company, but can accept proposals for life insurance policies by customers, as well as premiums, on the life insurance company's behalf. Once again, as no contract arises until the life insurance company accepts the proposal, there can be no liability in contract, although liability might arise in tort. This can be important, for instance, in situations where the life insurance agent absconds with the premium before paying it to the life insurance company.

It follows that, although liability for an agent in contract and tort intersect, there are circumstances in which liability might arise in one but not the other. Consequently, there is a valid role for tort law and a claimant should have the capacity to choose whether an action in tort or contract is more beneficial.[65]

IX. Conclusion

Agent strict liability was previously imposed under the label 'vicarious liability'. Such a label gave few clues as to the basis of the liability or its limits. By focusing on the one feature which the various relationships in which the courts impose strict liability for the tort of another have in common, it can now be seen that agent strict liability responds to the potential for abuse of authority vested in an agent to effect legal relations on a principal's behalf. Unlike previous explanations, the vesting of authority in an agent by a principal to effect legal relations on the principal's behalf is both necessary and sufficient for agent strict liability to be imposed. It can now also be seen that agent strict liability is more closely aligned with conferred authority strict liability, than it ever was with employee strict liability.

[65] *Henderson v Merrett Syndicates Ltd (No.1)* [1995] 2 AC 145.

PART III

Critique

7

The Boundaries between the Different Forms of Strict Liability for the Tort of Another

This book has proposed a new expositive framework within which strict liability for the tort of another can be understood. The framework is based on the one feature which the various relationships in which the courts currently impose such liability have in common – authority. It has been argued that there are three different forms of strict liability for the tort of another, each of which responds to the potential for the authority found in the relationships within which such liability is imposed to be abused.

Although it is possible to understand strict liability for the tort of another in terms of the authority present in each of the relationships in which the strict liability is currently imposed, it does not necessarily mean that it should. Compelling reasons for adopting the new expositive framework proposed by this book need to be identified. This chapter sets out the reasons why the new expositive framework for strict liability for the tort of another proposed by this book should be adopted. After outlining a number of broad arguments in favour of the new expositive framework, the chapter will focus on one in particular; its capacity to make clear the boundaries between the three different forms of strict liability for the tort of another.

I. Why Should the New Expositive Framework be Adopted?

The principal strength of the new expositive framework proposed by this book is that it provides a convincing basis for each form of strict liability for the tort of another that is both necessary and sufficient for that strict liability to be imposed. This book has shown that whenever the courts impose strict liability for the tort of another, the defendant is either vested with authority over the person who committed a tort against the claimant or has conferred a form of authority upon that person in respect of the claimant. This authority is significant because it has the potential to be abused. By dealing with such authority, a defendant consequently puts the claimant at risk of harm.

Conferred authority strict liability, for instance, is found in both the employment and school relationships and responds to the potential for abuse of the power relationship created by an employer or school conferring authority to direct the conduct of an employee or student upon another person. This potential for abuse of the power relationship exists because the power relationship enables the person upon whom authority has been conferred to direct the conduct of an employee or student and creates an expectation that the employee or student will obey.

In contrast, *employee strict liability* is limited to the employment relationship and responds to the potential for an employer, when exercising its authority to direct the conduct of an employee for its own benefit, to abuse that authority by putting the employee in a position that she unduly prioritises compliance with her employer's directions rather than give due weight to any alternate considerations that might reasonably lead the employee to conduct herself differently in the circumstances.

Finally, *agent strict liability* is limited to the agency relationship and responds to the potential for abuse of the power relationship created by a principal conferring authority upon an agent to effect legal relations on the principal's behalf. This potential for abuse of the power relationship exists because the power relationship enables the agent to effect legal relations on behalf of the principal in circumstances in which the party wishing to enter into legal relations with the principal is not expected to confirm with the principal the details of those legal relations.

A second reason why the new expositive framework proposed by this book should be adopted is that it accommodates the cases; especially some of the more unusual distinctions drawn by the cases. It explains, for instance, why a school might be held strictly liable to a student sexually assaulted by a teacher, but not by a janitor. With respect to the teacher, a school confers authority upon the teacher to direct the conduct of a student and in so doing creates a power relationship between the teacher and the student. This power relationship may provide the teacher with the means by which to commit a sexual assault. In contrast, no such authority is generally conferred upon a janitor so that the most that can be said is that the school provides an opportunity for the assault to occur. It has generally been recognised that this is insufficient for strict liability for the tort of another to be imposed.

The new expositive framework also explains why an employer is only held strictly liable for damage that results from a tort committed by an employee, and not for all damage caused by an employee. Employee strict liability does not arise because an employee causes damage, but because an employer may put an employee in a position that she unduly prioritises compliance with her employer's directions rather than give due weight to any alternate considerations that might reasonably lead the employee to conduct herself differently in the circumstances.

A third reason why the new expositive framework proposed by this book should be adopted is that it has the capacity to provide judges with greater guidance when deciding future cases. In the past, judges have found it difficult to determine both the scope of the different forms of strict liability for the tort of another and whether those different forms of strict liability for the tort of another should be extended to new factual situations. This was because the bases of the different forms of strict liability for the tort of another were confused and unclear. The difficulties that resulted can be seen in a case such as *Leichhardt Municipal Council v Montgomery*,[1] decided by the High Court of Australia. The question in that case was whether the Council should be held strictly liable for the negligence of a road contractor who had failed to adequately cover a hole in a footpath into which the plaintiff had fallen. All of the judges agreed that the Council should not be held strictly liable but gave separate judgments relying on different cases as to why.[2] The judges were unable to discern from the mass of often inconsistent and contradictory cases in both nuisance and negligence why a person might be held strictly liable for the tort of an independent contractor in some circumstances but not in others. What little guidance they had was reduced to labels such as a 'special kind of duty' or a 'special kind of vicarious responsibility',[3] which the judges did not think were 'normatively predictive'.[4] Should the judges have had the benefit of the new expositive framework proposed by this book, they would have seen that strict liability for the tort of another is generally only imposed on a defendant for the tort of an independent contractor where that independent contractor has either been conferred authority to direct the conduct of the injured claimant or conferred authority to effect legal relations on behalf of the defendant. As no such authority had been conferred by the Council on the road contractor in *Leichardt Municipal Council v Montgomery*, there was no basis upon which strict liability for the tort of another could be imposed.

The final reason why the new expositive framework proposed by this book should be adopted, and the focus of this chapter, is that it makes clear the boundaries between the three different forms of strict liability for the tort of another. There have been a number of cases in which different forms of strict liability for the tort of another have appeared to arise in the same factual situation. In the child sexual assault cases, for instance, strict liability for the tort of another might have been imposed by reason of either the employment relationship or the school

[1] (2007) 230 CLR 22.

[2] All except Crennan J, who agreed with the reasons of Gleeson CJ and Hayne JJ.

[3] See, eg, *Leichhardt Municipal Council v Montgomery* (2007) 230 CLR 22, 35 (Gleeson CJ): 'If the law were frankly to acknowledge that what is involved is not a breach by the defendant of a special kind of duty, but an imposition upon a defendant of a special kind of vicarious responsibility, a different problem would have to be faced. It would be necessary to identify and justify the exceptions to the general rule that a defendant is not vicariously responsible for the negligence of an independent contractor, and to provide a means by which other exceptions may be identified when they arise. That, in turn, would require an explanation of the general rule so as to account for the circumstances in which it yields to exceptions. It may be difficult to justify those circumstances in terms of fixed categories. Within those categories there may be individual cases some of which may be thought to merit making them an exception and others of which may not'.

[4] Ibid 74–75 (Hayne J).

relationship.[5] The potential for different forms of strict liability for the tort of another to arise in the same factual situation has led some commentators to question whether different forms of strict liability for the tort of another actually exist.[6] The new expositive framework proposed by this book, however, shows why different forms of strict liability for the tort of another have developed.

II. Making the Boundaries Clear

There are two points at which the three different forms of strict liability for the tort of another outlined by the new expositive framework proposed by this book potentially intersect. First, conferred authority strict liability and employee strict liability may both arise in situations in which the person upon whom authority has been conferred by an employer or school to direct the conduct of an employee or student is also an employee. Secondly, employee strict liability and agent strict liability may both arise in situations in which the agent is also an employee.

A. Conferred Authority Strict Liability v Employee Strict Liability

Employee strict liability is not the only form of strict liability for the tort of another that might be imposed on an employer for the tort of an employee. In certain circumstances, conferred authority strict liability might also be imposed. The question then is how best to determine which form of strict liability should be applied and in what circumstances.

The new expositive framework outlined by this book shows that conferred authority strict liability and employee strict liability differ in a number of respects. One point of distinction has already been noted; the two forms of strict liability respond to torts committed by different types of people. Conferred authority strict liability can respond to the tort of either an independent contractor or an employee. This is because it is not the status of the person who committed the tort that is important, but the fact that the person has been conferred authority by an employer or school to direct the conduct of the injured employee or student. Employee strict liability, on the other hand, only responds to a tort committed by an employee.

[5] See generally *New South Wales v Lepore* (2003) 212 CLR 511.

[6] See JG Fleming, *The Law of Torts* (9th ed, Sydney, Law Book Company, 1998) 434, who suggested that strict liability for the tort of another imposed under the label 'liability for breach of a non-delegable duty of care' was simply a disguised form of the strict liability for the tort of another imposed under the label 'vicarious liability'.

Another point of distinction is that the two forms of strict liability respond to different risks. Conferred authority strict liability responds to the risk of physical harm to an employee or student created by an employer or school conferring authority to direct the conduct of the employee or student upon another person. In contrast, employee strict liability responds to the risk of harm to a stranger to the employment relationship which exists because an employer can exercise its authority to direct the conduct of an employee for its own benefit and, in so doing, may put the employee in a position that she unduly prioritises compliance with her employer's directions rather than give due weight to any alternate considerations that might reasonably lead the employee to conduct herself differently in the circumstances.

Finally, and for these purposes more importantly, the two forms of strict liability differ in scope. The scope of conferred authority strict liability is not limited by the terms of the actual authority conferred by the employer or school upon another person to direct the conduct of an employee or student. Instead, it extends to circumstances in which the person upon whom authority has been conferred is acting with *apparent* authority. This is because an employee or student will interact with the person upon whom authority has been conferred on the basis of the apparent authority that has been conferred upon that person by the employer or school. One reason a student will go with a teacher into a storeroom, for instance, is because the teacher has the apparent authority to direct the student to do so.[7] It is the apparent scope of the authority, therefore, that shapes the power relationship between the person upon whom authority has been conferred and the employee or student and it is the potential for abuse of this power relationship that attracts the concern and intervention of conferred authority strict liability.

In contrast, the scope of employee strict liability is determined by reference to what it is an employee is *actually* (as opposed to apparently) authorised or, more appropriately,[8] directed by her employer to do. Employee strict liability can be imposed on an employer whenever an employee commits a tort in respect of a stranger to the employment relationship whilst acting within the course of her employment. In accordance with the *Salmond* test, a tort committed by an employee does not fall within the course of employment unless the conduct engaged in by the employee immediately prior to committing the tort was actually directed (either expressly or impliedly) by the employer. This is because where an employee is following her employer's actual directions, there is the potential for an employer to abuse its authority to direct the conduct of an employee by putting the employee in a position that she unduly prioritises compliance with her employer's directions rather than give due weight to any alternate considerations that might reasonably lead the employee to conduct herself differently in the circumstances. It is this potential for an employer to abuse its authority that attracts the concern and intervention of employee strict liability. Where an

[7] As happened in *New South Wales v Lepore* (2003) 212 CLR 511.

[8] Why 'directed' is a more appropriate term than 'authorised' in this context was explained in ch 5.

employee is acting outside her employer's actual directions (express or implied), the employee is no longer subject to her employer's authority and is free to make her own decisions about her conduct without risk of influence from the employer's exercise of authority.

As can be seen, conferred authority strict liability and employee strict liability are two very different forms of strict liability for the tort of another. The bases of the two forms of strict liability differ, as does their scope. Despite these differences, conferred authority strict liability and employee strict liability intersect in circumstances in which the person who commits the tort is an employee who has been conferred authority by her employer to direct the conduct of the claimant. It cannot be assumed, however, that just because the person who commits the tort is an employee who has been conferred authority by her employer to direct the conduct of the claimant that both forms of strict liability will apply.

Consider the child sexual assault cases. The question in the child sexual assault cases is whether a school or closely analogous institution can be held strictly liable for the sexual assault of a child within its care by an employee. In accordance with the new expositive framework proposed by this book, employee strict liability can only be imposed on an employer where the conduct engaged in by the employee immediately prior to the tort being committed was actually directed (either expressly or impliedly) by the employer. In the child sexual assault cases, the employees who committed the sexual assaults knew that they were not authorised to sexually abuse a child in their care or engage in conduct with the purpose of sexually abusing a child.[9] To the extent that the employees were driven by their own motivations when engaging in such conduct, it is very difficult to say that the employees were at risk of being influenced by an exercise of authority by the school or closely analogous institution. Any exercise of authority by the school or closely analogous institution in the circumstances would more than likely be done in a manner to discourage the employees from engaging in such conduct given the broader ramifications of such conduct for the operation of the school or closely analogous institution (not to mention the children). Without the potential in such circumstances for the school or closely analogous institution to abuse its authority to direct the conduct of an employee, there is no basis upon which employee strict liability can be imposed.

Although it was not possible for employee strict liability to be imposed in the child sexual assault cases, conferred authority strict liability could. This is because in the cases where schools or closely analogous institutions were held strictly liable for the sexual assaults, the people who committed the sexual assaults were not just employees, but employees who had been conferred authority to direct the conduct of the children in their care. In accordance with the new expositive framework

[9] It was acknowledged by the Supreme Court of New Zealand in *Dollars & Sense Finance Ltd v Rerekohu Nathan* [2008] 2 NZLR 557 (at 576) that acts knowingly done for the purpose of enabling wrongdoing to occur could not be considered to have been done within the actual authority of the wrongdoer.

proposed by this book, conferred authority strict liability is not limited by the actual terms of the authority conferred by an employer or school upon another person to direct the conduct of an employee or student but extends to circumstances in which the person upon whom authority has been conferred is acting with apparent authority. It was therefore not necessary in the child sexual assault cases for a claimant to show that the conduct engaged in by the employee immediately prior to the sexual assault was actually authorised or directed by the school or closely analogous institution. It was sufficient for the claimant to show that the employee was purporting to exercise the conferred authority immediately prior to engaging in the sexual assault. This was generally not difficult given that the employee typically had to use the authority conferred by the school or closely analogous institution to direct the claimant away from other children for the sexual assault to occur. It follows that the assaults in the child sexual assault cases could be viewed as an abuse of the power relationship created by the employer's conferral of authority upon the employee to direct the conduct of the child so that conferred authority strict liability could have been imposed.

Cases in which conferred authority strict liability could be imposed but employee strict liability could not, can also be found in the employment context. Consider cases in which one employee intentionally assaults another employee in the workplace.[10] As a general rule, employers are not held strictly liable for such assaults given that most employees know that they are not authorised to assault fellow employees or to engage in conduct with the purpose of assaulting a fellow employee.[11] To the extent that an employee is driven by her own motivations when committing such an assault, it is very difficult to say that the employee was at risk of being influenced by an exercise of authority by her employer. Any exercise of authority by the employer in the circumstances would more than likely be done in a manner to discourage the employee from engaging in such conduct given the broader ramifications of such conduct for the employer's business (not to mention the effect on the other employees).[12] Without the potential in such circumstances for the employer to abuse its authority to direct the conduct of an employee, there is no basis upon which employee strict liability can be imposed. Where the employee who commits the assault, however, has been conferred authority by the employer to direct the conduct of the other employee, conferred authority strict liability can be imposed if the employee was purporting to exercise the conferred authority immediately prior to the assault. This was the case in *MacMillan v Wimpey Offshore Engineers and Constructors Ltd*[13] where the foreman smashed the head of the plaintiff against a metal skip whilst in the process of giving the

[10] See eg *Gittani Stone Pty Ltd v Pavkovic* (2007) Aust Torts Reports 81–924 in which one employee shot a fellow employee sitting in his car outside his place of employment.

[11] eg when a fight occurs between employees at a staff lunch or for an employee prank. See further ch 4.

[12] In *Mohamud v VM Morrison Supermarkets plc* [2016] AC 677, for instance, the employee's supervisor physically tried to restrain the employee from committing the assault.

[13] [1991] SLT 515.

plaintiff directions.[14] It was also the case in *Bellman v Northampton Recruitment Limited*,[15] where the managing director had summoned the claimant in order to hear a lecture about arrangements within the workplace before brutally assaulting him at a social event.

As can be seen, although both conferred authority strict liability and employee strict liability can be triggered by the tort of an employee who has been conferred authority to direct the conduct of a student or a fellow employee, it does not necessarily follow that both forms of strict liability can always be imposed. This is particularly important in cases involving an employee who intentionally commits a tort. It is relatively unusual for an employer to actually authorise an employee to commit a tort. It is submitted, therefore, that it should also be relatively unusual for employee strict liability to be imposed on an employer in respect of an employee who intentionally commits a tort. In contrast, conferred authority strict liability can be imposed in respect of a tort intentionally committed by an employee provided that the employee engaged in the tort had been conferred authority by their employer to direct the conduct of a fellow employee or a student, and the employee was purporting to exercise the conferred authority immediately prior to the tort being committed. It follows that conferred authority strict liability is more likely to be imposed on an employer where an employee has intentionally committed a tort, than employee strict liability.

There are still some circumstances in which both conferred authority strict liability and employee strict liability might be imposed; namely, where an employee who has been conferred authority to direct the conduct of an employee or student has committed a tort in respect of the employee or student whilst acting within the actual scope of the conferred authority. This is most likely where the tort committed by the employee is negligent, rather than intentional. In *Ramsay v Larsen*,[16] for instance, either conferred authority strict liability or employee strict liability might have been imposed on the school in respect of the negligence of the teacher in directing a student to retrieve a set of keys from a tree in the school yard. This is because the teacher was acting within the actual scope of his authority immediately prior to giving the child the negligent directions. In such situations, a claimant may sue the employer for either conferred authority strict liability or employee strict liability. The claimant can choose which form of strict liability is more advantageous;[17] although it is not immediately apparent at this stage that there are any advantages to be obtained by pursuing one cause of action over the other.

[14] See further ch 4, s IV.
[15] (2018) EWCA Civ 2214.
[16] (1964) 111 CLR 16. See further ch 2.
[17] *Henderson v Merrett Syndicates Ltd (No.1)* [1995] 2 AC 145.

The new expositive framework proposed by this book makes clear, for the first time, the boundary between conferred authority strict liability and employee strict liability. That boundary can be diagrammatically represented as follows:

Figure 1 Overlap between Conferred Authority Strict Liability and Employee Strict Liability

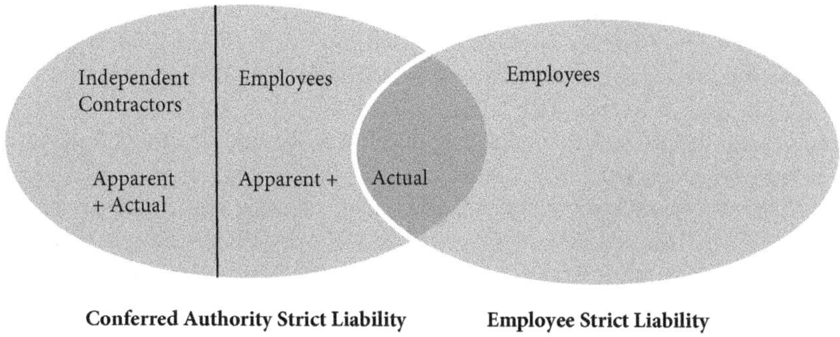

As can be seen, the only situation in which an employer might be sued for both conferred authority strict liability and employee strict liability is where the employer has conferred authority over an employee to direct the conduct of the claimant and the employee commits a tort in respect of the claimant whilst acting within the actual scope of the conferred authority. This will generally exclude instances of a tort intentionally committed by an employee unless the employee has been directed by her employer to commit such a tort.

Courts have long struggled to differentiate between the circumstances in which conferred authority strict liability and employee strict liability might be imposed. This was evident in the child sexual assault cases where judges could not decide whether to impose employee strict liability or conferred authority strict liability.[18] Although most judges chose to impose employee strict liability, this preference appears to have been driven more by difficulties in identifying a rational basis for conferred authority strict liability than any firm view that imposing employee strict liability was more appropriate. For instance, some judges were concerned that to

[18] eg McHugh J in *New South Wales v Lepore* (2003) 212 CLR 511 and Lord Hobhouse in *Lister v Hesley Hall Ltd* [2002] 1 AC 215 used conferred authority strict liability (or as it was then called, strict liability imposed under the label of 'liability for breach of a non-delegable duty of care'), whilst McLachlin CJ in *Bazley v Curry* (1999) 174 DLR (4th) 45 and Kirby J in *New South Wales v Lepore* used employee strict liability (or as it was then called, strict liability imposed under the label of 'vicarious liability').

impose conferred authority strict liability for the sexual assaults would remove the liability 'from any connection with the law of negligence'.[19] Alternatively, that to impose conferred authority strict liability for the sexual assaults would turn schools or closely analogous institutions into an 'insurer' of the children in their care.[20] Finally, there were concerns that to impose conferred authority strict liability for the sexual assaults would remove 'room for any operation of orthodox doctrines of [employee strict liability]'.[21]

The new expositive framework proposed by this book not only explains the boundary between conferred authority strict liability and employee strict liability, but does so in a way which addresses such concerns. It can now be seen that conferred authority strict liability has no more to do with the law of negligence than employee strict liability. Both forms of strict liability are imposed regardless of the defendant personally engaging in any conduct that might itself attract liability in tort. Nor does imposing conferred authority strict liability turn a school or analogous institution into an 'insurer' of the children in their care. First, such liability only arises in respect of those employees conferred authority by the school or analogous institution to direct the conduct of students. Secondly, the employee has to be acting within the actual or apparent scope of that authority for the liability to be imposed. Consequently, it is unlikely that conferred authority strict liability would be imposed on a school or closely analogous institution in the event that a teacher sexually assaulted a student at the teacher's home on the weekend.[22] There is also room for both conferred authority strict liability and employee strict liability to operate within the law of torts. The bases of both forms of strict liability differ and the extent to which they intersect can now be seen to be quite limited.

The new expositive framework proposed by this book also explains the boundary between conferred authority strict liability and employee strict liability in a way that does not risk the unprincipled expansion of either form of strict liability. To impose employee strict liability on the schools and closely analogous institutions in the child sexual assault cases, judges had to hold that such a deliberate and self-serving act as sexually assaulting a child could occur within the 'course of employment'.[23] To do this, they had to abandon the *Salmond* test and find that a tort committed by an employee could occur within the 'course of employment' whenever there was a sufficient connection between 'the nature of the employment and the particular tort'.[24] The risk with such an approach is that employee strict liability extends to cover torts intentionally committed by employees more generally. This risk is very real given that the sufficiency of the 'connection' necessary to impose employee strict liability remains an open question.

[19] *New South Wales v Lepore* (2003) 212 CLR 511, 601–02 (Gummow and Hayne JJ).
[20] Ibid.
[21] Ibid 602.
[22] As occurred in *Jacobi v Griffiths* (1999) 174 DLR (4th) 71.
[23] P Cane, 'Vicarious Liability for Sexual Abuse' (2000) 116 *Law Quarterly Review* 21, 21.
[24] *Lister v Hesley Hall Ltd* [2002] 1 AC 215, 229 (Lord Steyn).

Consider the decision of the England and Wales Court of Appeal in *Maga v The Trustees of the Birmingham Archdiocese of the Roman Catholic Church*.[25] In that case, employee strict liability was imposed on the church for the sexual assault of a boy by a priest, even though the boy was not a member of the congregation and the church had not sought to engage with the boy 'on any religious level'.[26] Although the judges found it difficult to distinguish the facts of *Maga* from the facts of the child sexual assault cases more generally, the new expositive framework proposed by this book indicates that the decision was more than likely incorrect. First, employee strict liability could not have been imposed on the church because the tort committed by the priest was intentional. Secondly, although there was scope to argue that the church had conferred authority upon the priest, such authority would have only extended to members of the congregation and not to the boy who was not a parishioner and had no reasonable grounds to think such authority extended to him given that he did not necessarily believe in God. Consequently, the church could not have created a power relationship between the priest and the boy which the priest subsequently abused. Unfortunately, the differences between the facts of *Maga* and the child sexual assault cases went undetected; giving rise to the risk that employee strict liability would extend to cover torts intentionally committed by employees more generally.

This risk has been fully realised following the recent decision of the Supreme Court of the United Kingdom in *Mohamud v WM Morrisons Supermarkets plc*.[27] The case currently stands as the high watermark for employee strict liability being imposed on an employer for the intentional tort of an employee. A customer at a Morrisons' petrol station had asked the employee at the payment kiosk for assistance in printing out a document. The employee refused the assistance, and ordered the customer out of the petrol station whilst shouting racial abuse. Not content with the customer leaving, the employee then followed the customer back to his car (which was parked in the petrol station forecourt) and physically assaulted him, causing serious physical injuries. The employee had resisted all attempts by his supervisor to stop the attack. Notwithstanding the apparent racial motivations for the assault, employee strict liability was imposed on Morrisons. In the Supreme Court's view, there was a sufficiently 'close connection' between the attack and the employment to justify the imposition of employee strict liability.[28] Specifically, the Supreme Court found that there was an 'unbroken sequence of events' between the attack and the 'field of activities' assigned to the employee, making it 'fair' and 'just' to impose employee strict liability for the assault 'under the principle of social justice'.[29]

[25] [2010] 1 WLR 1441.
[26] Ibid 1447.
[27] [2016] AC 677.
[28] Ibid [47].
[29] Ibid.

If the new expositive framework proposed by this book is adopted, it is difficult to see the decision of the Supreme Court in *Mohamud* as correct. Employee strict liability could not be imposed given the intentional nature of the assault. The employee in *Mohamud* was driven by his own motivations and not influenced by any exercise of authority by his employer. What evidence there was of the employer's authority being exercised suggested that it was to stop the attack given the actions of the employee's supervisor. Conferred authority strict liability could also not be imposed as Morrisons had not conferred any authority upon the employee to direct the conduct of the claimant.

It is the reasoning employed by the Supreme Court to reach the decision, however, that is most problematic. The Supreme Court made no attempt to identify what amounts to 'social justice' for the purposes of imposing employee strict liability or what limits should be placed on the imposition of such liability.[30] To therefore ask whether employee strict liability should be imposed on an employer 'under the principle of social justice' does nothing other than to invite expansion of the law.

The full impact of such reasoning in terms of its potential to expand employee strict liability can be seen by contemplating a slight change to the facts of *Mohamud*. Consider a situation in which the victim of a *Mohamud*-type attack was not a customer, but a fellow employee of equal standing. As explained in chapters 4 and 5, there is a consistent line of cases in which employers have avoided employee strict liability where an employee is injured as a result of a practical joke instigated by another employee.[31] An exception has been made in circumstances where the instigator of the practical joke was a supervisor of the injured employee and the practical joke occurred in the course of that supervision.[32] Under the approach of the Supreme Court in *Mohamud*, however, such a distinction is at risk of being overlooked. In both circumstances, the employees will be required to work together as part of their 'field of activities' and the practical joke may well form part of an 'unbroken sequence of events'[33] stemming from the commencement of that work. The question of the nature of the relationship between the two employees simply does not arise.

If, in accordance with the approach of the Supreme Court in *Mohamud*, little more than a causal connection is required to satisfy the 'close connection' test for establishing employee strict liability, there is effectively no limit on the imposition of employee strict liability other than the requirement that an employee be doing something connected with the tasks they are to perform as part of their employment. The previous case law under the *Salmond* test which sought to define

[30] A parallel might be drawn with the difficulties evident in containing the 'neighbourhood principle' after *Donoghue v Stevenson* [1932] AC 562.

[31] eg the well-known case of *Smith v Crossley Bros Ltd* (1951) 95 Sol Jo 65.

[32] eg *Chapman v Oakleigh Animal Products* (1970) 8 KIR 1063. In the harassment context, consider *Majrowski v Guy's and St Thomas' NHS Trust* [2007] 1 AC 224.

[33] [2016] AC 677, 693.

a limit on the imposition of employee strict liability is effectively swept aside. For this reason, the approach of the Supreme Court in *Mohamud* was extensively criticised by the High Court of Australia in *Prince Alfred College v ADC*.[34] In the High Court's view, the decision in *Mohamud* did not reflect any significant change in the underlying reason for imposing employee strict liability and could only be explained by an over-reliance on general principles such as 'fairness' and 'justice',[35] which the courts in Australia had to date resisted. To this end, the High Court of Australia opted to retain the *Salmond* test as the correct approach for determining whether employee strict liability should be imposed.

It is submitted that the High Court of Australia was correct in taking this approach. There was no need for the Supreme Court to risk the unprincipled expansion of employee vicarious liability by adopting the reasoning it did in *Mohamud*. The new expositive framework proposed by this book accommodates the existing cases and explains the boundary between conferred authority strict liability and employee strict liability in a way that does not risk the unprincipled expansion of either form of strict liability for the tort of another.

B. Employee Strict Liability v Agent Strict Liability

Just as conferred authority strict liability intersects with employee strict liability, employee strict liability also intersects with agent strict liability. Once again, this is because both forms of strict liability can arise in respect of a tort committed by an employee. It is necessary, therefore, to consider how best to determine which form of strict liability should be applied and in what circumstances.

Employee strict liability and agent strict liability can be distinguished in much the same was as conferred authority strict liability and employee strict liability. First, the two forms of strict liability respond to torts committed by different types of people. As mentioned earlier, employee strict liability only responds to torts committed by employees. In contrast, agent strict liability may respond to torts committed by an employee, an independent contractor or even a person acting gratuitously. As with conferred authority strict liability, it is not the status of the agent that is important, but the fact that the agent has been vested with authority by the principal to effect legal relations on the principal's behalf.

Another point of distinction is that the two forms of strict liability respond to different risks. Employee strict liability responds to the risk of harm to a stranger to the employment relationship which exists because an employer can exercise its authority to direct the conduct of an employee for its own benefit and, in so doing, may put the employee in a position that she unduly prioritises compliance with

[34] (2016) 258 CLR 134.

[35] Lord Neuberger, 'Some Thoughts on Principles Governing the Law of Torts', speech given at Singapore Conference on Protecting Business and Economic Interests, 19 August 2016 at www.supremecourt.uk/docs/speech-160819-03.pdf.

her employer's directions rather than give due weight to any alternate considerations that might reasonably lead the employee to conduct herself differently in the circumstances. In contrast, agent strict liability responds to the risk of harm to a party wishing to enter into legal relations with the principal (the *transactional party*) created by a principal vesting the agent with authority to enter into legal relations on the principal's behalf.

Finally, the two forms of strict liability differ in scope. As explained above, employee strict liability is determined by reference to what it is an employee is *actually* (as opposed to apparently) authorised or, more appropriately,[36] directed by her employer to do. This is because where an employee is following her employer's actual directions, there is the potential for an employer to abuse its authority to direct the conduct of an employee by putting the employee in a position that she unduly prioritises compliance with her employer's directions rather than give due weight to any alternate considerations that might reasonably lead the employee to conduct herself differently in the circumstances.

In contrast, agent strict liability is not limited by the terms of the actual authority vested by the principal in the agent. Instead, it extends to circumstances in which the agent is acting with *apparent* authority. This is because a transactional party will interact with an agent on the basis of the apparent authority that has been vested in the agent by the principal. One reason a transactional party will hand over money to an agent, for instance, is because the agent has the apparent authority to collect that money on the principal's behalf. It is the apparent scope of the authority vested in the agent, therefore, that shapes the power relationship between the agent and the transactional party and it is the potential for this power relationship to be abused that attracts the concern and intervention of agent strict liability. In this respect, agent strict liability is very similar to conferred authority strict liability.

As can be seen, employee strict liability and agent strict liability are two very different forms of strict liability for the tort of another. The bases of the two forms of strict liability differ, as does their scope. Despite these differences, employee strict liability and agent strict liability intersect in circumstances in which the person who commits the tort is both an employee and an agent. Once again, it cannot be assumed that just because the tort is committed by a person who is both an employee and an agent that both forms of strict liability will apply.

Consider the fraud cases.[37] The question in the fraud cases was whether an employer could be held strictly liable for the fraud of an employee. In accordance with the new expositive framework proposed by this book, employee strict liability can only be imposed on an employer where the conduct engaged in by the employee immediately prior to the tort being committed was actually directed (either expressly or impliedly) by the employer. In the fraud cases where such fraud

[36] Why 'directed' is a more appropriate term than 'authorised' in this context was explained in ch 5.
[37] See, eg, *Barwick v English Joint Stock Bank* (1867) II LR Exch 259.

was not of benefit to the employer,[38] the employees who committed the frauds knew that they were not authorised to commit the fraud or engage in conduct with the purpose of committing fraud. To the extent that the employees were driven by their own motivations when engaging in the fraud, it is very difficult to say that the employees were at risk of being influenced by an exercise of authority by the employer. Any exercise of authority by the employer in the circumstances would more than likely be done in a manner to discourage the employees from engaging in such conduct given the broader ramifications of such conduct for the legal transactions entered into by the employee on the employer's behalf (not to mention the effect on the transactional parties). Without the potential in such circumstances for the employer to abuse its authority to direct the conduct of an employee, there was no basis upon which employee strict liability could be imposed.

Although it was not possible for employee strict liability to be imposed in the fraud cases, agent strict liability could be. This is because in the cases where employers were held strictly liable for fraud, the people who committed the torts were not just employees but employees who had also been vested with authority to effect legal relations on behalf of their employer (that is, they were agents). The fraudulent conveyancing clerk in *Lloyd v Grace Smith & Co*,[39] for instance, had been vested with authority to collect the deeds on behalf of his employer. In accordance with the new expositive framework proposed by this book, agent strict liability is not limited by the actual terms of the authority vested in an agent by a principal but extends to circumstances in which the agent is acting with apparent authority. It was not necessary in the fraud cases therefore for a claimant to show that the conduct engaged in by the employee immediately prior to the tort being committed was actually authorised. It was sufficient for the claimant to show that the employee was purporting to exercise the authority conferred by the principal prior to the fraud being committed. Where this could be done, the fraud could be seen as an abuse of the power relationship created by the principal vesting the agent with authority to effect legal relations on the principal's behalf so that agent strict liability could be imposed.

As can be seen, although both employee strict liability and agent strict liability can be triggered by a tort committed by an employee who is also an agent, it does not necessarily follow that both forms of strict liability can be imposed in such circumstances. Once again, this is particularly important in cases involving an intentional tort committed by an employee. Where the tort is intentional and outside the scope of an employee's actual authority, employee strict liability will generally not arise. Agent strict lability, however, can be imposed for an intentional tort committed by an employee provided the employee engaged in the tort had been vested with authority by her employer to effect legal relations on the

[38] It was argued in ch 6 above that where the fraud was of benefit to the employer, such fraud might be viewed as being engaged in within the implied directions of the employer; eg *Barwick v English Joint Stock Bank* ibid.

[39] [1912] AC 716.

employer's behalf, and the employee was purporting to exercise the conferred authority immediately prior to the tort being committed. Outside cases of intentional wrongdoing, either employee strict liability or agent strict liability may be imposed provided the agent was acting within the scope of the actual authority vested in the agent by the principal immediately before the tort being committed. This is most likely where the tort committed by the employee is negligent, rather than intentional. In such circumstances, the claimant will have a choice as to which form of strict liability to pursue.

The new expositive framework proposed by this book makes clear, for the first time, the boundary between employee strict liability and agent strict liability. That boundary can be diagrammatically represented as follows:

Figure 2 Overlap between Employee Strict Liability and Agent Strict Liability

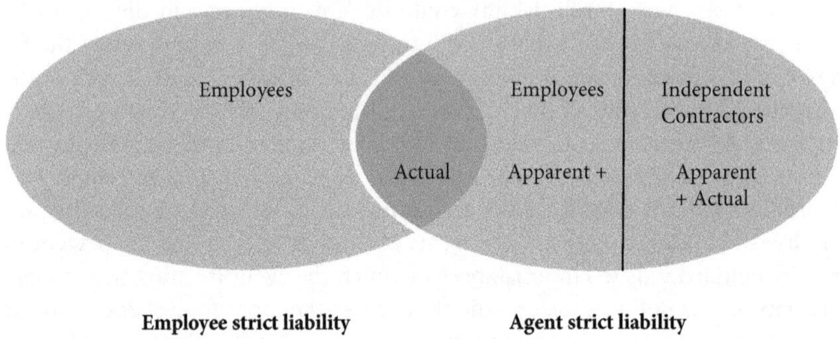

As can be seen, the only situation in which an employer might be sued for both employee strict liability and agent strict liability is where the employer has vested an employee with authority to effect legal relations on the employer's behalf and the employee commits a tort whilst acting within the actual scope of that authority. This will generally exclude instances of intentional wrongdoing unless an employee has been directed by her employer to engage in such conduct (either expressly or impliedly)[40].

The boundary between employee strict liability and agent strict liability has never really been clear. Judges often appear to resort to the concept of 'agency' in order to hold an employer strictly liable for a tort committed by an employee, particularly in cases of intentional torts; but they have done so within the framework of employee strict liability. This has once again risked extending the scope of employee strict liability to cover the intentional torts of employees more generally. It has also put pressure on the definition of 'agency' to the point that it has been

[40] As in *Barwick v English Joint Stock Bank* (1867) II LR Exch. 259.

suggested that both a 'bicycle courier'[41] and a 'pilot'[42] can be considered an agent. Such problems have arguably arisen due to the failure of the courts to distinguish accurately between the two different forms of strict liability for the tort of another. The new expositive framework proposed by this book has shown that employee strict liability and agent strict liability are two separate forms of strict liability for the tort of another. Although the two forms of strict liability intersect in respect of a tort committed by an employee who is also an agent, the bases of the two forms of strict liability differ as does their scope.

III. Conclusion

The existing explanations of strict liability for the tort of another are flawed.[43] They neither explain when such liability arises nor why. This book has sought to overcome such difficulties by proposing a new expositive framework to explain strict liability for the tort of another based on the one feature which the various relationships in which the courts currently impose such liability have in common – authority. This new expositive framework provides a convincing basis for the different forms of strict liability for the tort of another, makes clear the boundaries between those different forms of strict liability for the tort of another, accommodates more of the cases and has the capacity to provide judges with greater guidance when deciding future cases.

[41] See *Hollis v Vabu Pty Ltd* (2001) 207 CLR 21.
[42] See *Scott v Davis* (2000) 204 CLR 333.
[43] See generally ch 1.

8

Miscellaneous Categories of Strict Liability for the Tort of Another

This book has proposed a new expositive framework within which to understand strict liability for the tort of another and set out the reasons why the new expositive framework should be adopted. The final step is to see how the new expositive framework can assist in explaining what at present appear to be miscellaneous categories of strict liability for the tort of another.

This chapter will examine three such categories of strict liability: the strict liability imposed on the members of partnership for a tort committed by a partner; the strict liability imposed on a bailee for a tort committed by person upon whom authority has been conferred by the bailee to deal with the bailor's goods; and the strict liability imposed on the owner of a motor vehicle for a tort committed by a person driving the vehicle for the owner's purposes. It will show that whilst two of these categories fit comfortably within the new expositive framework proposed by this book, one does not. The exception is the strict liability imposed on the owner of a motor vehicle for a tort committed by a person driving the vehicle for the owner's purposes. Current cases indicate, however, that the courts are not as willing to impose such liability as they once were.[1]

I. Partner Strict Liability

Members of a partnership have long been held strictly liable for a tort committed by a partner in the course of carrying out the business of the partnership.[2] Although first recognised at common law, the liability was subsumed into legislation in the United Kingdom and each of the Australian states in the late nineteenth century.[3] Section 10(1) of the Partnership Act 1892 (NSW) is typical:[4]

> where, by any wrongful act or omission of any partner in a firm other than an incorporated limited partnership acting *in the ordinary course of the business of the firm*, or

[1] See *Scott v Davis* (2000) 204 CLR 333.

[2] Not including limited liability partnerships which have recently been allowed to incorporate. KL Fletcher, *The Law of Partnership in Australia* (9th ed, Sydney, LawBook Co, 2007) 6–8 and ch 6.

[3] Ibid 7–8.

[4] This section is based on s 10 Partnership Act 1890 (UK) c 39 and equivalent provisions exist in all the Australian states and territories (emphasis added).

> with the authority of the partner's co-partners, loss or injury is caused to any person not being a partner of the firm, or any penalty is incurred, the *firm is liable* therefor [sic] to the same extent as the partner so acting or committing to act.

Consequently, in *Polkinghorne v Holland*,[5] the High Court of Australia held a firm of solicitors strictly liable for a partner who negligently failed to advise a client where she could obtain accurate information about a company she was proposing to invest in.[6] Similarly, in *Walker v European Electronics Pty Ltd (in liq)*,[7] the New South Wales Court of Appeal held a firm of accountants strictly liable for a partner who misappropriated funds from a company to which the partner had been appointed as receiver.[8]

A. Basis of the Strict Liability

To determine the basis upon which members of a partnership are held strictly liable for a tort committed by a partner ('*partner strict liability*') it is necessary to examine why the partnership relationship exists and how it functions.

A 'partnership is the relation which subsists between persons carrying on a business in common with a view to profit'.[9] Partnerships are defined in such terms because, unlike a company, a partnership is not a separate legal entity. It is instead an association of individuals who pool resources and/or expertise to carry on a single business enterprise. The absence of a separate legal entity enables partners to avoid regulation under the company legislation. It does, however, mean that something else is required to legally bind the partners together. That something is authority. Each partner vests their fellow partners with authority to act as their agent. The vesting of such authority is evidenced by legislation. Turning once again to the Partnership Act 1892 (NSW), section 5 provides:[10]

> *Every partner … is an agent of the firm* and of the other partners for the purpose of the business of the partnership; and the *acts of every partner* who does any act for carrying on in the usual way business of the kind carried on by the firm of which the partner is a member *binds the firm and the other partners*, unless the partner so acting has in fact no authority to act for the firm in the particular matter and the person with whom the partner is dealing either knows that the partner has no authority or does not know or believe the partner to be a partner.

As can be seen, a partnership is essentially an agency relationship. Each partner is vested with authority to conduct the business of the partnership on behalf of their fellow partners as agent. The analogy is not precise in that a partner is not only an

[5] (1934) 51 CLR 143.
[6] Fletcher, *The Law of Partnership in Australia* (n 2) 187.
[7] (1990) 23 NSWLR 1.
[8] Fletcher (n 2) 186.
[9] See, eg, Partnership Act 1892 (NSW) s 1.
[10] Emphasis added.

'agent' but also a 'principal', each partner being entitled to a share of the proceeds of the partnership business. But the similarities are close enough that the 'rights, powers, duties, and obligations' of a partner 'are in many respects governed by the same rules and principles as those of an agent'.[11]

Because a partner is an agent, the basis of partner strict liability is closely associated with the basis of agent strict liability. A partner, just like an agent, is vested with authority to effect legal relations on behalf of the members of the partnership. This vesting of authority creates a power relationship which did not previously exist. That power relationship exists between the partner and any party wishing to enter into legal relations with the partnership (the *transactional party*) and enables the partner to effect legal relations on behalf of the members of the partnership in circumstances in which the transactional party is not expected to confirm with the other partners the details of those legal relations. The power relationship is therefore subject to abuse. A partner, for instance, can use the authority with which they have been vested by the other members of the partnership to misrepresent the partnership's assets to a transactional party. The members of a partnership consequently put a transactional party at risk of harm by vesting authority upon each of the partners to effect legal relations on behalf of the members of the partnership.

Additionally, a partner may have been vested with authority by the other members of the partnership to effect legal relations on behalf of clients of the partnership. This is not uncommon as many professionals, such as solicitors, brokers and accountants, conduct their business through a partnership structure due to historical restrictions on incorporation.[12] In such circumstances, the partner is again an 'agent' but an 'agent' in the exceptional sense that the employee of a solicitor who has been conferred authority to effect legal relations on behalf of the solicitor's clients was considered an 'agent' in chapter 6. When the members of a partnership vests a partner with authority to effect legal relations on behalf of clients of the partnership, a power relationship is created between that partner, the partnership's client and any third party wishing to enter into legal relations with the client. This power relationship is very similar to that created by the members of a partnership vesting a partner with authority to effect legal relations on behalf of the members of the partnership and is subject to abuse because neither the partnership's clients nor the third parties wishing to enter into legal relations with the partnership's clients are expected to confirm details of the legal relations with one another. A partnership consequently puts both their clients and third parties wishing to enter into legal relations with their clients at risk of harm when they vest a partner with authority to effect legal relations on behalf of the partnership's clients. This risk of harm would not exist but for the power relationship created by the vesting of authority by the members of the partnership upon the partner.

Partners not only vest each other with authority to effect legal relations on behalf of the members of the partnership or their clients, but vest authority to

[11] J Story, *Commentaries on Partnership* (Boston, CC Little and J Brown, 1859) 1.
[12] Fletcher (n 2) 5.

conduct the business of the partnership more generally. Such authority is not something to which agent strict liability ordinarily responds. In *Sweeney v Boylan Nominees Pty Limited*,[13] for instance, the owner of a fridge escaped strict liability for a tort committed by an independent refrigeration mechanic even though the refrigeration mechanic was repairing the fridge on the fridge owner's behalf.[14] Partnerships, however, are a special case. Partners not only conduct business on each other's behalf but hold themselves out as conducting a *single business enterprise*. Having associated for this purpose, it is contrary to the public interest to allow partners to subsequently dissociate when it is in their interests to do so. As Joseph Story explained:[15]

> in ordinary partnerships, there is a universal mandate and a joint *proepositura*, by which each partner is *institor* of the whole trade to an unlimited extent, each being liable *in solido* for the company debts.

The peculiarities of the partnership relationship mean that partner strict liability extends somewhat beyond agent strict liability. Legislatures have confirmed that partners, having held themselves out as such, '*should not be able to associate and dissociate at will*'.[16] Consequently, the legislation governing partnerships requires that the members of partnerships are not only held strictly liable for a tort committed by a partner which occurs in the course of effecting legal relations on behalf of the partnership, but are held also strictly liable for a tort committed by a partner that occurs in the course of carrying on the business of the partnership more generally. Such liability is imposed by way of legislation as a matter of public policy and is *peculiar* to the partnership relationship.

Although the legislation governing partnerships means that the basis of partner strict liability extends somewhat beyond the basis of agent strict liability, at their core the two forms of strict liability are very similar. Partner strict liability can therefore be seen as an extended form of agent strict liability (having been extended by way of legislation). As with agent strict liability, it is not an absolute form of liability; it is not imposed in the absence of any tort being committed.[17] Partner strict liability is instead imposed *regardless* of whether the other members of the partnership either individually or collectively committed a tort. What the liability does is relieve a claimant from having to prove that the vesting of authority by the members of a partnership in a partner contributed to the damage suffered by the claimant. In so doing, partner strict liability provides claimants with a degree of protection from an abuse of the authority vested in a partner by the members of a partnership.

[13] (2006) 226 CLR 161.

[14] See further ch 6.

[15] Story, *Commentaries on Partnership* (n 11).

[16] See, eg, Partnership Act 1892 (NSW) s 10.

[17] P Cane, 'Responsibility and Fault: a Relational and Functional Approach to Responsibility' in P Cane and J Gardner (eds), *Relating to Responsibility* (Oxford, Hart, 2001) 81, 99.

B. In What Circumstances Does the Strict Liability Arise?

Legislation provides that partner strict liability can be imposed on the members of a partnership whenever a partner commits a tort whilst acting within the ordinary course of the business of the partnership.[18]

Three points can be made about the general circumstances in which partner strict liability arises. First, because there are different bases upon which partner strict liability can be imposed, the types of damage which may be recovered under partner strict liability vary. For instance, in circumstances in which a partner commits a tort in the course of effecting legal relations on behalf of the partnership or clients of the partnership, partner strict liability mirrors agent strict liability and is generally limited to economic loss. As the authority vested in a partner by the other members of the partnership is an authority to effect legal relations on behalf of the partnership or the partnership's clients, the potential for abuse of the power relationship created by the vesting of such authority is typically limited to harm to the contractual expectancies of a transactional party wishing to enter into legal relations with the partnership or the partnership's clients. Such harm generally materialises in the form of economic loss, although in certain circumstances, it may also extend to property loss, given that a transactional party may hand over property to a partner in the course of effecting legal relations with the partnership or the partnership's clients with which the partner may subsequently abscond.

As noted in the previous section, a partner is not only vested with authority by the members of a partnership to effect legal relations on behalf of the partnership and potentially the partnership's clients, but is vested with authority to conduct the business of the partnership more generally. In order to prevent partnerships associating and dissociating at will, legislation governing partnerships requires that the members of a partnership are not only held strictly liable for a tort committed by a partner in the course of effecting legal relations on behalf of the partnership or the partnership's clients, but are also held strictly liable for the a tort committed by a partner in the course of carrying on the business of the partnership more generally. To the extent that the members of a partnership can be held strictly liable by way of legislation for a tort committed by a partner in carrying out the business of the partnership more generally, there is no real basis upon which to limit the types of damage for which partner strict liability may be imposed. This is because partnerships undertake a broad range of business activities which may harm persons dealing with the partnership in a variety of different ways. It follows that the members of partnerships have been held strictly liable for different types of damage including physical damage suffered as a result of the negligent operation of a mine[19] and economic loss suffered as a result of negligent advice.[20]

[18] Above n 4.
[19] *Mellors v Shaw* (1861) 1 B & S 437; 121 ER 778.
[20] As occurred in *Polkinghorne v Holland* (1934) 51 CLR 143.

A second, and closely associated point, is that there are few restrictions on who can sue for partner strict liability given the different bases upon which such liability may be imposed. Where a partner commits a tort in the course of effecting legal relations on behalf of the partnership or the partnership's clients, partner strict liability once again mirrors agent strict liability so that an action to hold the members of a partnership strict liability for a tort committed by a partner is ordinarily restricted to transactional parties wishing to enter into legal relations with the members of the partnership or a client of the partnership. Because legislatures have extended partner strict liability to circumstances in which a partner commits a tort whilst carrying out the business of the partnership more generally, however, any person against whom a tort has been committed by a partner can potentially bring an action for partner strict liability.

A final point that can be made about the general circumstances in which partner strict liability arises is that it only arises in respect of a tort committed by a partner. Whether a person is a partner is to be determined in accordance with the various Partnership Acts. The vagaries of determining the existence of a partnership are beyond the scope of this book.[21]

C. Scope of the Strict Liability

Before partner strict liability can be imposed, it needs to be shown that the partner was acting within the ordinary course of the business of the partnership.[22] Although there are different bases upon which partner strict liability can be imposed, the courts appear to adopt a similar approach to determining whether a tort committed by a partner occurred within the ordinary course of the business of the partnership.

In circumstances in which a partner commits a tort in the course of effecting legal relations on behalf of the partnership or the partnership's clients, partner strict liability mirrors agent strict liability and extends to circumstances in which the partner is acting with *apparent* authority. Provided the transactional party wishing to enter into legal relations with the members of the partnership or the partnership's client reasonably believes that the partner is purporting to exercise the authority vested in the partner by the partnership immediately prior to the tort being committed, partner strict liability can be imposed. This is best demonstrated by cases involving fraud.

There are numerous cases in which the members of a partnership have been held strictly liable for the fraud of a partner which occurred whilst the partner was purporting to effect legal relations on behalf of the partnership or the partnership's clients.[23] One of the earliest cases was *Clayton's Case*.[24] A customer had

[21] See generally Fletcher (n 2) ch 2.
[22] Above n 4.
[23] F Pollock, *A Digest of the Law of Partnership* (4th ed, London, Stevens, 1888) 53–56.
[24] *Devaynes v Noble* (1816) 1 Mer. 572.

left securities with a banking partnership for safe keeping. When two of the partners sold those securities without the permission of the customer, the members of the partnership were held strictly liable for the fraud even though the remaining partners were innocent of any conduct which could of itself constitute a tort.[25] A more recent example is the decision of the House of Lords in *Dubai Aluminium Co Ltd v Salaam*.[26] In that case, a firm of solicitors was held strictly liable when the senior partner dishonestly assisted a client perpetrate a fraud by drawing up sham legal documents, again in circumstances in which the remaining partners were innocent of any conduct which could of itself constitute a tort.[27] No liability would have been imposed in either of those cases if partner strict liability was limited by the terms of the actual authority conferred by the members of a partnership upon a partner to effect legal relations on behalf of the partnership or the partnership's clients. This is because the partners involved in those cases knew they had no actual authority to commit fraud or engage in conduct with the purpose of committing a fraud. As with agent strict liability, however, it is submitted that strict liability was nonetheless imposed because the partners in those cases were purporting to exercise the authority conferred by the partnership immediately prior to the frauds occurring.

The reason partner strict liability is not limited by the actual terms of the authority vested in a partner by the members of the partnership in circumstances in which a partner is purporting to effect legal relations on behalf of the partnership or the partnership's clients is that a transactional party wishing to enter into legal relations with the partnership or the partnership's clients will interact with the partner on the basis of the apparent authority they reasonably purport to exercise. One reason the partners in *Clayton's Case* were able to sell the securities, for instance, is because they had been vested with apparent authority by the members of the partnership to dispose of assets on behalf of the partnership's clients. The power relationship between a partner and a transactional party is therefore shaped by the authority which the partner reasonably purports to exercise, not the terms of the actual authority vested in the partner by the members of the partnership. It is the potential for this power relationship to be abused which puts transactional parties at risk of harm.

Cases involving fraud typically arise in circumstances in which a partner is purporting to effect legal relations on behalf of the partnership or the partnership's clients. It might have been open to the courts to adopt a different approach to determining whether a partner was acting within the ordinary course of the business of the partnership in circumstances in which the partner was not purporting

[25] Case described by Pollock, *A Digest of the Law of Partnership* (n 23) 53–54. Today the case would be handled under a specific section of the Partnership Acts which deals with the misapplication of money or property left in the custody of a partnership. See, eg, Partnership Act 1892 (NSW) s 11.

[26] [2003] 2 AC 366.

[27] At least, it was assumed that the partner had engaged in dishonest assistance, the point not being contested at trial. Ibid 390–91 (Lord Millett).

to effect legal relations on behalf of the partnership or the partnership's clients, but was purporting to conduct the business of the partnership more generally. In interpreting the partnership legislation which imposes such liability, however, the courts have been prepared to use the same approach on the basis of the policy concern that partners should not be allowed to associate and dissociate at will. It follows that, even where a partner is not purporting to effect legal relations on behalf of the members of partnership or the partnership's clients, the courts will use the apparent authority vested by the partnership in the partner to conduct the business of the partnership more generally to determine whether the partner was acting within the ordinary course of the business of the partnership immediately prior to the wrongdoing occurring.

Consider *Hamlyn v John Houston & Co.*[28] In that case, the England and Wales Court of Appeal held the members of a partnership strictly liable when a partner offered the employee of a competitor a bribe to find out information about the competitor's business. Although the partner had no actual authority to pay bribes, the partner was conducting legitimate business on behalf of the partnership with the competitor immediately prior to paying the bribe and was therefore acting within the apparent scope of his authority immediately before the fraud. Similarly, in *Proceedings Commissioner v Ali Hatem*[29] the New Zealand Court of Appeal held a partnership which conducted a motor vehicle garage business strictly liable when a partner sexually harassed a woman applying for a job at the garage. Once again, although the partner had no actual authority to engage in sexual harassment, the partner was conducting a job interview on behalf of the members of the partnership immediately prior to the harassment and was again found to be acting within the apparent scope of his authority immediately prior to the harassment.[30] Admittedly, the approach of the courts can be difficult to reconcile with the new expositive framework put forward by this book since the partners in the cases were not acting in their capacity as agent for the partnership or the partnership's clients immediately prior to committing the torts. Unlike the other relationships examined in this book, however, the partnership relationship is governed by legislation and subject to the broader public policy concern that partners should not be allowed to associate and dissociate at will.

Using apparent authority to determine the scope of partner strict liability does not mean that the members of a partnership will be held strictly liable for all torts committed by a partner. It still has to be shown that a partner was purporting to act within the apparent scope of the authority vested in the partner by the partnership immediately prior to the tort being committed. Where this cannot be done, strict liability will not be imposed.

[28] [1903] 1 KB 81.

[29] [1999] 1 NZLR 305.

[30] Alternatively, liability in such cases could be seen as an example of strict liability for the wrongdoing of a person upon whom authority has been conferred in relation to another as in *Petrou v Hatzigeorgio* (1991) Aust Torts Reports 81–071. See further ch 4.

Consequently, partner strict liability was not imposed on a firm of solicitors in *Flynn v Robin Thompson & Partners*[31] when a partner at a firm of solicitors physically assaulted the husband of a plaintiff who had brought legal proceedings against the firm for negligence. Although the partner had been defending the claim brought against the partnership prior to the assault and the assault took place outside the judge's chambers after proceedings for the day had finished, the partner had run into the plaintiff's husband quite by chance and was not purporting to further the legal proceedings immediately prior to the assault occurring. A different decision might have been reached if the partner was in a meeting with the plaintiff and her husband and was trying to settle the legal proceedings at the time the assault occurred. Similarly, the firm of solicitors in *Harman v Johnson*[32] escaped partner strict liability when a client gave one of the partners a sum of money to invest at the partner's discretion and the partner later absconded with it. Although the members of a firm of solicitors can vest each other with authority to make specific investments on behalf of clients, they do not generally vest each other with authority (and had not done in this case) to accept funds in order to undertake general investment activities since solicitors are not financial advisers or brokers. As the partner had no apparent authority to engage in such investment activities in the first place, the partner was found not to be acting within the apparent scope of the authority vested in him by the members of the partnership immediately prior to the tort being committed.

As can be seen, the new expositive framework for understanding strict liability for the tort of another put forward by this book can assist in explaining the partner strict liability. The liability can be described as an extended form of agent strict liability, such liability having been extended by legislatures as a matter of public policy, on the basis that partners vest each other with authority as agents to conduct the business of the partnership.

II. Strict Liability for a Tort Committed by a Person upon whom Authority has been Conferred to Deal with a Bailor's Goods

A less well-known example of strict liability for the tort of another is the strict liability imposed on a bailee for a tort committed by a person upon whom authority has been conferred by the bailee to deal with a bailor's goods.

A bailment arises when one person (the *bailee*) 'voluntarily takes' another person's goods (the *bailor*) into her possession and holds or deals with those goods on the bailor's behalf.[33] As a bailor no longer has possession of her goods,

[31] (2000) 97(6) LSG 36.
[32] (1853) 2 E&B 61 cited by Pollock (n 23) 54.
[33] *The Pioneer Container* [1994] 2 AC 324, 342 (Lord Goff of Chieveley).

stringent obligations are placed on a bailee to protect the bailor's interests. A bailee, for instance, is obliged to keep the bailor's goods safe.[34] A bailee is also obliged to deal with those goods in a manner consistent with the bailor's rights of ownership.[35] To this extent, a bailee owes a positive duty to protect a bailor's goods from theft.[36] Furthermore, a bailee bears the onus of proving that she took reasonable care of the bailor's goods or that any failure by the bailee to take reasonable care of the bailor's goods was not a cause of those goods being damaged.[37]

Although a bailee owes a duty to keep a bailor's goods safe, a bailee may confer authority upon another person to deal with the bailor's goods. For instance, a bailee may create a sub-bailment by transferring possession of the goods to another person (the *sub-bailee*) without relinquishing the role of bailee.[38] Where a sub-bailment is created, the sub-bailee will face the same prospective liability in respect of the bailor's goods as the bailee. A bailee may also give custody or temporary control of the bailor's goods to an employee. In such circumstances, it is unusual for an employee to become a sub-bailee and the employee will consequently not owe the same duties in respect of the bailor's goods as the bailee.[39] There are also circumstances in which an independent contractor can be given custody or temporary control of a bailor's goods by a bailee without the independent contractor becoming a sub-bailee. A security guard given access to a bailee's premises for the purposes of conducting random security checks, for instance, is not usually given sufficient possession of the goods stored in the premises to be construed as a sub-bailee of those goods.[40] Once again, as the independent contractor does not become a sub-bailee, they will not owe the same duties in respect of the bailor's goods as the bailee.

When a bailee confers authority upon another person to deal with the bailor's goods, the courts have found that the bailee may be held strictly liable for a tort committed in respect of the bailor's goods by that person. The most well-known example is the decision of the England and Wales Court of Appeal in *Morris v C W Martin & Sons Ltd*.[41] In that case a furrier forwarded a mink stole to a cleaner on behalf of his customer.[42] The cleaner was subsequently held strictly liable for the theft of the stole by an employee who had been given the stole for cleaning purposes. The England and Wales Court of Appeal also suggested in *British Road*

[34] Salmon LJ in *Morris v C W Martins & Sons Ltd* [1966] 1 QB 716, 738.

[35] Ibid.

[36] N Palmer, *Palmer on Bailment* (3rd ed, London, Sweet & Maxwell, 2009) 47–52.

[37] Ibid 52–55.

[38] Ibid 1240.

[39] *Vincent v State Bank of NSW Ltd*, Unreported, New South Wales Supreme Court, Young J, 20 July 1993, cited by Palmer ibid 458.

[40] eg there was no suggestion in *British Road Services Ltd v Arthur V. Crutchley & Co Ltd* [1968] 1 Lloyd's Rep 271 that the security guard appointed to provide security services in respect of the bailee's warehouse was a sub-bailee.

[41] [1966] 1 QB 716.

[42] No case was brought against the furrier in respect of the stolen fur.

Services Ltd v Arthur V. Crutchley & Co Ltd[43] that the owner of a warehouse could be held strictly liable for the negligence of a security firm hired to patrol the warehouse when 200 cases of whisky were stolen.[44] The whisky was being held by the warehouse owners for a road carriage company and was awaiting shipping at the time of the theft.

Although the basis of the strict liability for the tort of another imposed on a bailee has yet to be formally identified,[45] the courts have made it clear that a bailee will not be held strictly liable whenever a third person commits a tort in respect of bailor's goods, but only for a tort committed by a person upon whom authority has been conferred by the bailee to deal with the bailor's goods.[46] As Salmon LJ explained in *Morris v C W Martin & Sons Ltd*:[47]

> A bailee for reward is not answerable for a theft by any of his servants but only for a theft by such of them as are deputed by him to discharge some part of his duty of taking reasonable care. A theft by any servant who is not employed to do anything in relation to the goods bailed is entirely outside the scope of his employment and cannot make the master liable. So in this case, if someone employed by the defendants in another depot had broken in and stolen the fur, the defendants would not have been liable. Similarly in my view if a clerk employed in the same depot had seized the opportunity of entering the room where the fur was kept and had stolen it, the defendants would not have been liable. The mere fact that the master, by employing a rogue, gives him the opportunity to steal or defraud does not make the master liable for his depredations.

The distinction is borne out by numerous cases in which bailees have escaped strict liability because the person who committed a tort in respect of the bailor's goods had not been conferred sufficient authority to deal with the bailor's goods by the bailee.[48] The decision of the Queen's Bench Division in *Swiss Bank Corporation v Brink's-MAT Ltd*[49] provides a good example. Brink's-MAT had been charged with transporting a significant sum of Bank of England notes from three banks in England to the Swiss Bank Corporation in Zurich. An employee at Brink's-MAT with criminal connections provided information with respect to the movement of the notes enabling them to be stolen. Although the employee worked at the Brinks-MAT vaults where the notes were at the time they were stolen, the employee had not been 'entrusted with the care and custody of these notes' and had not been involved with the handling of the shipment.[50] As a result, Brinks-MAT avoided strict liability for the theft.

[43] [1968] 1 Lloyd's Rep 271.

[44] As the owner of the warehouse had also been negligent, however, it was not necessary to impose liability for the wrongdoing of the security firm.

[45] Palmer, *Palmer on Bailment* (n 36) 816–21.

[46] Or indeed by a sub-bailee.

[47] *Morris v C W Martins & Sons Ltd* [1966] 1 QB 716, 740–41 (Salmon LJ).

[48] Palmer (n 36) 834–35. See more recently *Brink's Global Services In v Igrox Limited* [2010] EWCA Civ 1207.

[49] [1986] 2 Lloyd's Rep 79.

[50] Ibid 87.

A. Basis of the Strict Liability

When a bailee confers authority upon another person to deal with a bailor's goods, the bailee puts the person upon whom such authority has been conferred in a position of power with respect to the bailor's goods which did not previously exist. This is because the conferral of authority by the bailee not only gives the person conferred authority custody or possession of the bailor's goods, but enables the person upon whom authority has been conferred to deal with those goods without being questioned. For instance, if the bailee confers authority upon a courier to deal with the bailor's goods, the courier will be able to drive away with those goods without being questioned. As the person upon whom authority has been conferred is not necessarily subject to the same stringent duties in respect to those goods as the bailee,[51] there is significant potential for this position of power to be abused. A bailee consequently puts the bailor's goods at risk of physical harm whenever they confer authority upon another person to deal with those goods.

The authority conferred by a bailee upon another person to deal with a bailor's goods is very similar in nature to the authority conferred by an employer or school upon another person to direct the conduct of an employee or student, there being no real distinction in this respect between circumstances in which a defendant confers authority over a person or a person's goods. It is submitted, therefore, that the strict liability for the tort of another imposed on a bailee is a form of conferred authority strict liability. The liability responds to the potential for abuse of the position of power created by the conferral of authority by a bailee by holding the bailee liable regardless of the bailee having personally engaged in any conduct in respect of the bailor's goods which might itself attract liability in tort. It is not an absolute form of liability; it is not imposed in the *absence* of any tort being committed.[52] The strict liability is instead imposed *regardless* of any tort being committed by the bailee. What the liability does is relieve a bailor from having to prove that the conferral of authority by the bailee upon another person to deal with the bailor's goods contributed to the damage suffered by bailor. In so doing, the liability provides the bailor with a degree of protection from an abuse of the authority conferred by the bailee upon another person to deal with the bailor's goods.

B. In What Circumstances Does the Strict Liability Arise?

Strict liability for the tort of another can be imposed on a bailee whenever a bailee confers authority upon another person to deal with a bailor's goods and that person commits a tort in respect of those goods whilst purporting to exercise the conferred authority.

[51] Particularly in respect of an employee or independent contractor who receives custody or temporary control of the bailor's goods, but does not become a sub-bailee. See above.

[52] Cane, 'Responsibility and Fault' (n 17) 81, 99.

Two points can be made about the general circumstances in which strict liability for the tort of another may be imposed on a bailee. First, as with conferred authority strict liability, the strict liability imposed on a bailee for a tort committed by a person upon whom authority has been conferred by the bailee to deal with the bailor's goods is restricted to physical loss of or damage to the bailor's goods.[53] The reason is that the authority conferred by a bailee is an authority to physically deal with the bailor's goods. The risk created by a bailee when conferring authority upon another person to deal with the bailor's goods is therefore a risk of physical loss or damage only. It follows that the only person who can seek to impose strict liability for the tort of another on a bailee is the bailor.

Secondly, strict liability for the tort of another can be imposed on a bailee in respect of a tort committed by an employee, an independent contractor or even someone acting gratuitously. This is because it is not the status of the person who has committed the tort which is important, but the fact that they have been conferred authority by the bailee to deal with a bailor's goods.

On this point, there is an outstanding question as to whether a bailee can be held strictly liable for a tort committed by a person upon whom authority has been conferred to deal with the bailor's goods in circumstances in which the person upon whom such authority has been conferred has become a sub-bailee of the bailor's goods. There are as yet no cases in which strict liability for the tort of another has been imposed on a bailee in respect of a tort committed by a sub-bailee.[54] In principle, there is no obvious reason why the liability should not extend to a tort committed by a sub-bailee. A sub-bailee, by definition, is conferred authority by the bailee to deal with the bailor's goods; but the point is yet to be considered by the courts.

One reason for the absence of cases is that a bailor is entitled to proceed directly against the sub-bailee.[55] This is what occurred in *Lotus Cars Ltd v Southampton Cargo Handling plc.*[56] In that case, Lotus had delivered a number of new cars to stevedores at the Southampton docks in order for the cars to be shipped to Canada. The stevedores placed the cars in a secure compound kept by the port authority from which one of the cars was stolen when thieves cut through the wire fence. Lotus brought proceedings against the stevedore as bailee and the port authority as sub-bailee. Both were found personally liable to Lotus on the basis that they had both failed to use reasonable care in the storage of the vehicle.

A second and related reason for the absence of cases is that because a sub-bailee is subject to the same duties as the bailee in respect of the bailor's goods, the risk of a sub-bailee abusing the authority conferred to deal with the bailor's goods is potentially less than the risk of a person who does not become a sub-bailee abusing the authority conferred to deal with the bailor's goods. Since this is the very risk to

[53] Including damage consequential upon such physical damage.
[54] Palmer (n 36) 1240.
[55] Palmer (n 36) 1240.
[56] '*The Rigoletto*' [2000] 2 All ER 705.

which the strict liability for the tort of another responds, the courts may question whether it is appropriate to impose strict liability on a bailee for a tort committed by a sub-bailee conferred authority to deal with the bailor's goods in circumstances where the sub-bailee is under the same duties in respect of the bailor's goods as the bailee. This assumes, however, that there is never any advantage to a bailor in proceeding against the bailee, as opposed to the sub-bailee.

One case in which such an advantage presented itself was the decision of the Privy Council in *The Pioneer Container*.[57] The principal issue in *The Pioneer Container* was whether a sub-bailee could invoke the contractual terms of a sub-bailment against a bailor even though the bailor was not privy to such terms. The sub-bailee in that case was a ship owner who sought to rely on an exclusive jurisdiction clause in a sub-bailment contract whilst defending claims brought by cargo owners after the ship had sunk. It was in the sub-bailee's interests to be able to rely on such a term, because if they were unable to do so, they would have had to defend claims in respect of the sinking in a number of different jurisdictions. The Privy Council found that the ship owner could rely on the exclusive jurisdiction clause because the cargo owners had allowed the bailee to sub-bail the goods 'on any terms'.[58] As a result, the cargo owners were subjected to terms of a sub-bailment to which they were not party. If a bailee can be held strictly liable for a tort committed by a sub-bailee, as the reasoning in this book suggests, the cargo owners might have avoided this position by suing the bailees rather than the sub-bailees. The cargo owners' claim against the bailees would then have been governed by the contractual terms of the bailment and the bailees could then sue the sub-bailees to recover their loss in accordance with the contractual terms of the sub-bailment.[59] If, however, the duties imposed on a sub-bailee in respect of their dealings with the bailor's goods are deemed sufficient to protect the interests of a bailor when a bailee confers authority upon the sub-bailee to deal with the bailor's goods, the decision reached in *The Pioneer Container* can be considered correct. It will take an appropriate case to find out which view is correct.

C. Scope of the Strict Liability

The strict liability for the tort of another imposed on a bailee is generally limited to circumstances in which the person upon whom authority has been conferred by the bailee commits a tort in respect of the bailor's goods whilst *purporting to exercise the conferred authority*. This is because the liability responds to the potential for abuse of the position of power created when a bailee confers authority upon another person to deal with the bailor's goods and such potential only exists where

[57] [1994] 2 AC 324.

[58] Ibid 333.

[59] This is ultimately the result reached in cases like *Simaan General Contracting Co v Pilkington Class Ltd (No.2)* [1988] QB 758 where courts have denied claims for economic loss in tort and required parties to sue down a chain of contracts.

the person upon whom authority has been conferred is purporting to exercise the conferred authority immediately prior to the tort being committed.

Importantly, the strict liability for the tort of another that might be imposed on a bailee is not limited by the terms of the actual authority conferred by a bailee upon a person in respect of the bailor's goods. As with conferred authority strict liability more generally, the scope of the strict liability for the tort of another that might be imposed on a bailee extends to circumstances in which the person upon whom authority has been conferred is acting with *apparent* authority. Provided third parties reasonably believe that the person upon whom authority has been conferred is purporting to exercise the authority conferred by the bailee immediately prior to the tort being committed, strict liability might be imposed on the bailee in respect of a tort committed by the person upon whom authority has been conferred over a bailor's goods. This is best demonstrated by cases involving theft. There are numerous cases in which a bailee has been held strictly liable for the theft of a bailor's goods by a person upon whom authority has been conferred by the bailee to deal with those goods. *Morris v C W Martin & Sons Ltd*[60] is the most well-known example, but there are many others.[61] In such cases, no liability would have been imposed if the strict liability for the tort of another that might be imposed on a bailee was limited by the terms of the actual authority conferred by the bailee. This is because in each of those cases the person upon whom authority has been conferred to deal with the bailor's goods knew they had no actual authority to steal the bailor's goods or engage in other conduct which enabled the bailor's goods to be stolen. It is not, however, the actual scope of authority which is important in determining whether strict liability for the tort of another might be imposed on a bailee, but the apparent scope of authority. A person upon whom authority has been conferred by a bailee to deal with a bailor's goods is able to deal with those goods without being questioned because of the apparent authority that has been conferred upon that person by the bailee. To return to the example of the courier, one reason a courier can drive away with goods without anyone raising the alarm is because the courier has apparent conferred authority to do so. It is the apparent scope of the authority, therefore, which shapes how the person upon whom authority has been conferred by the bailee can deal with the bailor's goods and it is the capacity to deal with the bailor's goods which presents the risk of physical harm to which the strict liability for the tort of another that might be imposed on a bailee responds. Provided that the person upon whom authority has been conferred by the bailee to deal with the bailor's goods was purporting to exercise the conferred authority immediately prior to the tort being committed, strict liability for the tort of another can be imposed.

As with conferred authority strict liability more generally, using apparent authority to determine the scope of the strict liability for a tort of another that might be imposed on a bailee does not mean that a bailee will be held strictly liable

[60] [1966] 1 QB 716.
[61] Palmer (n 36) 833–35.

for all torts committed by a person upon whom authority has been conferred by the bailee to deal with the bailor's goods. It still has to be shown that the person was purporting to act within the apparent scope of that authority so that there was the potential for the position of power created by the bailee's conferral of authority to be abused. The most common situation in which a person conferred authority to deal with a bailor's goods has been found to be acting outside the apparent scope of the authority conferred by the bailee is where the person upon whom authority has been conferred is an employee and has returned to their place of employment after business hours to deal with the bailor's goods. Consequently, the bailee in *Sanderson v Collins*[62] escaped liability when an employee coachman returned to work after garaging the coach for the night and took it for a joyride.[63] Similarly, in *Darling Ladies Wear Ltd v Hickey*[64] the bailee escaped liability when an employee returned to work after hours to steal a car which he had been working on. As the apparent authority of the employee to deal with the bailor's goods ceased at the end of the working day, so too did the bailee's liability.

The strict liability for the tort of another that has been imposed on a bailee can therefore be seen to fit comfortably within the new expositive framework for strict liability for the tort of another proposed by this book. To the extent that it is imposed when a bailor confers authority upon another person to deal with a bailor's goods, the liability can be seen as a form of conferred authority strict liability.

III. Strict Liability for a Tort Committed by a Person Driving a Car for the Owner's Purposes?

The final category of strict liability for the tort of another to be examined by this book is the strict liability imposed on the owner of a motor vehicle for a tort committed by a person driving the vehicle for the owner's purposes. In the days of the horse and carriage, carriage owners were held strictly liable for torts committed by the driver of the carriage whilst driving.[65] Initially, such liability was limited to circumstances in which the carriage owner was in the carriage at the time the tort was committed,[66] but was later extended to circumstances in which the driver was using the carriage for the owner's purposes even though the owner was absent.[67] With the arrival of the motor vehicle, the principle was extended yet again. For instance, in *Ormrod v Crosville Motor Services Ltd*[68] the England and

[62] [1904] 1 KB 628.
[63] Ibid 631.
[64] [1950] 1 DLR 720.
[65] A brief history of the liability can be found in *Soblusky v Egan* (1959–60) 103 CLR 215, 229–31 (Dixon CJ, Kitto and Windeyer JJ).
[66] See *Chandler v Broughton* (1832) 1 C&M 29, 149 ER 301.
[67] See *Booth v Mister* (1835) 7 Car & P 66, 173 ER 30.
[68] [1953] 1 WLR 1120.

Wales Court of Appeal found the owner of a racing car strictly liable for the negligence of a friend who was driving the car from England to Monte Carlo so that it could be used in the famous race. Similarly, in *Soblusky v Egan*,[69] the High Court of Australia found the owner[70] of a car strictly liable for the negligence of a friend whom he had asked to drive to a meeting they were both attending because the owner 'had a stiff neck and he preferred not to drive long distances'.[71]

Traditionally, the courts have explained the strict liability imposed on the owner of a motor vehicle for a tort committed by a driver of the motor vehicle on the basis that the driver was acting as the owner's 'agent' at the time the tort was committed, hence the requirement for the vehicle to be being used for the owner's purposes. As Denning LJ noted in *Ormrod v Crosville Motor Services Ltd*:[72]

> It has often been supposed that the owner of a vehicle is only liable for the negligence of the driver if that driver is his servant acting in the course of his employment. But that is not correct. The owner is also liable if the driver is his agent, that is to say, if the driver is, with the owner's consent, driving the car on the owner's business or the owner's purposes.

Throughout this book, the term 'agent' has been used in the narrow contractual sense of a person vested with authority by a principal to effect legal relations on the principal's behalf. This definition was adopted because, outside the motor vehicle cases, agent strict liability has generally been restricted to situations in which the person who committed the tort was vested with such authority.[73] In contrast, Denning LJ used the term 'agent' in the above statement as meaning one person doing something on behalf of another person. This broader sense of the term 'agent' appears to have been adopted in an effort to side-step the general rule that strict liability for the tort of another cannot be imposed in respect of an independent contractor. This was acknowledged by Lord Wilberforce in *Morgans v Launchbury*:[74]

> I accept entirely that 'agency' in context such as these is merely a concept, the meaning and purpose of which is to say 'is vicariously liable', and that either expression reflects a judgment of value – respondeat superior is the law saying that the owner ought to pay.

It is not possible in such circumstances to see the strict liability imposed on the owner of a motor vehicle for a tort committed by a person driving the vehicle for the owner's purposes as a form of agent strict liability in accordance with the new expositive framework put forward by this book.

[69] (1959–60) 103 CLR 215.

[70] This case was complicated by the fact that the transfer of registration on sale had not been completed, leaving the defendant technically a bailee.

[71] *Soblusky v Egan* (1959–60) 103 CLR 215, 225.

[72] [1953] 1 WLR 1120, 1122.

[73] See generally ch 6.

[74] [1973] AC 127, 135.

If the strict liability imposed on the owner of a motor vehicle for a tort committed by a person driving the vehicle for the owner's purposes is not a form of agent strict liability, is there any other basis upon which such strict liability might be imposed? To answer this question it is necessary to consider the particular features of the relationship between the motor vehicle owner, the driver and an injured third party to see how else the strict liability might be explained.

One feature of the relationship is that when strict liability for the tort of another is imposed, the defendant is either the owner or bailee[75] of the motor vehicle. It is difficult, however, to attribute any significance to the ownership of the motor vehicle since the owners of other chattels, such as a firearm or a bicycle,[76] are not held strictly liable for torts committed by the users of those chattels with the owner's consent.[77] It is also not clear why ownership of the motor vehicle might itself be a source of liability. One explanation could be the retention of some type of control over the vehicle even though it was being used by someone else.[78] It is difficult, however, to assess what type of actual control the owner of a motor vehicle might be able to exert over its use when the owner is not present,[79] other than calling for the return of the vehicle. Such difficulties with the concept of 'control' are now well recognised and control has been abandoned as a basis for other forms of strict liability for the tort of another.[80] Alternatively, it might have something to do with the role of the owner in maintaining the vehicle or the limited opportunity of the driver to check the soundness of the vehicle before driving. This is unlikely, however, as the owner of the vehicle is held strictly liable even where the injury to the third party has nothing to do with the condition of the vehicle.

Another feature of the relationship between a motor vehicle owner, the driver and an injured third party is that the driver is acting for the 'owner's purposes'.[81] This is the feature which most judges have focused on to date. It seems to have been

[75] As in *Soblusky v Egan* (1959–60) 103 CLR 215. Use of the term 'owner of a motor vehicle' should also be taken to include a reference to a 'bailee of a motor vehicle'.

[76] Examples discussed by MacKinnon LJ in *Hewitt v Bovin* [1940] 1 KB 188, 192–93. He says at 193, referring to a question put by Bennett J in the course of argument: 'Suppose a son says to his father: "I have been invited to shoot next Saturday in the country; will you kindly lend me your gun, and will you lend me your car to get down there?" The father agrees to both requests. If at the shoot the son maladroitly peppers a beater, can his victim sue the father for damages? And if, coming home in the car, the son knocks down a pedestrian, can that second victim sue the father for damages? I can see no valid distinction between the two cases'.

[77] Although there have been attempts to extend the vicarious liability of a car owner to the owners of other forms of motorised transport (see below).

[78] In *Samson v Aitchison* [1912] AC 845, the Privy Council said (at 850) in a case on appeal from New Zealand: 'In the opinion of their Lordships this amounts to a finding of fact that the appellant had not abandoned the control which they think prima facie belonged to him … And if the control of the car was not abandoned, then it is a matter of indifference whether Collins, while driving the car, be styled the agent or the servant of the appellant in performing that particular act, since it is the retention of the control which the appellant would have in each case that makes him responsible for the negligence which caused the injury'.

[79] Except where the driver is an employee.

[80] eg it is no longer used to support vicarious liability for employees. See further ch 1.

[81] Lord Wilberforce in *Morgans v Launchbury* [1973] AC 127.

thought that, because the driver is doing something for the purposes of the owner, the owner should be held strictly liable for any torts committed by the driver in performing the task. Elsewhere in the law, however, arranging for another person to do something the defendant could have done themselves has not generally been enough to invoke strict liability for the tort of another.[82] Such reasoning also leads to the drawing of some potentially fine distinctions. Take, for example, the situation of a real estate agent selling a house for a vendor. If the real estate agent drove a prospective purchaser to the house whilst using the real estate agent's own car and negligently caused an accident injuring the prospective purchaser, the vendor would not be held strictly liable for the negligence of the real estate agent even though the real estate agent was acting for the purposes of the vendor at the time the accident occurred.[83] If, however, instead of driving the real estate agent's own car, the real estate agent was driving the vendor's car, the vendor would be strictly liable for the negligence of the real estate agent. It is difficult to explain the different results in these two situations without resorting to ownership of or right to use the motor vehicle which, as shown, is also incapable of adequately explaining the outcomes of these cases.

Another feature of the relationship between a motor vehicle owner, the driver and the injured third party is that damage sustained by the third party typically involves personal injury. This suggests that what the law might be concerned with is the need to compensate people injured in road accidents. This was a policy championed by Lord Denning, as Lord Pearson explained in *Morgans v Launchbury*:[84]

> Lord Denning MR, with the object of ensuring that compensation will be available for injured persons, has sought to extend the liability of a car owner for negligent driving of his car by other persons, because the car owner is the person who has or ought to have a motor insurance policy.

The limiting of strict liability for a tort committed by a driver to circumstances in which the driver is acting for the owner's purposes, however, would seem to defeat this aim. Access to the owner's insurance may be needed to compensate the injured claimant irrespective of whether the vehicle was being used for the owner's purposes, the purposes of the driver, or even if the vehicle was being driven by a thief at the time of the accident. For this reason, legislation has now been introduced in all Australian states and territories extending compulsory motor vehicle insurance schemes to indemnify not only the owner but also the driver of the motor vehicle in cases of personal injury.[85] A concern with compensating personal injury also does not explain why the strict liability imposed on a motor vehicle owner for

[82] Hence the general rule against vicarious liability for independent contractors.
[83] See further ch 6 for limitations on the liability of a home owner for the tort of a real estate agent.
[84] [1973] AC 127, 141.
[85] See, eg, Motor Accidents Compensation Act 1999 (NSW) s 112. See generally GE Dal Pont, *Law of Agency* (2nd ed, Sydney, LexisNexis, 2008) 619, fn 173.

a tort committed by a person driving the vehicle for the owner's purposes can be relied upon to recover property damage as well as damages for personal injury.[86]

The only other possible feature of the relationship between a motor vehicle owner, the driver and the injured claimant that might have some bearing on the strict liability imposed on the motor vehicle owner for a tort committed by the driver is the nature of the activity being engaged in by the driver; that is, the driving of a motor vehicle. Driving a motor vehicle is commonly regarded as a risky activity. As Lord Wilberforce commented in *Morgans v Launchbury*:[87]

> My Lords, I have no doubt that the multiplication of motor cars on our roads, their increasing speed, the severity of the injuries they may cause, the rise in accidents involving innocent persons, give rise to problems of increasing social difficulty with which the law finds it difficult to keep abreast.

It is possible, therefore, that in imposing strict liability on a motor vehicle owner for a tort committed by a person driving the vehicle for the owner's purposes, the law is responding to the riskiness of the activity being undertaken or instigated by the owner of the vehicle and perhaps the limited opportunity to other road users to take measures to protect themselves from such risks.[88] Similar concerns have been expressed elsewhere in the law. Chapter 2 explained, for instance, how land owners were held strictly liable at the end of the nineteenth century for torts committed by an independent contractor engaged to perform work threatening support or common walls given that such work was thought to involve an inherent danger to an adjoining property. The strict liability of a carriage owner for a tort committed by a driver of the carriage was recognised around the same time. A concern with the risks associated with driving a carriage or a motor vehicle would explain both why ownership of or a right to use the vehicle was necessary for strict liability to be imposed, as well as the requirement for the driver to be pursuing the owner's purposes at the time the tort was committed.[89]

More recently, however, there seems to have been a trend towards dismantling or limiting forms of strict liability for the tort of another that have been based on the undertaking or instigating of risky activities. The courts appear to have realised that there are actually very few things that contain an inherent risk of danger that cannot be controlled by the person doing or managing the thing or

[86] See, eg, *Jordan v Gosson Industries Pty Limited* (1963) 82 WN (Pt 1) (NSW) 157, where a tow truck was driven into a shop.

[87] [1973] AC 127, 136.

[88] *Ormrod v Crossville Motor Services Ltd* [1953] 1 WLR 1120, 1123 (Denning LJ): 'The law puts an especial responsibility on the owner of a vehicle who allows it out on to the road in charge of someone else, no matter whether it is his servant, his friend, or anyone else'.

[89] Millward LJSC emphasised the importance of both these features in *Pawlak v Doucette* [1985] 2 WWR 588, [35]: 'Thus, an extension of the principle beyond automobiles to chattels, such as a motor boat, where the principal furnishes the chattel, meets the concern that the principle is not a general principle for vicarious liability of agents, yet retains liability where the causal connection establishes a relationship of the *use of the principal's property for the principal's purpose*' [emphasis added].

the activity.[90] As demonstrated in chapter 2, strict liability for the tort of another no longer seems to be imposed on adjoining land owners for work done by an independent contractor even where such work might affect support or common walls. Similarly, the courts no longer seem as willing as they once were to hold the owner of a motor vehicle strictly liable for a tort committed by the driver of the vehicle. This is best demonstrated by the decision of the High Court of Australia in *Scott v Davis*[91] which was discussed in chapter 6. In that case, the High Court not only refused to extend strict liability for the tort of a driver to other modes of transport, specifically aeroplanes, but challenged the very foundations of the strict liability. This can be seen quite clearly in the following statement by Gummow J:[92]

> A more fundamental reason for denying any extension of *Soblusky* is that, for the reasons detailed earlier in this judgment, it rests upon insecure and unsatisfactory foundations in principle.

Even those judges who appeared to approve strict liability for a tort committed by a driver in its narrow sense as limited to motor vehicles[93] can be seen to have had such concerns. As Giles J recently noted in the decision of the New South Wales Court of Appeal in *Gutman v McFall*,[94] if the 'principle were good law, Gleeson CJ [in *Scott v Davis*] would not have confined it to motor vehicles'.[95] Similar concerns about the foundations of the strict liability imposed on the owner of a motor vehicle for a tort committed by a person driving the vehicle for the owner's purposes were expressed by members of the House of Lords in *Morgans v Launchbury*.[96]

There has been an occasional lower court decision in which strict liability has been imposed on the owner of a motor vehicle for a tort committed by a person driving the vehicle for the owner's purposes. In *Candler v Thomas (T/A London Leisure Lines)*,[97] for instance, two judges of the England and Wales Court of Appeal applied *Morgans v Launchbury*,[98] by which they were bound, to find the owner of a van strictly liable for the negligence of a friend who was driving the van to deliver a parcel on behalf of the owner. A single judge of the British Columbia Supreme Court was also prepared in *Pawlak v Doucette*[99] to extend the strict liability of a motor vehicle owner for a driver to other forms of transport including motor boats.[100] It is difficult to put much weight on such decisions, however, given

[90] See, eg, *Read v J Lyons & Company* [1947] AC 156, 181–82 (Lord Simonds): 'I would reject the idea that, if a man carries on a so-called ultra-hazardous activity on his premises, the line must be drawn so as to bring him within the limit of strict liability for its consequences to all men everywhere'. See further ch 2.
[91] (2000) 204 CLR 333.
[92] Ibid 421.
[93] Gleeson CJ and McHugh J.
[94] (2004) 61 NSWLR 599.
[95] Ibid 609.
[96] [1973] AC 127, 135 (Lord Wilberforce) and 141–42 (Lord Pearson).
[97] [1998] RTR 214.
[98] [1973] AC 127, 135.
[99] [1985] 2 WWR 588.
[100] cf *Gutman v McFall* (2004) 61 NSWLR 599.

the concerns expressed about the liability by judges of both the High Court of Australia and the House of Lords, the broader trend away from imposing strict liability for the tort of another on the basis of risky activities and the absence of any other clear basis on which the owner or bailee of a motor vehicle might be held strictly liable for a tort committed by a driver. Unfortunately, there is unlikely to be another opportunity for either the High Court of Australia or the Supreme Court of the United Kingdom to formally resolve such concerns about the foundations of the liability as the advent of compulsory motor vehicle insurance has made the liability of limited practical significance. As it stands, there has not been an opportunity for a higher court in Australia or England and Wales to assess the continued validity of the strict liability now for over 30 years. In such circumstances, perhaps it is now finally time to recognise that the cases supporting the liability are little more than 'historical oddities that have outlived their usefulness'.[101]

IV. Conclusion

As can be seen, the new expositive framework for strict liability for the tort of another proposed by this book can assist in explaining what presently appear to be miscellaneous categories of strict liability for the tort of another. Partner strict liability, for instance, can be seen as an extended form of agent strict liability. Similarly, the strict liability for the tort of another imposed on a bailee can be seen as an example of conferred authority strict liability. The only apparently miscellaneous example of strict liability for the tort of another that does not seem to fit with the new expositive framework proposed by this book is the strict liability imposed on the owner of a motor vehicle for a tort committed by a person driving the vehicle for the owner's purposes. Current cases indicate, however, that the courts are not as willing as they once were to impose such liability.

[101] F Trindade, P Cane and M Lunney, *The Law of Torts in Australia* (4th ed, Melbourne, OUP, 2007) 783.

9

Conclusion

This book has argued that strict liability for the tort of another can be reconceptualised as a response to the potential for abuse of the authority found in each of the three main types of relationships in which the courts currently impose such liability. On this basis, a new expositive framework has been devised within which three main forms of strict liability for the tort of another have been identified: conferred authority strict liability; employee strict liability; and agent strict liability. Each form of strict liability has been shown to reflect differences in the nature of the authority present in each of the relationships in which strict liability for the tort of another is imposed.

I. The Importance of the Book

By focusing on the common features of the relationships in which strict liability for the tort of another is currently imposed, this book has been able to reveal, for the first time, the internal consistency of strict liability for the tort of another. The book has shown not only why there are different forms of strict liability for the tort of another, but how they interrelate.

Conferred authority strict liability is found in both the employment and school relationships and responds to the potential for abuse of the power relationship created by an employer or school conferring its authority to direct the conduct of an employee or student upon another person. The potential for abuse of the power relationship exists because the power relationship enables the person upon whom authority has been conferred to direct the conduct of an employee or student and creates an expectation that the employee or student will obey.

Employee strict liability is limited to the employment relationship and responds to the potential for an employer to abuse its authority to direct the conduct of an employee for its own benefit. The potential for abuse exists because an employer may discipline an employee for failing to follow directions, putting the employee in a position that the employee may unduly prioritise compliance with the directions of the employer rather than give due weight to alternate considerations that might lead the employee to conduct herself differently in the circumstances.

Agent strict liability is limited to the agency relationship and responds to the potential for abuse of the power relationship created by a principal conferring authority upon an agent to effect legal relations on the principal's behalf. The potential for abuse of the power relationship exists because the power relationship enables the agent to effect legal relations on behalf of the principal in circumstances in which the party wishing to enter into legal relations with the principal is not expected to confirm with the principal the details of those legal relations.

The differences between the various forms of strict liability for the tort of another can be summarised as follows:

Table 1 Comparison of the Three Different Forms of Strict Liability for the Tort of Another

	Conferred Authority Strict Liability	**Employee Strict Liability**	**Agent Strict Liability**
Who can sue?	Persons over whom authority has been conferred to a third party to direct the conduct of that person (typically employees and students)	Strangers to employment relationship	Transactional party effecting legal relations with principal through agent
Who can be sued?	Person conferring authority (typically employers and schools)	Employers	Principals
For whose tort does liability arise?	Employee, independent contractor or volunteer	Employee	Employee, independent contractor or volunteer
Type of damage	Physical damage	Unrestricted	Economic or property loss resulting from damage to contractual expectancies
Scope of liability	Conduct within actual or apparent scope of authority conferred upon third party (can extend to intentional misconduct if third party purporting to exercise apparent authority over claimant immediately prior to tort being committed)	Limited to conduct within actual scope of authority or, more appropriately, directions issued by employer (either express or implied) (does not typically extend to intentional misconduct)	Conduct within actual or apparent scope of authority vested in agent (can extend to intentional misconduct if agent purporting to exercise apparent authority immediately prior to tort being committed)

An understanding of the differences between the various forms of strict liability for the tort of another can assist judges to overcome some of the difficulties previously experienced in imposing such liability. For instance, it can now be seen that there was no need in the child sexual assault cases to find that the deliberate and self-serving act of sexually assaulting a child could occur within the 'course of employment'. The strict liability imposed in those cases did not arise by reason of the employment relationship, but by reason of the relationship between the school or closely analogous institution and the child in its care. Employee strict liability could not be imposed because it is limited by what it is an employee is *actually* authorised, or more appropriately, directed to do[1] and does not typically extend to intentional misconduct unless that intentional misconduct has been directed by the employer.[2] In contrast, conferred authority strict liability could be imposed in the child sexual assault cases because it arises in circumstances in which the person upon whom authority has been conferred by an employer or school is acting within the *apparent* scope of that authority immediately prior to the sexual assault and can extend to intentional misconduct.

Understanding the differences between the various forms of strict liability for the tort of another can also help resolve the historical difficulties in determining who is both an 'employee' and an 'agent' for the purposes of strict liability for the tort of another. Fixing upon a single definition of who is an 'employee' has always been difficult due to the range of circumstances in which the term is applied; tax, pensions, workplace health and safety legislation etc.[3] But it is not essential to fix upon a single definition. The definition of an 'employee' will most likely vary depending on the task to which the term is put. It is, however, now possible to fix a definition of who is an 'employee' for the purposes of strict liability for the tort of another.

It has been argued in this book that employee strict liability responds to the potential for an employer to abuse its authority to direct the conduct of an employee by putting an employee in a position that the employee may unduly prioritise compliance with the directions of the employer rather than give due weight to alternate considerations that might lead the employee to conduct herself differently in the circumstances. By definition, an 'employee' must therefore be someone who does not have sufficient freedom of action to determine her own conduct and is therefore at risk of altering her conduct in accordance with an exercise of authority by another person given the threat of disciplinary action for failing to so act.[4] Defining an 'employee' in such terms requires courts to consider the specifics of a particular relationship before determining whether employee

[1] Those directions being express or implied.

[2] In which case the employer may be seen to have itself committed a tort; MA Jones, JF Clerk and WHB Lindsell, *Clerk and Lindsell on Torts* (21st ed, London, Sweet & Maxwell, 2018) [5.76].

[3] *Hollis* v *Vabu Pty Ltd* (2001) 207 CLR 21.

[4] See further chs 3 and 5.

strict liability might apply. That is, the definition of an 'employee' will need to be assessed on a case by case basis. To this extent, the definition of 'employee' does not necessarily reflect workers previously classified as an 'employee' as opposed to an 'independent contractor'. The distinction remains valid, but the boundary between an 'employee' and an 'independent contractor' can now be more firmly grasped. The is because the limits of the process for determining who is an 'employee' for the purposes of employee strict liability are set by the risk to which the liability can now be seen to respond. It follows that the courts do not have an open invitation to extend employee strict liability to relationships 'akin' to employment.[5] There was no basis for the Supreme Court of the United Kingdom to make such an extension and the extension should now be reversed.

Greater assistance can also be derived in determining who is an 'agent'. Traditionally, agent strict liability was associated with employee strict liability; the two forms of strict liability were described using the same label and were thought to be justified on similar grounds. This association was difficult, however, as it enabled agent strict liability to be used to side-step the general rule that an employer could not be held strictly liable for the tort of an independent contractor. It can now be seen that agent strict liability is much more closely associated with conferred authority strict liability than employee strict liability. As a result, the definition of who is an agent is much more confined, being restricted to a person who is conferred authority to effect legal relations on behalf of the principal.[6] It follows that the scope of agent strict liability is similarly confined, leaving the general rule of no strict liability for the torts of an independent contractor (or, at the very least, a person who is not an employee) largely intact.

II. Authority

The new expositive framework put forward by this book for understanding strict liability for the tort of another is based upon the concept of authority.

'Authority', in this respect, is distinct from the concept of 'authorisation' that historically underpinned the Salmond 'course of employment' test. 'Authorisation' refers, in general terms, to whether an employee has permission to engage in the particular conduct that resulted in harm to the claimant. Its focus is the association between the directions issued by the employer to the employee and the tort committed by that employee. In contrast, the concept of 'authority' is much broader and refers, in general terms, to a capacity to exercise the power to direct another person's conduct. Its focus is not the actions engaged in by the person who committed the tort and whether such conduct was permitted by the defendant, but the vulnerability of the claimant or the person who committed the tort to an

[5] *Various Claimants* v *Catholic Child Welfare Society* [2013] 2 AC 1.
[6] See further ch 6.

exercise of the power vested in the defendant to direct the conduct of that person and, in some circumstances, to confer that power upon a third party. To avoid confusion, the consequence of an exercise of authority by an employer has been described in this book in terms of what an employer has 'directed', as opposed to 'authorised', an employer to do (either expressly or impliedly).

Note that the concept of 'authority' is also distinct from 'control'. 'Authority' refers to the *capacity* to direct the behaviour of another person or location of a thing,[7] whereas 'control' refers to the *actual exercise* of that capacity.[8] 'Control' failed as the basis of employee strict liability because it was not always present; consequently, it was neither necessary nor sufficient for employee strict liability to be imposed. 'Authority' though is always present in the identified relationships; and there is always an inherent risk that the authority present in each of the relationships in which strict liability for the tort of another is imposed will be abused. This risk appears sufficient for strict liability for the tort of another to be imposed.

The concept of 'authority' is not without difficulty. There is no one settled meaning which applies in all circumstances. Authority does, however, generally connote some type of power held by one person over another person or thing. The question then is the extent of the power required before one person might be held strictly liable for the tort of another. This is something for which an understanding can be developed over time from the facts of the cases. At present the cases indicate that the standard required is quite high. For instance, in cases of conferred authority strict liability or employee strict liability, the authority consists not only of a power to direct the conduct of another person, but also the right to discipline that person in the event of non-compliance. In cases of agent strict liability, the authority consists of a power to effect legal relations on behalf of another person. The question in subsequent cases will be whether the type of authority present is sufficiently analogous to justify imposing strict liability for the tort of another. This will be a particularly important question in cases involving the potential liability of a church for a sexual assault committed by a priest or other church official.[9]

III. Normative Underpinnings

The new expositive framework put forward by this book has explained both the basis of the various forms of strict liability for the tort of another and the circumstances in which those various forms of liability arise. What it has not explained is *why* strict liability for the tort of another is imposed. Although an important question, there has been insufficient space within the scope of the book to fully explore the normative justification of the liability.

[7] JAH Murray, *The Oxford English Dictionary* (Oxford, Clarendon Press, 1923) v 1, 572.
[8] Ibid v 2, 927.
[9] See generally ch 4.

There is space, however, to speculate briefly as to what that justification might be. The book has shown that what attracts the concern and intervention of the law in cases of strict liability for the tort of another is the potential for abuse of the authority present in each of the relationships in which such liability is imposed. Such a concern with an abuse of authority or power can be seen elsewhere in private law. For example, the doctrine of undue influence in contract law enables transactions to be set aside where a person in a position of influence over another person takes advantage of that influence whilst transacting. Similarly, the doctrine of unconscionability enables transactions to be set aside where a transaction has been procured with a person who was at a special disadvantage.[10] Both these doctrines respond to the potential for a position of power between transacting parties to be abused, although they can be distinguished from strict liability for the tort of another on the basis that evidence of conduct personally engaged in by the defendant (as opposed to a third party) needs to be shown for both doctrines before a transaction can be set aside.

A form of liability which is closer in nature to strict liability for the tort of another is the strict liability imposed in equity for breach of a fiduciary duty. A fiduciary is in a position of power with respect to the beneficiary of the duty and is entrusted to act not in her own interests, but in the interests of the beneficiary.[11] Where a fiduciary puts herself in a position of conflict or potential conflict with the interests of the beneficiary or puts the interests of the beneficiary in conflict or potential conflict with the interests of another person and the beneficiary suffers damage as a result, the fiduciary can be held strictly liable to the beneficiary for any damage the beneficiary suffers as a result.[12] It does not matter for this purpose whether the fiduciary was 'well-intentioned' or 'acting in good faith'; the existence of the conflict or potential conflict is sufficient for strict liability to be imposed.[13] A fiduciary is also generally required to exercise her duties as a fiduciary personally. This means that in certain circumstances where a fiduciary delegates the exercise of any such duties to another person, the fiduciary can be held strictly liable for any conduct engaged in by that person which attracts liability in respect of the beneficiary.[14]

As can be seen, strict liability for breach of fiduciary duty shares a number of features with strict liability for the tort of another; both forms of strict liability respond to the potential for abuse of a power relationship and both forms of liability can be imposed, in certain circumstances, regardless of the defendant personally engaging in any conduct which might attract liability in and of itself.

[10] At least in Australia; *Commercial Bank of Australia* v *Amadio* (1983) 151 CLR 447. cf the position in England and Wales; *Lloyds Bank Ltd* v *Bundy* [1975] QB 326.

[11] GE Dal Pont and DRC Chalmers, *Equity and Trusts in Australia* (4th ed, Sydney, LawBook Co, 2007) 100–02.

[12] Ibid 92.

[13] Ibid 95.

[14] Particularly where the fiduciary is a trustee; JD Heydon and MJ Leeming, *Jacobs' Law of Trusts in Australia* (7th ed, Sydney, LexisNexis Butterworths, 2006) 391–92.

It is possible therefore that the justification for strict liability for the tort of another might also be similar to the justification for strict liability for breach of a fiduciary duty. Justice Mason of the High Court of Australia outlined the justification for the fiduciary duty in *Hospital Products Ltd v United States Surgical Corporation*:[15]

> The critical feature of these relationships is that the fiduciary undertakes or agrees to act for or on behalf of or in the interests of another person in the exercise of a power or discretion which will affect the interests of that other person in a legal or practical sense. The relationship between the parties is therefore one which gives the fiduciary a special opportunity to exercise the power or discretion to the detriment of that other person who is accordingly vulnerable to abuse by the fiduciary of his position. The expressions 'for', 'on behalf of', and 'in the interests of' signify that the fiduciary acts in a 'representative' character in the exercise of his responsibility.

The authority to which strict liability for the tort of another responds does not precisely mirror the authority found in a relationship in which a fiduciary duty arises. The biggest difference is that the authority to which strict liability for the tort of another responds may sometimes be exercised by a party in its own interests (as with an employer), whereas a fiduciary is always required to act in the interests of the beneficiary. Notwithstanding this difference, the two forms of liability are sufficiently similar to give rise to the possibility that they might be justified on similar grounds. That is, strict liability for the tort of another might be justified in terms of the authority entrusted to and accepted by a defendant and the vulnerability of a claimant to a potential abuse of such authority.

There is also the possibility that strict liability for the tort of another may be justified on the basis that a defendant's dealings with authority may have itself contributed to a claimant's damage. This is because the authority present in the relationships within which strict liability for the tort of another is imposed has the potential to enable or facilitate the tort in respect of which the claimant is suing. For example, where an employer or school confers authority upon another person to direct the conduct of an employee or student, they not only create an opportunity for a tort to occur but may actually provide the means by which the tort can occur. A teacher, for instance, can use the authority conferred upon them by a school to direct a student into a private room in order to perpetrate a sexual assault. Strict liability for the tort of another might, therefore, not just respond to the potential for abuse of the authority present in the relationships within which strict liability for the tort of another is imposed, but seek to hold a defendant accountable to the extent that its dealings with such authority may actually have contributed to the commission of the tort. In this way, tort law effectively places the onus on the defendant to prove that its dealings with authority did not contribute to the tort complained of by the claimant. This onus can be discharged through separate indemnity or contribution proceedings brought by the defendant against the person who committed the tort against the claimant.

[15] (1984) 156 CLR 41, 96–97.

Evidently, there are a number of grounds upon which strict liability for the tort of another might be justified and identifying an appropriate justification for the liability will be a considerable project. A suggestion for how such a project might be approached is set out in the postscript to this chapter. This book has, however, assisted in this task by developing a clearer understanding of the basis of strict liability for the tort of another and the circumstances in which such liability is imposed.

IV. Personal Liability v Strict Liability

The focus of this book was strict liability for the tort of another. Personal liability, however, is also imposed within the various relationships which were examined. It is possible, therefore, that the authority present in the relationships examined by this book may have an impact not only on the imposition of strict liability for the tort of another but also the imposition of personal liability.

Consider the employment relationship. It is well established that an employer owes an employee a duty of care, so that an employer must take reasonable steps to prevent an employee coming to any reasonably foreseeable harm. Historically, this duty has been expressed as a number of specifically enumerated duties, such as a duty to provide a safe place of work, safe tools and equipment with which to work and a safe system of work to operate under. Outside the employment relationship, however, it is unusual in modern tort law for specific duties to be enunciated in this way. When describing the liability of car drivers, for instance, a car driver is said to owe a duty to use reasonable care. It has not been suggested that a car driver owes a specific duty to select an appropriate vehicle, ensure the vehicle is adequately maintained or to keep their driving skills up-to-date.

The reason modern tort law does not generally enunciate a specific duty of care is because the formulation of the duty in this way suggests a certain conclusion on liability.[16] When a specific duty is enunciated, breach of that duty is more easily determined because delineation of the duty specifically dictates what should have been done, directing attention away from the issue of whether the holder of the duty behaved reasonably or not. Specifically enumerated duties of care also enable courts to side-step or divert attention away from many of the concerns generally focused upon when assessing liability in tort. In particular, such duties allow liability for omissions to be established more easily because the unreasonable conduct of a defendant can be described as a positive act, rather than an omission. For example a failure by an employer to install a safety guard on a piece of dangerous equipment, a clear omission, can be described as the installation of unsafe

[16] See Jane Stapleton's comment on Lord Hoffmann's attempt to specifically enumerate a duty of care in *South Australia Asset Management Company v York Montague* [1997] AC 191 in 'Negligent Valuers and Falls in the Property Market' (1997) 113 *Law Quarterly Review* 1.

equipment,[17] a positive act. This feature of specifically enumerated duties was particularly significant at the time the duties of an employer were devised because such liability was being steadfastly denied in other categories of case.[18]

The question then is why tort law has persisted in enumerating these specific employers' duties. The historical difficulties faced by an employee in suing her employer, such as contributory negligence being a complete defence, are of limited explanatory force because many of these difficulties have since been removed.[19] A concern with the safety of employees also does not offer much assistance. There are many occasions where safety is in issue but tort law does not resort to the enumeration of specific duties, for instance, when determining the liability of road users. Nor can it be a concern simply with risks being created by the employer for the employee, there being very few instances of human conduct that do not result in the creation of some type of risk. Perhaps then it can be explained in terms of the authority vested in an employer to direct the conduct of an employee. The potential for an employer to abuse its authority to direct the conduct of an employee by putting an employee in a position that the employee unduly prioritises compliance with the directions of the employer rather than give due weight to alternate considerations that might lead an employee to conduct herself differently in the circumstances not only puts strangers to the employment relationship at risk of harm, but the employee herself. Authority, therefore, may not only explain strict liability for the tort of another, but the enhanced personal liability which is typically found in the same relationships.

V. Where to from here?

This book has sought to make sense of strict liability for the tort of another as that liability is currently imposed by the courts. It has identified several key features of the liability, the most significant of which is arguably that the liability is relational.

[17] eg Russell LJ said of the defendant employers in *Calder v H. Kitson Vickers & Sons (Engineers) Ltd* [1988] ICR 232, 239: 'They provided the plaintiff with *unsafe equipment* whilst condoning what was plainly an unsafe system of working' (emphasis added). See also more generally on the potential to blur the line between misfeasance and non-feasance: P Cane, *Atiyah's Accidents, Compensation and the Law* (5th ed, CUP, Cambridge, 1993) 63–67.

[18] See, eg, *Meux v Great Eastern Railway Company* [1895] 2 QB 387, 392 (Kay LJ): 'The law as to such a state of things has been summed up in *Taylor v Manchester, Sheffield and Lincolnshire Ry. Co.* [1895] 1 QB 134. That was an action for personal injuries to the plaintiff, and the general doctrine is stated thus by Lindley L.J: "It appears to me that this is an action founded on tort, and the conclusion to which I have arrived is based upon the following reasons. That which caused the injury was not an act of omission, it was not a mere non-feasance; it was not merely the not taking such care of the plaintiff as by the contract the defendants were bound to take, but it was an act of misfeasance – it was positive negligence".'

[19] The apportionment of contributory negligence was introduced by the Law Reform (Contributory Negligence) Act 1945 (UK) c 28. The House of Lords also held in *Smith v Baker* [1891] AC 325 that an employee could no longer be taken to have voluntarily assumed the risks of employment.

It has been shown that strict liability for the tort of another arises by reason of a relationship between either the defendant and the person who committed the tort or the defendant and the claimant. To qualify as a basis upon which to impose strict liability for the tort of another, it must be a feature of that relationship that one person has the authority to direct the conduct of another person.

Evidently, the language adopted by this book does not match the language currently used by the courts. Adopting the new terminology and underlying reasoning can though provide judges with considerable assistance when determining cases of strict liability for the tort of another. The recent decision of the England and Wales Court of Appeal in *Barclays Bank v Various Claimants*[20] provides a good example. The case concerned the practice of Barclays Bank to require new employees to undergo a medical test as a condition of their employment. Barclays had contracted with a GP in Newcastle to examine the new employees and provide a report. The examinations were conducted at a surgery in the GP's home. In the course of the examinations, the GP sexually abused a number of the female employees. It was accepted at trial that the GP was not an employee of Barclays Bank but an independent contractor. Nonetheless, in accordance with recent advancements in 'vicarious liability' in the courts in England and Wales, the Court of Appeal found that the GP was in a position 'akin' to employment and that Barclays Bank could be held strictly liable for the sexual abuse suffered by the employees.[21]

The willingness of the Court of Appeal to disregard the traditional restriction on imposing 'vicarious liability' in respect of the torts of independent contractors can be better appreciated with a closer examination of the facts of the case:[22]

> The Claimants were all young, some very young, at the relevant time. If they wished to be employed by the Bank they had no option but to undergo the examination, and in respect of the minority who were existing employees, they were instructed to comply as part of their employment.

The critical factor here is that the employees were required by the employer to attend at the surgery and undertake the examination.[23] These facts suggest it was not the relationship between Barclays Bank and the GP which was the relevant relationship for the determination of strict liability but the relationship between Barclays Bank and its employees. The case is therefore an example of conferred authority strict liability and not employee strict liability. It is for this reason that it was not a bar to recovery that the GP was an independent contractor. Nor was it problematic that the tort committed by the GP was intentional.

For too long the courts have stumbled around in the dark when imposing strict liability for the tort of another, reaching justifiable decisions but without an adequate theoretical framework by which to explain such decisions. In order to reach those decisions, judges have had to adapt the existing, ill-fitted framework;

[20] *Barclays Bank plc v Various Claimants* [2018] EWCA Civ 1670.
[21] Ibid [58]–[60].
[22] Ibid [10].
[23] Cf *Brayshaw v Aspley Surgery* [2018] EWHC 3286 (QB).

for instance, by extending employee strict liability to the torts of an independent contractor as occurred in *Barclays Bank v Various Claimants*. As explained in this book, there is no basis for such an extension.

The unprincipled expansion of the law of strict liability for the tort of another is not inevitable. The recent relaxation of tests for imposing strict liability for the tort of another, particularly evident in the courts in England and Wales, is the result of confusion as to the differences between the various types of that liability. The new expositive framework proposed by this book provides the means to overcome that confusion and set the law back on track.

Postscript

Any attempt to understand strict liability for the tort of another in and of itself is necessarily limited. The liability forms part of the law of torts and indeed private law more generally. To this extent, efforts to determine the normative underpinnings of strict liability for the tort of another must be informed by a wider understanding of the law of torts. In turn, the expositive framework proposed by this book can provide insights into the structure and operation of the law of torts more generally.

What the expositive framework proposed by this book has shown to be significant when imposing liability in tort is the existence and features of specified pre-existing relationships. It is not just that there is a correlative relationship between the parties to the legal action in the sense that a determination of the legal action will require a consideration of the respective positions of each of the parties to the legal action.[24] The pre-existing relationship between the parties and/or other relevant actors has been shown to have a direct bearing on the process adopted by the courts to determine liability in the law of torts.

Liability in the law of torts has historically been viewed as a function of certain formulas or recipes that prescribe when liability might arise.[25] Many of those formulas or recipes have changed little over time. The use of such formulas or recipes has arguably inhibited the development of a more holistic view of liability in the law of torts. As Maitland famously noted: 'The forms of action we have buried, but they still rule us from their graves'.[26] The ghosts of the writs of trespass, case, assumpsit and nuisance are ever present in the law of torts today.

Over time, strict liability for the tort of another has come to be viewed as a more isolated form of liability operating at the margins of this framework of formulas or recipes.[27] There has consequently not been the same need to explain strict liability for the tort of another in the same terms as what are now seen to

[24] P Cane, *The Anatomy of Tort Law* (Oxford, Hart, 1997) 10–15.
[25] Ibid 2–10.
[26] FW Maitland, *The Forms of Action at Common Law* (Cambridge, CUP, 1909) Lecture I.
[27] Particularly since *Donoghue* v *Stevenson* [1932] AC 562.

be the more mainstream forms of tort liability. Consider the prevailing trend to explain the law of torts in terms of corrective justice. Corrective justice theorists have struggled to explain strict liability for the tort of another given the liability is imposed regardless of the defendant personally engaging in any conduct which may attract liability in tort and therefore in the absence of any 'wrong' in need of correction. One response of corrective justice theorists to such difficulties has been to rebadge strict liability for the tort of another as a form of fault-based liability.[28] Another has been to disregard strict liability for the tort of another as an anomaly and focus on explaining the more mainstream forms of tort liability.[29]

It cannot be denied that strict liability for the tort of another is today an exceptional form of liability. It does not necessarily follow, however, that strict liability for the tort of another is an anomaly. Like other areas of tort, strict liability for the tort of another is relational. It is possible that a relational view of the law of torts might be of more general use in explaining the liability imposed by the courts. One question posed by this book therefore is whether a more convincing explanation of the different types of liability in the law of torts can be derived by shifting the focus from the historical formulas or recipes to the absence or presence of certain pre-existing relationships.

Viewing tort law in relational terms suggests an alternate classification of the law of torts. That classification can be depicted diagrammatically as follows:

Figure 1 A Relational Classification of Tort Law

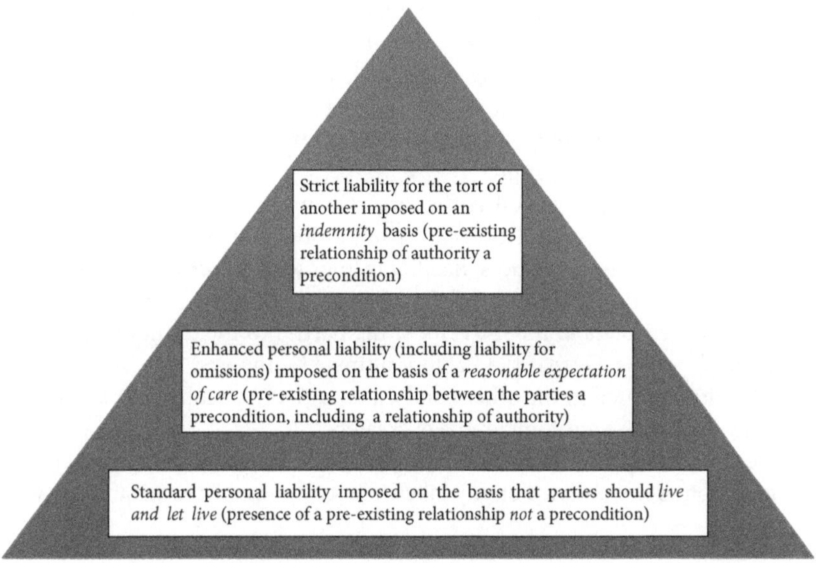

[28] See eg E Weinrib, *The Idea of Private Law* (Oxford, OUP, 2005) 185–187.

[29] Discussed in P Cane, 'Corrective Justice and Correlativity in Private Law' (1996) 16 *Oxford Journal of Legal Studies* 471, 485–587.

At the peak of the pyramid, reflecting the more limited range of circumstances in which liability might arise, is strict liability for the tort of another. A pre-existing relationship of authority is a precondition to liability being imposed (typically, an employment, school or agency relationship) and the liability effectively takes the form of an *indemnity* for a tort committed by another person. It has been argued in this book that the law of torts responds to the risk of that power relationship being abused.[30]

In the middle of the pyramid is a broader band of liability for which a pre-existing relationship is also a precondition. The liability imposed in this band, however, is liability arising by reason of the defendant's own conduct within the course of the relationship. The presence of the relationship is therefore not of itself sufficient to impose liability on the defendant. In addition to the presence of a particular type of pre-existing relationship, the claimant must show that the defendant has personally engaged in conduct to which liability in tort might attach. The set of pre-existing relationships which attracts this band of liability in the law of torts is broader than, but also includes, the set of pre-existing relationships which attract strict liability for the tort of another. As noted earlier in this chapter the same relationships which give rise to strict liability for the tort of another also give rise to enhanced personal liability in the law of torts. That enhanced liability specifically includes liability for omissions. The relationship between a hospital and patient is an example of a relationship that might fall within this middle band, but not within the top band of the pyramid. This is because although hospitals are regularly held liable for negligent omissions in respect of their patients, they are not subject to strict liability for the tort of another.[31] It might be argued that liability in the law of torts in this middle band responds to a *reasonable expectation of care* being taken by reason of these pre-existing relationships and that the relevant relationships are those which engender such an expectation.

At the base of the period is the largest band of liability in the law of torts for which a pre-existing relationship is not a precondition for the imposition of liability. In these circumstances, liability is imposed regardless of any relationship between the parties; as in the case of road users. In this band, it can be argued that the liability responds to the interests of the parties to the claim being allowed to '*live and let live*' such that the liability ultimately imposed is less extensive than the liability imposed in the other bands, although the circumstances in which the liability might arise are comparatively greater.

At first glance, this picture of liability in the law of tort appears unfamiliar. One reason is the absence of any labels currently associated with liability in the

[30] It having been shown that there is no need for a claimant to prove that the power relationship has actually been abused.

[31] See ch 2.

law of the torts. Were those labels to be added, the pyramid might look something like this:

Figure 2 Relationships Matched with Forms of Liability

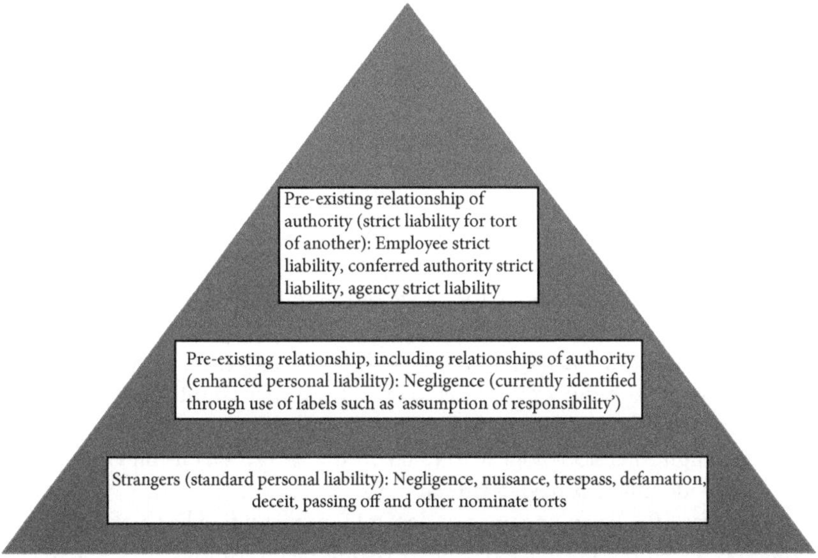

Another reason this picture of liability in the law of tort might appear unfamiliar is that it does not appear to respond to or reflect any of the rules (or formulas or recipes) that have been used by the courts in determining whether to impose liability in the law of torts. The classification looks beyond the form of any individual tort to the substantive process used by the courts when determining liability and how that process changes in the presence or absence of certain pre-existing relationships. On close examination, that process appears to be one of balancing. When determining liability in the law of torts, it can be argued that the courts examine and weigh the respective interests of the parties as members of the broader community and those of any other relevant actors.[32] This balancing is not unprincipled. The relevant interests[33] and the weight to be attached to those interests when balancing has been slowly developed by the courts over time.[34] The nature of the balance to be achieved can be seen, however, to differ depending on the presence or absence of specified pre-existing relationships.

[32] See more generally C Beuermann, 'Are the Torts of Trespass to the Person Obsolete? Part 1: Historical Development (2017) 25(3) *Tort Law Review* 103; and C Beuermann, 'Are the Torts of Trespass to the Person Obsolete? Part 2: Continued Evolution' (2018) 26(1) *Tort Law Review* 6.

[33] Which may be internal or external, depending on the type of relationship in question.

[34] And can be adapted to meet more modern conditions.

It is for this reason that a distinction is made in the above diagram between three discrete outcomes of the different balancing processes undertaken by the courts when determining liability in the law of torts: 'live and let live'; reasonable expectations and indemnity.

To explain further. A finding of 'no liability' in the law of torts generally indicates a determination by the courts that the imposition of liability would unduly interfere with the freedom to act. In the balancing process depicted at the base of the pyramid (identified as 'live and let live'), the courts are carefully trying to balance the interests of defendants in freedom of action and the interests of claimants in freedom from harm in the absence of a relevant pre-existing relationship. Although different labels have been used to describe this balancing process (compare nuisance and negligence, for instance), those labels can be seen to reflect differences in the nature of the interests being interfered with rather than a difference in approach. For example, the range of interests to be balanced in nuisance cases is arguably narrower than in negligence cases more generally given nuisance is a tort that protects only land and land does not move. As people are mobile, there are a broader range of interests to be taken into account when determining liability in torts that protect bodily integrity, such as negligence. The balancing processes might therefore appear to differ in the two torts, but on closer inspection, can be identified as having similar aims.

In contrast, the balancing process depicted in the middle band of the pyramid is different given the presence of a pre-existing relationship that can change the expectation of the parties as to how they will interact. By virtue of such a relationship, a claimant not only expects a defendant not to interfere, but to possibly deliver some type of benefit. The courts therefore take such expectations into account and are more prepared to tip the balance in favour of the claimant's freedom from harm and away from the defendant's freedom to act when determining liability. For example, an employer is required to provide an employee with a safe system of work and safe tools and equipment notwithstanding the cost implications for the employer in making such provision.

In the balancing process depicted at the peak of the pyramid, the fact of the relationship and the presence of a sufficient connection between the tort committed and that relationship is sufficient in and of itself for liability to be imposed so that the defendant is effectively required to hold the claimant harmless and pursue its own claims against the tortfeasor. As evident from the examination of strict liability for the tort of another in this book, any balancing in this band of liability is largely limited to determining whether the requisite relationship and a sufficient connection with that relationship exists.

The classification outlined above with necessary brevity is radical. It does not reflect any existing classification of the liability imposed in the law of torts. The classification has been made possible by starting with one of the more exceptional forms of liability in the law of torts, as opposed to the tort of negligence. Searching for alternate classifications would not be necessary if a convincing explanation of liability in the law of torts had been derived which was capable of providing judges with adequate assistance when deciding cases. Unfortunately, tort law remains bound by the historical forms of action and has made little progress in escaping such bonds. Adopting a relational view of the law of torts, as suggested by the expositive framework of strict liability for the tort of another proposed by this book, might just provide fertile ground for reconstructing tort liability in order to provide the assistance most clearly sought by the courts. Future projects will pursue this goal.

BIBLIOGRAPHY

Articles/Books/Reports

Atiyah, PS, *Vicarious Liability in the Law of Torts* (London, Butterworth & Co, 1967)
Balkin, RP and Davis, JLR, *Law of Torts* (4th ed, Sydney, LexisNexis, 2009)
Banks, RC I'Anson, *Lindley & Banks on Partnership* (16th ed, London, Sweet & Maxwell, 1990)
Barker, K, 'Unreliable Assumptions in the Modern Law of Negligence' (1993) 109 *Law Quarterly Review* 461
Beuermann, C, 'Vicarious Liability: A Case Study in the Failure of General Principles' (2017) 33 *Journal of Professional Negligence* 197
——, 'Are the Torts of Trespass to the Person Obsolete? Part 1 – Historical Development' (2017) 25 *Tort Law Review* 103
——, 'Are the Torts of Trespass to the Person Obsolete? Part 2 – Continued Evolution' (2018) 26 *Tort Law Review* 6
——, 'Do Hospitals Owe a so-called "Non-Delegable Duty of Care" to their Patients?' (2018) 26 *Medical Law Review* 1
——, 'Up in *Armes:* The Need for a Map of Strict Liability for the Wrongdoing of another in Tort' (2018) 25(1) *Torts Law Journal* 1
——, 'The abstraction of form and the associated dangers for the English courts: the case study of vicarious liability', paper presented at Obligations IX, Melbourne Law School, 18 July 2018
Blackstone, W, *Commentaries on the Laws of England* (3rd ed, Clarendon Press, 1768) Vol 3 429
Burns, F, 'The Future of Prescriptive Easements in Australia and England' (2007) 31 *Melbourne University Law Review* 3
Cane, P, *Atiyah's Accidents, Compensation and the Law* (5th ed, Cambridge, CUP, 1993)
——, 'Corrective Justice and Correlativity in Private Law' (1996) 16 *Oxford Journal of Legal Studies* 471
——, *The Anatomy of Tort Law* (Oxford, Hart, 1997)
——, 'Vicarious Liability for Sexual Abuse' (2000) 116 *Law Quarterly Review* 21
——, 'Responsibility and Fault: a Relational and Functional Approach to Responsibility' in P Cane and J Gardner (eds), *Relating to Responsibility* (Oxford, Hart, 2001) 81
Cardozo, BN, *The Nature of the Judicial Process* (New Haven, YUP, 1921)
Collins, H, 'Independent Contractors and the Challenge of Vertical Disintegration to Employment Protection Laws' (1990) 10 *Oxford Journal of Legal Studies* 3
Commission to Inquire into Child Abuse, Parliament of Ireland, *Report* (Sydney, LawBook Co, 2009)
Dal Pont, GE, 'Agency: Definitional Challenges through the Law of Tort' (2003) 11 *Torts Law Journal* 6
—— and Chalmers, DRC, *Equity and Trusts in Australia* (4th ed, Sydney, LawBook Co, 2007)
——, *Law of Agency* (2nd ed, Sydney, LawBook Co, 2008)
Fleming, JG, *The Law of Torts* (9th ed, Sydney, LBC Information Services, 1998)
Fletcher, KL, *The Law of Partnership in Australia* (9th ed, Sydney, LawBook Co, 2007)
Giliker, P, *Vicarious Liability in Tort: A Comparative Perspective* (Cambridge, CUP, 2010)
Heuston, RFV and Buckley, RA, *Salmond and Heuston on the Law of Torts* (19th ed, London, Sweet & Maxwell, 1987)
Heydon JD and Leeming, MJ, *Jacobs' Law of Trusts in Australia* (7th ed, Sydney, LexisNexis Butterworths, 2006)
Holmes, OW, Jr, 'Agency Part II' (1891) 5 *Harvard Law Review* 1
Honore, T, *Responsibility and Fault* (Oxford, Hart, 1999)

Jaumotte, F, 'Female Labour Force Participation: Past Trends and Main Determinants in OECD Countries' OECD Economics Department Working Papers, No 376, (2003)

Jones, MA, Clerk, JF and Lindsell, WHB, *Clerk and Lindsell on Torts* (21st ed, London, Sweet & Maxwell, 2018)

Lunn, S, 'Sexual abuse apology welcomed', *The Australian*, 21 July 2008

Maitland, FW, *The Forms of Action at Common Law* (Cambridge, CUP, 1909) Lecture I.

McCarry, GJ, 'The Employee's Duty to Obey Unreasonable Orders' (1984) 58 *Australian Law Journal* 327

Murphy, J, 'The Liability Bases of Common Law Non-Delegable Duties – A Reply to Christian Witting' (2007) 30(1) *University of New South Wales Law Journal* 86

——, 'Juridical Foundations of Common Law Non-Delegable Duties' in J Neyers, S Pitel and E Chamberlain (eds), *Emerging Issues in Tort Law* (Oxford, Hart, 2007) 369

Murray, JAH, *The Oxford English Dictionary* (Oxford, Clarendon Press, 1923)

Neuberger (Lord), 'Some Thoughts on Principles Governing the Law of Torts', speech given at Singapore Conference on Protecting Business and Economic Interests, 19 August 2016 at www.supremecourt.uk/docs/speech-160819-03.pdf

Newark, FH, 'The Boundaries of Nuisance' (1949) 64 *Law Quarterly Review* 480

Neyers, JW, 'A Theory of Vicarious Liability' (2004) 43 *Alberta Law Review* 287

Palmer, N, *Palmer on Bailment* (3rd ed, London, Sweet & Maxwell, 2009)

Pollock, F, *A Digest of the Law of Partnership* (4th ed, London, Stevens, 1888)

Reynolds, FMB, *Bowstead and Reynolds on Agency* (18th ed, London, Sweet & Maxwell, 2006)

Sappideen, C, O'Grady, P, Warburton, G with Eastman, K, *Macken's Law of Employment* (6th ed, Sydney, LawBook Co, 2009)

Spencer, JR, 'Motor-cars and the Rule in *Rylands* v *Fletcher*: a Chapter of Accidents in the History of Law and Motoring' (1983) 42 *Cambridge Law Journal* 65

Stallybrass, WTS, *Salmon's Law of Torts* (9th ed, London, Sweet & Maxwell, 1936)

Stapleton, J, *Product Liability* (London, Butterworths, 1994)

——, 'Negligent Valuers and Falls in the Property Market' (1997) 113 *Law Quarterly Review* 1

Stauffer, IR and Hyde, CB, 'The Sins of the Fathers: Vicarious liability of Churches' (1993) 25 *Ottawa Law Review* 561

Stevens, R, 'Why Do Agents "Drop out"?' [2005] *Lloyd's Maritime and Commercial Law Quarterly* 101

——, 'Non-Delegable Duties and Vicarious Liability' in J Neyers, S Pitel and E Chamberlain (eds), *Emerging Issues in Tort Law* (Oxford, Hart, 2007) 331

——, 'Vicarious Liability or Vicarious Action' (2007) 123 *Law Quarterly Review* 30

——, *Torts and Rights* (Oxford, OUP, 2007)

Story, J, *Commentaries on Partnership* (Boston, CC Little and J Brown, 1859)

Trindade, F, Cane, P and Lunney, M, *The Law of Torts in Australia* (4th ed, Melbourne, OUP, 2007)

Underhill, A, Hardy Ivamy, ER and Jones, DR, *Underhill's Principles of the Law of Partnership* (12th ed, London, Butterworths, 1986)

Weinrib, E, *The Idea of Private Law* (Oxford, OUP, 2005)

Williams, G, 'Vicarious Liability: Tort of the Master or of the Servant' (1956) 72 *Law Quarterly Review* 522

——, 'Liability for Independent Contractors' (1956) *Cambridge Law Journal* 180

INDEX